Cultural Text Studies 2:

Transatlantic

Edited by:

Camelia Elias & Andrea Birch

Aalborg University Press • 2006

Cultural Text Studies 2:
Transatlantic

Edited by:
Camelia Elias & Andrea Birch

© The Authors and Aalborg University Press, 2005

Cover: Camelia Elias
Layout: Bente Vestergaard
Printed by Narayana, 2006
ISBN 87-7307-754-2
ISSN 1901-1911

Distribution:
Aalborg University Press
Niels Jernes Vej 6B
9220 Aalborg Ø
Denmark
Phone: (+45) 96 35 71 40, Fax (+45) 96 35 00 76
E-mail: aauf@forlag.aau.dk
Homepage: http://www.forlag.aau.dk

All rights reserved. No part of this book may be reprinted or reproduced or utilized in any form or by any electronic, mechanical, or other means, now known or hereafter invented, including photocopying and recording, or in any information storage or retrieval system, without permission in writing from the publishers, except for reviews and short excerpts in scholarly publications.

Table of Contents

Camelia Elias and Andrea Birch:
Introduction — 5

Camelia Elias and Bent Sørensen
Transatlantic: New Perspectives — 19

Bent Sørensen:
Images of Europe: Readings in the Literary Topography of Generational Writings — 21

Dovile Budryte and Charles Perrin:
The Idea of Europe in Selected American World History Textbooks — 41

Camelia Elias:
Passage-way to Culture and Writing – Literature of Transit: Codrescu, Federman, Hoffman, and Simic — 55

Lene Yding Pedersen:
Atlanticized: Joseph O'Connor's Irish America — 79

Steen Christiansen:
Continuity Breach: The British Revision of the American Superhero — 109

Marian Dolan and Kay J. Keels:
Song of the Silenced: American Performance of Baltic Choral Music — 133

J. Kay Keels:
Entrepreneurship in Lithuania: Embracing a Western Tradition — 147

Heather Gollmar Casey:
The Transatlantic Flow of Morality: A Case Study of Abortion Politics — 161

Mary Beth Looney:
'Dove sono le donne artisti?'…and Other Questions Regarding Revisionist Art History and Italian Women — 171

Jean Westmacott:
Travels with Merrill (and the Athena Project) — 183

Søren Hattesen Balle:
'Crossing a Bare Common': Emerson's Ironic Negotiation of the Sublime — 195

Brian Barlow:
Anxiety between Europe and America: Reinhold Niebuhr and His Use of Søren Kierkegaard's Concept of Anxiety — 215

Contributors — 223

Introduction

CAMELIA ELIAS AND ANDREA BIRCH

This volume of interdisciplinary scholarship brings together explorations of transatlantic perspectives in arts, literature, history, philosophy and law. In the individual essays the transatlantic perspective opens up comparative aspects of phenomena within these fields, but this perspective also allows for a new type of engagement with the phenomena themselves, which can be analyzed in new historical, transnational contexts. The present volume is itself an expression of a transatlantic exchange. The contributors are all affiliated with either Aalborg University or Brenau University, two small research and educational institutions which over a number of years have experimented with transatlantic exchanges of students, faculty and scholarship. Out of these exchanges came the idea to commission essays exploring the transatlantic aspects of the contributors' core fields. The ensuing essays have been grouped to further highlight the interplay between different scholarly fields and approaches. The scholarship is therefore hopefully presented in such a way that the whole is greater than the sum of its individual parts.

~~~

The transatlantic connection is at its clearest in the investigation of what is representational in the relation here vs. there. The representation of place, space, and belonging is a process of registering differing mentalities. These mentalities help create the emergence of some binary dichotomies: home vs. abroad, us vs. them, ideal vs. real, motivation vs determinacy, cultural exchange vs. negotiation, being in transit vs. settling, adaptation vs. assimilation, exile vs. expatriotism and invasion (cultural hegemony or imperialism), historicity vs. belonging. Crossing the Atlantic thus involves some economies of representation and the essays presented in this volume aim at disclosing the implications of the notion of transatlantic for the way in which we read the significance of cultural texts. The transatlantic connection explored by the essays in *Transatlantic* emphasizes not only a desire to explain different cultures, but also to focus on the mechanisms of representing difference and heterogeneity in literature. The representation of place can be said to be mediated in terms of both an imaging of place and an imagining of it, while space can be considered in terms of the sublime in which the experience alone of being abroad is rendered in terms of greatness. Greatness is linked with anticipation, and anticipation is something that all subjects involved in a transatlantic crossing share. Whether territorial or cultural displacement is induced by coercion or follows the will of a subject, the transatlantic crossing always opens up a space for communication across influence, dominance, interactions, exchanges, master and local narratives. A sense of belonging springs out of the need to re-articulate one's anticipation of a place and expectation to understand a different culture.

In the following each essay will be discussed in terms of its specific contribution and situated in its transatlantic context, as well as in its place within the scheme of the volume:

Bent Sørensen's essay "Images of Europe: Readings in the Transatlantic Topography of Generational Texts" is oriented by his observation that Europe has functioned as a counter-image in American intellectual thought and debate at least since the 1920s and onward. Insofar as any representation of place usually takes place after the fact, after the arrival to a certain place, it is noteworthy to observe that before a place is visited or chosen for longer settling some mental images are always conjured up not necessarily by what constitutes factual information about the said place, but by imagination, by the way in which the place is being imagined. These imaginary images often find their way in descriptions which present themselves as objective. Sørensen's essay looks not only at how place is represented but also offers insights into the semiotics of place as it is linked to experience. The central argument revolves around the idea that Europe has been imaged by American intellectuals and writers as carrier of an element of Bohemianism and greater tolerance towards deviation. Yet, as Sørensen contends, experience also has darker aspects, as Europe is considered by writers (both exiled and travelers) as a "free space" for drugs and the uninhibited unfolding of sexuality. Opposed to the representation of Europe as a decadent place, Europe is also an 'old' continent, which has implications for the way in which Europe is both imagined and experienced. Here Sørensen makes an assumption and raises a central question: "one thing is to go into exile, another is to write about it. How do we get from the writer being located in a foreign locale to even talking about a representation of this place as something different from any other textual construct? How is foreign place or even place as such present in texts?" Sørensen places under scrutiny texts from four generations: from Ernest Hemingway's *The Sun Also Rises*, via selected Beat and Blank Generation texts, to Douglas Coupland's *Shampoo Planet*, and analyzes signifiers and key concepts such as "Eurotrash", and "Bohemian or machismo Paradise" in the light of cultural exchange which is dependent on the imaginary construction of place in general and the significance of age, conservatism and modernity in particular.

Another essay which emphasizes an imaginary idea behind the representation of place and the cultural negotiation of meaning in a historical dimension is Dovile Budryte and Charles Perrin's essay "The Idea of Europe in Selected American World History Textbooks". This essay analyzes two textbooks that are currently used in world history classes in the United States: *World Civilizations: Their History and Culture* (Philip Lee Ralph, et al., 1997) and *Traditions & Encounters: A Global Perspective on the Past* (J.H. Bentley and H.F. Zeigler, 2003). Each case study is organized around the following questions: what is the unit of analysis within each textbook, how prominent is the "European" theme, how do the authors describe the development of European societies before 1500, how do they explain the rise of Europe after 1500, and how do the authors describe European interactions with other parts of the world? Ralph and the other authors of *World Civilizations* use the term "civilization" as the unit of analysis and conceptualize a civilization as a real entity with more or less distinct borders and characteristics. The text has a European focus. In the first part of volume one, the image of a European civilization emerges after the survey of the Mesopotamian, Egyptian, and Hebrew civilizations. Their vision of Europe sets the stage for a dualistic approach to transatlantic relations. Europe is one entity and the United States will remain the "other". In the second part of volume one, titled "The World of the Classical Era", the authors elaborate on the European theme. In volume two the European nation-states play a central role. The non-Western, non-European civilizations are marginalized until the rise of a "new" post-World War II "world civilization". Europe is then merely one of several regions (but still the authors describe post-World War II developments in Europe in more detail than developments in other geographic areas). Interestingly, although the authors of the text claim that the current world civilization is characterized by US dominance, they do not pursue the consequences of that observation. Instead, they try to identify common global issues (such as, the environmental crisis) that unite the common world civilization. However, given their geographic approach to the world and their emphasis on the fragmented, nation-state system, Budryte and Perrin argue that the authors do not convince readers that there *are* any common, shared global issues.

In contrast to the first textbook analyzed, Bentley and Zeigler clearly want their text *Traditions & Encounters* to be free of Eurocentrism. In their preface they explicitly state that "it…is impossible to understand the world's history by viewing it through the lenses of any particular society". They claim that their textbook will include expanded treatments of several non-European societies. To support their efforts to avoid privileging any one society, Bentley and Zeigler try to avoid using the word "civilization". Instead, they use "complex societies" as their unit of analysis. The term European civilization is absent; it is replaced with the more unfamiliar and ambiguous term "European society". The first complex society which they identify as European is western Europe during the middle ages. Only two of the twenty-two chapters on the pre-modern era deal exclusively with western Europe. China is the subject of three chapters. However, in contrast to the chapters on the pre-modern era, Europe does figure prominently in the chapters on the modern era. Even more surprisingly, Bentley and Zeigler seem to have no reservations about introducing the idea of European exceptionalism. However, they conclude that the Europe of today is not a superpower. In a textbook that is 1,169 pages long, the European Union receives one paragraph and a table shows that Europe is the only area of the world whose population is projected to decline over the next fifty years. Europe is merely one actor (and not a very strong actor) among many. The hidden message is that Europe is not capable of challenging the power of the United States.

Both texts ultimately have the consequence of de-emphasizing Europe. *World Civilizations* does so by ending with the concept of a world civilization that must face common global issues. *Traditions & Encounters* is more overt in showing that Europe is just part of the complex mosaic of societies; it is not the centerpiece. With either textbook, students in the US are left wondering: Where does the United States fit into this mosaic? Does the United States even fit into the mosaic at all or is it isolated? What are the consequences of this isolation? Does it lead to world dominance or to a form of marginalization? Are there ways to bridge the divide between the United States and other parts of the world? In particular, are there ways to cross the transatlantic divide and partner with Europe, long admired by the US (if only secretly) as so central to civilization and world society?

Camelia Elias's essay "Passage-way to Culture and Writing" takes its point of departure in what can be termed the transatlantic experience and the literature of transit insofar as the texts she analyzes are all written by immigrant writers. Andrei Codrescu, Raymond Federman, Eva Hoffman, and Charles Simic's quasi autobiographical writings themselves link the idea of crossing borders and the Atlantic with the kind of writing which is rendered crossed – in a metaphorical sense – by notions of belonging, being in transit, and strategic positioning vis-à-vis cultural understanding. Elias's paper foregrounds the idea that what makes the literature of transit transatlantic is its ability to turn writing into a sort of religion which observes and subverts the customs of new territories.

The essay explores, on the one hand, the notion of transatlantic through a consideration of the concept of belonging and develops the idea of neutrality as a strategy in dealing with the sense of belonging in the context of shifting nationalities and cultural backgrounds. Insofar as the examined texts themselves anchor their narrative in cultural observations that have a specific double perspective and transnational import, Elias's text considers how writing which uses the metaphor of border-crossing forms the basis of successful integration in a society which invokes mentality as a differing factor in its reasons for acknowledging or dismissing the presence of foreigners. On the other hand, the essay sees the notion of transatlantic as a metaphor of in-between-ness through which the literary value of the literature of transit can be assessed. Here Elias makes the point that when the authors analyzed seem to ask the question as to how they can translate their life stories into fictional ones, they also ask the question of how geographical displacement can be translated into a geography of emotion characterized by a desire to go against norms of conventionality. The transatlantic experience is thus rendered as the site of non-conformity insofar as it settles in the paradox of belonging. Some aspects of American culture emerge against such a background, and places such as New York, San Francisco, and Chicago are shown to function as transatlantic spaces where creativity happens because and in spite of belonging.

Another example of the literature of transit which "atlanticizes" the very space where it takes place is Lene Yding Pedersen's essay "Atlanticized: Joseph O'Connor's America". Her arguments constitute a significant contribution to the idea that spaces and places are negotiated by crossings in their "atlanticized" form. The suggestion is that crossings always involve an economy of representation. She thus distinguishes between economies of space and economies of writing as they are manifested in contemporary Irish writer Joseph O'Connor's writings which offer representations of America and the Atlantic that are shown to be in an interdependent relationship with each other. Following critics such as Robert James Scully who claimed that ever since the 1840s Ireland has undergone a process of 'Atlanticizing' itself, Yding Pedersen examines two works by O'Connor. In her reading of *Star of the Sea* (2002) she explores the novel's problematic representation of the Famine against the background of themes dealing with history and history writing. Her reading of *Sweet Liberty: Travels in Irish America* (1996) examines the 'Atlanticized' idea in a contemporary context. The idea of crossing is significant here insofar as it stands for the formation of compounds: Ireland is not Ireland without America. What is at stake is the idea that the transatlantic crossing determines and predicates identity. Thus, Yding Pedersen uses this premise to investigate the meaning of O'Connor's 'Irish America' and she shows how *Sweet Liberty* depicts America in the 1990s by portraying as well an image of the 'Atlanticized' author. In her readings of both books she points out O'Connor's use of literary genres (the historical novel and travel writing) for his thematization of the Famine and Irish America, and she points out how both of O'Connor's books relate to these genre conventions in a paradoxical way. Yding Pedersen's essay furthermore suggests that the challenging of literary conventions from an atlanticized point of view has a direct implication for the ways in which identity can be re-fashioned. The author is who he is not only because he writes, but also because he crosses cultural boundaries in writing and in life.

Elias and Yding Pedersen's essays share an interest in the specific function of the notion of transatlantic: to actively change and determine a writer's prerogatives. Exile and travel writing is here seen not only as part of a negotiating process in cultural exchange but also as an investment in making the personal narrative inherently transatlantic regardless of the borders crossed.

Insofar as the notion of transatlantic emphasizes not only exchange but also the way in which exchanges are interpreted by both sides, it is interesting to note how processes of adaptation, assimilation, and invasion also trigger a revisionist approach. Steen Christiansen's essay: "Continuity Breach: The British Revision of the American Superhero" takes stock of how the genre of comic books is first invaded, and then revised according to new marketing strategies and new creative modes of thinking. Christiansen's essay is an examination of the way a number of British comicbook writers entered the US comics field and altered several of the key conventions of the comicbook and particularly the superhero genre. Christiansen argues that the British writers' invasion of the American genre and premise in the 80s, and the subsequent revision of it on their own terms, unlike other transatlantic crossings, constituted a revitalizing move within the field since especially the mid 80s faced a period of transition due to the poor sale of comicbooks.

Drawing on Harold Bloom's notion of the anxiety of influence, Christiansen offers a semiotic account of the intertextual connections and discontinuities between the work of British writers (Alan Moore, Neil Gaiman, and Grant Morrison) and that of the superhero genre. The essay then looks at the reception of comicbooks and notes the shift to their being accepted into mainstream culture. Christiansen's essay not only looks at the current status of the comicbook genre but also links the paratextual reading of a number of comicbook covers with the problems associated with adaptations and revisions, such as the translations of the mentioned writers' comicbooks into fiction and film. The transatlantic perspective is here made explicit as Christiansen contextualizes the idea of cross aesthetics by looking at how the examined authors not only crossed the Atlantic to come to the US, but also opened a space in their work for a crossing over in other areas.

Another essay which emphasizes a crossing over in its more metaphorical sense is Marian Dolan and Kay Keels's essay "Song of the Silenced: American Performance of Baltic Choral Music". In this case, the crossing involves having an American choir learn and perform Baltic musical scores. Dolan (the conductor) and Keels (one of the singers) describe three challenges the American conductor and the American singers must face. First, the Baltic music that had been silenced in Estonia, Latvia, and Lithuania by the Soviets is to be re-presented by Americans who have no experience of this silencing.

Time and effort must be spent on getting the Americans to almost spiritually cross over into the Baltic composers' cultural context.

Second, the American singers, who like most Americans are uni-lingual, must learn a foreign language in such a way that they do not merely mouth the words but sing them with meaning. In a world where English is becoming the common language, the American singers had to gain a sensitivity to why a language, such as Estonian, spoken by only a few, is significant. For nations with small populations, language is a great unifier and promotes a sense of identity. During the years of Sovietization, the languages of the Baltic countries were silenced and replaced by Russian. The Americans in the choir learned that silencing a language is culturally shattering and learning the Baltic languages became almost a cultural study.

Third, so they could convey the message convincingly to listeners on the American side of the Atlantic, the American singers had to capture how important communal singing is to the Balts. This was a challenge because Americans are individualistic and choral singers often try to impose their individual voices on the ensemble. Moreover, for most Americans singing is merely a pleasant, entertaining pastime. So, how was an American choir to sing as one (as a Baltic choir would) and how would the American singers understand that to represent the Baltic composers' intent they had to feel the power inherent in communal singing? One solution was to tell the Americans about the history of the national song and dance festivals of Estonia, Latvia, and Lithuania, show them video footage of the huge Baltic song festivals, and impress them with statistics (if one-third of the Estonian population attended the 1998 *Laulupidu*, the equivalent 33% of the 1988 US population was 83 *million* people!) Yes, Dolan and Keels prove in their account that Americans can sing with understanding if they make the investment in crossing over into a new cultural context, another language, and the ideals of community.

Just as Americans can cross over to embrace the spirit of the Baltic countries, an almost complementary article by Kay Keels, "Entrepreneurship in Lithuania: Embracing a Western Tradition", shows that citizens of the Baltic country of Lithuania have made a decision to cross over to the west as the model for their society. Societies are texts that we can read. We read the US, a western country, as a land of rugged individualists. It has become a commonplace to assume that individualism is the necessary prerequisite to entrepreneurship. (Entrepreneurship can be defined as the creation of new enterprises by free-thinking risk takers who identify unmet needs, charge money for the satisfaction of those needs, and so generate wealth.) How did Lithuania, a country that had been squeezed into the sphere of the Soviet planned socialist economies and with an historic communal tradition, transform itself into an entrepreneurial society?

If we read Lithuanian society, we can actually identify beneath the communal text some sub-texts that reveal qualities that are assets to entrepreneurs. For example, the communal national song festivals of Lithuania grew into rallies of cultural pride during Soviet occupation. These rallies, which became known as the Singing Revolution, bore witness to the fact that Lithuanians have the fierce self-confidence and determination needed to become successful entrepreneurs. Indeed, by 2003 the World Bank had listed Lithuania among the top twenty countries known for ease of starting a new business. Because so few people are familiar with the languages of the Baltics (except, perhaps, the American choral singers referred to above!), the peoples of Lithuania have not only had to literally hone their foreign language skills, they have had to metaphorically cross over and adopt positive associations with the language of western capitalism. For Lithuanians, no longer is entrepreneurship a dirty word; they are no longer ambivalent toward capitalism; and, they no longer are resentful of those who accumulate wealth.

In an intriguing footnote, Keels does point out a warning to the citizens of the Baltic countries. In the rush toward gaining individual recognition for their own accomplishments, each Baltic country wants to be evaluated as a separate entity. However, as Keels advises, the Baltic countries should not lose the spirit of cooperation that helped to bring about their independence from the Soviet system. Keels's suggestion that the Baltic countries should retain a communal spirit among themselves points out the secret of US (and increasingly European Union) success: the creativity of individuals is fostered within the united strength of united states (or, in the case of the EU, united countries). The paradoxes of cross cultural, transatlantic exchanges multiply. Individualistic Americans learn about community from the Balts and the historically communal Balts can learn about individualism and cooperation from the Americans across the Atlantic.

The challenge of uncovering the direction of transatlantic exchanges becomes very obvious in Heather Gollmar Casey's essay, "The Transatlantic Flow of Morality: A Case Study of Abortion Politics". Historically, the transatlantic crossing of social policies has been from Europe to the US, with the US diluting the innovative (liberal) policies before implementing them on the American side of the Atlantic. Casey's close examination of abortion legislation and abortion discourse in the United States, United Kingdom (excluding Northern Ireland), France, and Germany suggests that rather than the US adopting European policies, the countries are apparently arriving simultaneously at increasingly more restrictive abortion legislation, while using different discourse to justify the fairly similar outcomes. Specifically, in the US, discussion of women's rights focuses on individual rights. More restrictive abortion legislation is then justified on the grounds that prioritizing women's concerns limits the rights of others (future citizens, the fetus, etc.). In the European countries, discussion of women's rights tends to focus on government responsibility to support mothers by creating environments in which women can afford to raise children. More restrictive abortion legislation can then be justified on the grounds that the government is providing public health care and other humanitarian services for women so there is no need for a woman to have an abortion. Casey speculates that the current US administration wants to claim that more restrictive abortion legislation is an example of the reversal in the direction of transatlantic crossings. Whereas liberal policies once came from Europe to America, now conservative gales are originating in the US and blowing toward Europe. Still, even if that is so, Casey demonstrates that the discourse does not flow neatly from east to west, nor west to east across the Atlantic, but remains rooted in American or European rhetoric of justification. How can there be exchanges of ideas, true dialogue, and questioning of policies if discourse is almost manipulated to appeal to specific audiences?

One solution might be to move beyond metaphorical crossings to literal physical crossings of the Atlantic as Mary Beth Looney describes in *"Dove sono le donne artisti...*and Other Questions Regarding Revisionist Art History and Italian Women". In one week in March 2004, Looney guided under-graduate level students from her Special Topics in Art History class to three Italian cities. The course content focused on women as art makers in the Renaissance and Baroque eras and the students embarked on their trip with the expectation of viewing works by the women artists so celebrated in their English language texts. Of course, the students were aware of the rarity of women artists and history's treatment of them. Still, it was impossible to completely prepare 21st century American students, so conditioned to consider the "other" in all aspects of life and exposed to revisionist historical practices in the US, for what they would find or, rather, not find in Italian museums and churches. Not only were the works of the Italian women artists difficult to locate, but when they did find them the students had to bring their own fanfare. Italian museum literature does not identify where unique works are and wall text is rare. Perhaps mirroring the model of Italian feminists who are unobtrusive renegades, the works of the women artists wait silently to make their impact. The students eagerly and painstakingly searched nooks and crannies and repeatedly experienced the joy of discovering for themselves the works by women artists, such as Giovanna Garzoni's paintings in the Pitti Palace. The students' active involvement in museum exploration resulted in excitement that is often lacking when meanings are spelled out. Museum goers generally expect comfort and convenience and viewers in the US are told what is important. Literal transatlantic crossings can change the way travelers experience the other country and their home country upon their return. If they communicate their experiences, they can change the behavior of others, even those in the country they had traveled to. In Looney's example, Italians may be able to see their own museums through new lenses. The lessons from cross cultural travelers are powerful: we must all make efforts to become actively engaged with the world around us. Lived experience, however it is interpreted, is never easy, but it can be exhilarating!

You can feel the exhilaration in Jean Westmacott's essay "Travels with Merrill (and the Athena Project)" as she describes her travels in Italy in the summer of 1995 as part of the Athena Project. Westmacott explains the reason for her trip. In 1994 a group of citizens from Athens, Georgia, USA, decided their city needed a public sculpture to celebrate its classical origins. Westmacott was awarded the sculpture commission for an image of Athena, to be eight feet tall and carved from Italian Carrara marble. Brenau University student, Lara Magzan, born in Sarajevo, in former Yugoslavia, served as the model. Westmacott hired another Brenau University student, Merrill Hayes, as studio assistant for the project. So, in June 1995, Westmacott and Hayes were off to the Nicoli Studios in Carrara, Italy. Signor Carlo Nicoli wanted Westmacott to collaborate on the finishing details of the marble Athena enlarged from the cast. Citizens, living and dead, of several countries (e.g., English writers, French philosophers, and a nurse from Tripoli) make their way into Westmacott's account. Her descriptions are so vivid that readers will feel their feet moving across the 16th century covered wooden bridge in the early morning and taste the freshly baked apricot brioche and cappuccino. Most importantly, readers will start to experience on a visceral level the excitement of physically crossing over into new places, forging friendships, telling one's own stories, and listening to the stories of others. The statue of Athena now stands serenely resolute in front of the Classic Center in Athens, Georgia, USA, as an embodiment of European and American collaboration and a celebration of the ongoing benefits of transatlantic interrelationships.

Even if a crossing is literal, the writing about it becomes metaphorical. Søren Hattesen Balle's essay "'Crossing a Bare Common': Emerson's Ironic Negotiation of the Sublime" unpacks the metaphor of crossing by offering a microanalysis of the term and its relations to the literary tropes of hyperbole, metalepsis, catachresis and chiasmus. Hattesen Balle suggests that Emerson's crisscrossing of tropes causes the sublime to hypertrophy. By looking at Emerson's travel book *English Traits*, in which the transatlantic relations between Britain and America are seen as less oppositional than mutually imitative and splitting, Hattesen Balle demonstrates how cultural difference is both a function of hybridity and mimicry. Difference and imitation are two sides of the transatlantic coin which is used in the exchange of perspectives that have a double character. Following Homi Bhaba, Hattesen Balle's essay is also an exploration in postcolonialism and its emphasis on duplicity and the double interaction between the voice of authority and the sublime. What is at stake is the fact that imitation never comes alone, as it were, but is always accompanied by a form of resistance. Emerson's America, while imitating the values and norms of the colonial Britain, also resists them. The result is however the product of a double signification. As Hattesen Balle argues, it only makes sense to talk of Emerson's postcolonial discourse at the juncture between imitation and resistance when they mutually enforce each other. One of the important points that the essay makes is that in a transatlantic relation the sublime is estranged from itself causing the upheaval of transcendentalist ideals. By way of making references to Wallace Stevens and Harold Bloom, Hattesen Balle's essay furthermore suggests that the double-crossing of imitation into resistance and vice-versa can also be seen as a revisionist pattern thus creating a moment of anxiety.

Brian Barlow's essay, "Anxiety between Europe and America: Reinhold Niebuhr and His Use of Søren Kierkegaard's Concept of Anxiety", offers a specific example of how any transatlantic crossing, besides being associated with anticipations, imitations, and revisions, can also be the opportunity for making a leap of faith. In the winter of 1937, Niebuhr was invited to deliver the prestigious Gifford Lectures at the University of Edinburgh in

1939. The invitation filled him with self-doubt and even anger. He saw the Gifford Lectures as a form of slavery that kept him from his usual mode of communication, extemporaneous speaking, as in sermons and political speeches. His discovery and use of Søren Kierkegaard's concept of anxiety enabled Niebuhr to creatively adapt to and transcend the anxieties of his life and mind in writing and delivering the Gifford Lectures. Of course, Niebuhr's anxiety was not miraculously healed. This is consistent with Kierkegaard's view that even persons of faith suffer from anxiety. Human beings are free. We must deal with the anxiety of freedom as we face the possibility of sinning (we will sin if we have the prior sin of unbelief) and the possibility of not sinning (we have the opportunity not to sin if we have faith). In either case, anxiety is never completely resolved or transcended. Niebuhr picked up this message from Kierkegaard and applied it on a personal level (so he could face the anxiety of writing the lectures) and on the theoretical level (so he could analyze freedom and sin). Niebuhr has become well known for his short prayer seeking serenity in an age of anxiety, which is really every age, because human beings, even believers, are never completely free of anxiety. So, there is still anxiety in America and in Europe and between them. The lesson we can learn from Niebuhr and Kierkegaard is that in this apocalyptic age of anxiety we can still face uncertainty with faith, hope, and disciplined action. Anxiety will never disappear, but it does not have to paralyze us. Niebuhr, while still experiencing anxiety every step of the way, was able to make a leap of faith and deliver his Gifford Lectures, which have become his most famous book, *The Nature and Destiny of Man*.

As inspiration for the contributors Bent Sørensen and Camelia Elias have written a small manifesto, entitled "Transatlantic - New Perspectives", trying to pinpoint some of the advantages of the transatlantic approach to scholarship within and across many fields. The volume commences with this short piece, which sets the tenor for the spirit of open exchanges within scholarship as well as between scholars – a spirit we also hope readers of this volume will feel that the individual pieces will communicate to them.

Aalborg and Brenau, May 2005

Transatlantic: New Perspectives

CAMELIA ELIAS AND BENT SØRENSEN

The transatlantic perspective in scholarship opens up for new approaches to comparative studies in the fields of literature, culture, history, politics, law, philosophy etc. Core problematics in all these fields lend themselves to readings of the type we dub cultural text studies: an approach that focuses on textual manifestations of identities, mentalities and cultural phenomena, and which offers specific contextualizations of these phenomena, whether these contexts be historical, economic, political or aesthetic.

The specifically transatlantic view means a step beyond comparison for comparison's own sake, in that the concept of the transatlantic entails a focus on mobility, flow, change, exchange, transit and transformation. This means that comparisons can be performed that are historically motivated (development over time), that trace influences (seen as processes of negotiation of meaning), and are geographically specific (situating the impact of the countries and regions involved in the exchange).

An examination of the two constituent parts of the compound 'transatlantic' may be illuminating: The syllable "trans" invites us to think in movements across, to speak in terms of passages, travels and crossings. Movement always involves agency: "Who moves?" An object: "Who moves what?" A destination: "Who moves what, whereto?" Historicity: "Who moves what, when?" Motivation: "Who moves what, why?" The component "Atlantic" invites us to think in terms of the scene of exchange, to see the Atlantic as a shared stage between continents and between specific cultural and political entities. The Atlantic is simultaneously a divide we need to cross, and a connector that facilitates this crossing. The ocean is historically invested in as a medium of passage, whether the passage is inscribed in a tale that is fatal for the individuals crossing the ocean, or whether the voyage holds out great promise for freedom, salvation and empowering change.

Taken as a whole, the transatlantic view on exchange in cultural text studies specifically privileges an engagement with and analysis of processes of negotiation and mediation, whether the objects of analysis are cultural parameters, concepts or ideas, or more specific and concrete objects such as goods, persons etc. The transatlantic perspective is particularly suited for the traveler who personally traverses the Atlantic and brings along the conditioned view from 'home', whether that be the Americas or the Euro-African side of the transatlantic equation. The personal narrative of cultural exchange is therefore inherently transatlantic in that all 'readings' of the 'other' culture is filtered by the notions that are homegrown in the author of the text produced. In transatlantic scholarship one of the most employed strategies is to combine the personal narrative with a self-reflexive meta-consciousness of being involved in intercultural negotiation and reading/text-production. The transatlantic scholar makes a virtue out of employing the personal experience of the cultural transaction and exchange, and draws a comparison that might otherwise remain understood and implicit out in the open.

Transatlantic scholarship should always consider that whatever the object of study is, there are two mindsets or mentalities involved in the negotiations and mediations of meaning attached to the object of study. The task of the scholar observing the phenomena from the transatlantic perspective is always to make explicit what makes the paper transatlantic, or in other words to mobilize the self-reflexive, meta-language that poses itself in the set of questions: What makes my paper transatlantic, what is gained thereby, how can I communicate to my reader what new vistas and what limitations my transatlantic focus lends me?

Images of Europe: Readings in the Literary Topography of Generational Writings

Bent Sørensen

This paper is part of an on-going work on generating a type of analysis of the semiotics of place in American generational novels. The frame of this work is to chart how generational fictions operate with the establishment of potential 'free spaces' where the cultural choices of the characters can unfold, and of potential utopian ideas concerning ways of making life in the USA of the 1980s and '90s liveable. The generational novels share the feature of illustrating intercultural encounters where generational representatives formulate their own subcultural consciousness and identities in topographical terms, where the USA is compared and contrasted with counter-images of other locations. This can be Bohemian myths of Europe (typically Paris), or machismo arenas such as Spain, or conventional escape areas for outlaws (real as well as fictional) such as Mexico or Canada, or 'exotic' topoi such as Northern Africa or Japan, where the local culture forms an object of fascination for the characters in a constant tension between machismo/samurai ethics and a drug related drop out/mañana life style.

Here I focus specifically on images of Europe in generational novels: Why are representations of Europe developing from ones of Bohemia or a machismo Paradise toward a wasteground for Eurotrash? Europe has always functioned as a counter-image in American intellectual thought and debate, not just in the 20th Century. From at least the 1920s and onward this has meant that Europe has been imaged by American intellectuals and writers as carrier of an element of Bohemianism and greater tolerance towards deviation, apparently supported by the fact that novels which were unpublishable in America sometimes were printable in Europe (typically France) and read there. For that reason Europe has seemed well suited as a free space for young (predominantly male) authors' (literary and real) experiments with sexuality and drugs, but has also been a reservoir of darker experience of war and death, often coupled with cultural decadence. Closely related to this is the experience of Europe as an 'old' continent, which naturally triggers off a dichotomy in the imaging of it. On the one hand there are traditions and values here that 'new' America cannot offer in any form; on the other hand the age may carry with it a lethargy and conservatism which can be hard to accept for young progressive Americans. During the 1980s the pendulum in this dichotomy has swung towards the critical side, which is encapsulated in the signifier 'Eurotrash', which has become a more and more frequently used label for (particularly) younger Europeans, whether the American culture meets this phenomenon in Europe, or whether the Eurotrash comes to the USA as a form of nemesis as in Coupland's novel, *Shampoo Planet*.

Representations of Place

To investigate images of Europe in American texts one must invoke the tradition of mutual dependence and antagonism between the two continents, a heady stew of ingredients of economic, political and cultural philosophical nature. For centuries the relationship seen from the American side of the Atlantic was one of inferiority constructs. North America consisted of colonies subservient to European states, were poor materially and culturally, lacking the advanced institutions of education and dissemination of cultural products and values that were found in Europe. As a result of this, Americans who could, would look to Europe for their taste ideals as well as for a real place to go to for education, whether formal or aesthetic-cultural.

During the 19th century, even after the political independence from Europe had been long won for the USA, the practice of intellectuals and artists of going to Europe for a great *Bildungsreise* continued to blossom. Writers and other cultural operators instituted the practice of voluntary and temporary expatriation which was crucial in the construction of the 'Lost Generation' ethos and writings. By the beginning of the 20th century there were various motives for this choice of location for the practicing of one's art, including sentimental longings for a more original artistic 'climate', overt protests at the home-grown provincialism of America and American thought and ideas, and more pragmatic choices dictated by economic considerations, publishing strategies, or strategies of acquiring suitably 'other' raw material for writing. A figure like Ernest Hemingway seems to combine all of the above reasons in his choices of exile/expatriation. We shall take our point of departure for an investigation of images of Europe in generational texts in his novel *The Sun Also Rises*.

However, one thing is to go into exile, another is to write about it. How do we get from the writer being located in a foreign locale to even talking about a representation of this place as something different from any other textual construct? How is foreign place or even place as such present in texts?

J. Gerald Kennedy has a preliminary discussion of this problematic in his *Imagining Paris: Exile, Writing, and American Identity* (1993). The beginning of the solution of the problem of representation lies in this observation, for Kennedy:

> A real environment becomes intelligible - and comparable - only after it enters language as an instance of place; yet as geographical theorists have suggested, all conceptions of place are inherently and inescapably subjective. (Kennedy, 1993: 5)

Thus we have the statement that place is an intangible construct until it enters discourse, and only after it has done so can we compare this construct of language with other constructs, whether they be of place, time or an emotion. Can one then compare the language construct of place with the 'real' place? According to contemporary theories of signification and language the answer is no. Kennedy:

> [T]he notion of place implies the projection of human sensibility upon the natural or built environment. Hence one cannot compare an "actual" place with its literary representation, since there is literally no "place" apart from an interpreting consciousness. The only possible comparison for the critic is thus between a personal, readerly concept of place (perhaps informed by knowledge of an existent site) and a textual, writerly image. (5)

In other words we are left with language constructs on different levels as the only material for comparisons of place and for interpretation of place. If we wish to represent place as writers, we engage in a process of representation first as readers, then as writers. If we want to interpret place we are automatically readers. Kennedy sums up:

> This distinction forces a rethinking of the status of literary topography, for the salient difference lies not in the relation between real and fictive environments

> but between textual scenes and the symbolic experiences of place which they inscribe. (5)

Thus representations of place are safely relocated back in the textual universe where the interpreter can bask in connotative and denotative decoding of signs, which activity can be supplied with a superstructure of mythological interpretation or psychological interpretation as one sees fit (Kennedy suggests: "Perhaps every textual construction of place implies just such a mapping or symbolic re-presentation of an interior terrain" (5-6). If anyone is reminded of the so-called pathetic fallacy, which sees place and other 'natural' phenomena as metaphors for psychological states, whether of authors or of characters, this is not surprising). What remains is that a reading strategy which treats representations of place as over-determined textual sites is possible and often fruitful. This paper performs analyses that amply document this claim by not focusing on characterization or thematic analysis as one might expect from the generic perspective of the *Bildungsroman* (of which the generational novel is a subcategory), but on these apparently marginal textual loci. This incidentally suits the present writer's predilection for taking the long way around and looking for the devil in the detail.

Thomas Carmichael discusses the general question of representation of place, specifically the city, in postmodern texts in his article, "Buffalo/Baltimore, Athens/Dallas: John Barth, Don DeLillo and the Cities of Postmodernism" (*The Canadian Review of American Studies*, Fall 1991, vol. 22, No. 2: 241–249). As his subtitle indicates he does not discuss generational writers, but his observations still have some validity for the works of such generational authors of the 1980s and 1990s as Bret Easton Ellis, Jay McInerney and Douglas Coupland. Carmichael agrees with Kennedy that "the setting as metaphor is a function of the discourse within which it is situated" (241). The discourse of generationality, I would argue, determines the choice of setting in surprising ways, as I have tried to outline in the above list of typical localities, and as I will try to document in the ensuing analyses.

Carmichael continues in a discussion of some ambiguities specific for postmodern textual representations of place:

> Barth [in "The Spirit of Place" from *The Friday Book: Essays and Other Nonfiction* (1984), BS] insists, that the proper function of the trope of place in contemporary fiction is to be found in postmodern reconciliation of competing claims: "realism and anti-realism, linearity and nonlinearity, continuity and discontinuity". (241)

This is alignable with Ihab Hassan's

> [A]ssertion of a postmodern "ambilectic" or the "double tendency" of postmodernism to celebrate indeterminacy on the one hand and immanence on the other, though the latter is often an ultimately despairing chase through the empty signs of a hyper-real and thoroughly commodified culture. (242)

The feeling of being lead a "chase" as a reader is recognizable as a response to both the cityscapes of Ellis and McInerney and the culturalized landscapes of Douglas Coupland. However, whereas Ellis plumps on the side of indeterminacy and despair (after all "Everything means less than zero"), Coupland oscillates towards the side of a belief in the immanence to the extent where he transcends (or regresses from) these postmodern positions in the representation of place.

Thus in postmodernist texts we find surprising contradictions in the use of representation in general and specifically representations of place, but the basic metaphoricity of place is maintained, and even foregrounded within a postmodern stylistics: "[T]he site of the narrative unfolding is always the sign and context of a particular postmodern attitude" (241), namely the context that "in postmodern fiction we also confront the ironic encoding of the city as a positive site of resistance to the master tropes of cultural authority" (241). Again we are reminded of Ellis (specifically in *American Psycho*) and McInerney's labyrinthic cityscapes in which anything can happen, but nothing usually does.

Images of Europe: from Bohemia to Eurotrash

Ernest Hemingway's *The Sun Also Rises* is readable as an oscillation between the city as a Bohemian trap which foregrounds the impotence and futility of the characters' lives, and the country or village settings which foreground the freedom from sexual pressure and relative happiness of the characters, specifically Jake Barnes. J. Gerald Kennedy has given a very detailed reading of how places in Paris are located with specific degrees of sexual significance in the mating rituals of Jake and Brett (and her other lovers). Here it suffices to say that Paris in general serves to remind Jake on numerous different levels of his wound and incapability of attaining sexual completeness. Kennedy sums up the scene where Brett is joined by Mike in Paris, and where she is the centre of attention at the Select (*The Sun Also Rises*, 84–86):

> This third scene in the Select crystallizes a meaning inherent in the previous two: that as a centre of libidinal activity, a scene of erotic intrigue, Montparnasse recurrently forces upon Jake the realization that he is out of the game, relegated to a spectatorial role, excluded from the sexual play unfolding around him. (Kennedy, 1993: 115)

Thus Paris becomes a metaphoric locus for the frustrated libido of Jake Barnes. However, Jake has the means of sublimating this frustration into *aficion* for various manly pursuits. This is first seen when he goes on a fishing trip into the Basque country with Bill Gorton. The transition from city to country is described in loving detail, as are the workings of the financial transactions with the local population. The bus ride is described as a slow progression towards the top of the mountain crest, through a forest and then revealing the sight of:

> [T]he red roofs and white houses of Burguete ahead strung out on the plain, and away off on the shoulder of the first dark mountain was the grey metal-sheathed roof of the monastery of Roncesvalles.
> 'There's Roncevaux,' I said. (Hemingway, 1926: 113–114)

This is the first glimpse of the scene of the future male bonding between Jake and Bill, and the geography of a potential, promised "away off on the shoulder" monasterial peace and insight into matters beclouded by the pressures of Paris. The first night in Burguete functions as a form of purification for Jake and Bill, because of the unexpected cold they encounter. Bill comments six times on the climate in the space of three pages, and it is only with the help of the ministrations of the local food and drink and a warm bed that the Americans struggle through the first night. After this rite they wake up, in a purer state of mind, to a good day of talking and fishing. Here Jake's rod is inspected by a *gendarme*, who when questioned "Is that all right?" replies "Yes. Of course" (115). This is something that cannot normally be said about Jake's impotent "rod", so the purification has well and truly begun.

This scene is followed by a comic interlude where Bill dazzles Jake with a number of language jokes that presuppose a current knowledge of the American literary and cultural scene. Jake has a hard time with some of the references, and Bill satirizes Jake's ignorance in terms of his being an expatriate:

> 'Don't you read? Don't you ever see anybody? You know what you are? You're an expatriate. Why don't you live in New York? Then you'd know these things. What do you want me to do? Come over here and tell you every year?' [...]
>
> 'You're an expatriate. You've lost touch with the soil. You get precious. Fake European standards have ruined you'. (120)

The point is of course that Bill does not mean these evaluations, but is just parodying American attitudes of original belonging ("You have lost touch with the soil"), attitudes that were current in the debate of the '20s over whether expatriatism would not lead to a loss of American identity. And still further the point is that, when spoken in these surroundings where, if anything, the two Americans are in touch with the soil and are not being "spoiled" by anybody's standards, other than possibly their own, Bill's words are shown to represent false fears. Europe figured as the primitive, but pure pleasure-haven of Burguete is better for Jake than anyplace else. The provincial restraints of New York are referred to later by Bill: "Listen. You're a hell of a good guy, and I'm fonder of you than anybody on earth. I couldn't tell you that in New York. It'd mean I was a faggot" (121). Thus Europe is shown to be liberating for the emotional bonding between the two men, yet the bonding and tranquility is also later shown to be temporary and transient.

A darker image of Europe is that conjured up by the circumstances of Jake's wounding during the first World War. The scene of the wounding occurs "flying on a joke front like the Italian. In the Italian hospital we were going to form a society. It had a funny name in Italian" (38). This reiteration of the word "Italian" and its persistent linkage to something funny or jokey is highly significant to the general thematics of the novel. Here it is clear that Italian, both as language and topography is being bitterly ridiculed, which comes to a climax in the speech given to Jake by an Italian colonel: "'You, a foreigner, an Englishman' (any foreigner was an Englishman) 'have given more than your life'" (39). Thus, the Italians are stereotyped as having little sense of the reality principle, but a lot of sense for drama - another unserious trait, linked to the jokey-ness of this European locus.

After the ugly scenes of jealousy in Pamplona, Jake once again retreats from the company of his friends and spends some time recuperating and swimming in San Sebastian. This locality is figured thus:

> Even on a hot day San Sebastian has a certain early-morning quality. The trees seem as though their leaves were never quite dry. The streets feel as

though they have just been sprinkled. It is always cool and shady on certain streets on the hottest day. I went to a hotel [...] There was a green mountainside beyond the roofs. Spain had not changed to summer-time, so I was early. I set my watch again. I had recovered an hour by coming to San Sebastian. (237–238)

Thus the locality of San Sebastian is figured in metaphors of renewal and recovery. Everything is fresh, cool, shady and "early" or more primordial than the previous locale frequented by Barnes. The mountainside that harbored the monastery of Roncevalles reappears symbolically green, beckoning here to Jake, holding out a promise of redemption.

Nevertheless it is also a Spanish locality that signals the next descent into hell for Jake, when he goes to fetch Brett after the failure of her relationship with Romero: "The Norte station in Madrid is the end of the line. All trains finish there. They don't go on anywhere" (244). Similarly Madrid is the end of the line for Jake and Brett. They cannot go on, and yet they go on. Their relationship ends in a taxi, as it re-commenced within the telling of the novel in a cab scene in Paris. Thus the two large European cities become connected and both aligned with the impotence and frustration that Brett brings out in Jake. The "mounted policeman" in the final cab scene in Madrid signals to Jake that no matter how many times he fetches Brett out of trouble he can never again rise to the occasion: "He raised his baton" (251). A simple act that the impotent Jake can never repeat, which triggers his bitter rejection of redeemed love between him and Brett.

Thus, images of Europe in Hemingway's novel have a number of possible polarities, either as the originator of a jokey tragedy, or of a confining impotence (there are many things about Paris that make Jake very angry), or of a potential healing free space, positively contrasted with American narrowness. These complex valorizations of European localities, explicitly contrasted with more unambiguous negative valorizations of America, are typical of the early 20th century representations of Europe as Bohemian free spaces, with all the attendant psychological complications this can raise in the American mind.

Jack Kerouac's novel *On the Road* is completely circumscribed by motion on the American continents, and thus contains no scenes where characters are portrayed in a European setting. Nevertheless images of Europe play a small but pivotal role in the novel. At the dead centre of the novel, Sal Paradise, who has hitherto followed blindly where Dean Moriarty leads him in his mad pursuit of 'kicks', takes over as director of events. Dean has come to yet another end of a relationship, and the boys "racked our brains for where to go and what to do" (Kerouac, 1957: 178), when Sal has an epiphany: "I realized it was up to me. [...] 'I have here the sum of eighty-three dollars and change, and if you come with me let's go to New York - and after that let's go to Italy'" (178).

This proposal sparks off a moment of crisis between the two friends. Dean the con-man now has to decide whether he will trust Sal enough to follow him to Italy, and be in his care and keep. Sal reiterates the proposal in the following terms: "'We'll go dig all the crazy women in Rome, Paris, all those places; we'll sit at sidewalk cafés; we'll live in whorehouses. Why not go to Italy?'" (178) Thus it is clear that for Sal (in order to sell the idea of going there to Dean) Europe is linked (in positively Hemingway-esque terms) with sexuality, women and specifically whores. Europe is a sexualized locus, one of leisure and pleasure – at a price, of course: "'I'll make some money, I'll get a thousand dollars from the publishers'" (178). No Europe without paying the dues, much the same way Barnes found Europe: "It felt comfortable to be in a country where it is so simple to make people happy. [...] Everything is on such a clear financial basis in France. [...] If you want people to like you you have only to spend a little money" (Hemingway, 1926: 237). A simple place to be an American, indeed. The preoccupations of Americans with how Europeans relate to money is a recurrent feature in several other fictional representations of Europe as we shall see.

We turn now to another of Kerouac's texts to see images of Europe, playing themselves out in representations of actual European loci. In 1966 Kerouac published a short account of his voyage to France to search for his mythic Celtic ancestry, entitled *Satori in Paris*. The book claims to be autobiographical, but is indistinguishable from his usual fictional style of writing, with the exception that he uses his real name for the protagonist. The book depicts the disorientation Kerouac experiences when he arrives in Paris and is given wrong directions by the natives, whom he insists on addressing in Quebec French, which he claims is the authentic, preserved French "still understood in the streets of Paris" (Kerouac, 1966: 7). In a touching but hilarious scene, Kerouac describes how he is sitting in a church, hat in hand, listening to music, when "a woman with kids and husband comes by and lays twenty centime (4¢) in my poor tortured misunderstood hat (which I was holding upsidedown in awe)" (6). Wherever he goes in his supposedly native land, speaking his supposedly native original tongue, he is misunderstood and misguided.

The disappointment comes to a head, in a scene that again combines money matters and fears with sex:

> I get so mad I go down to the whore districts. A million Apaches with daggers are milling around. I go in a hallway and I see three ladies of the night. I announce with an evil English leer *'Sh'prend la belle brunette'* (I take the pretty brunette) - The brunette rubs her eyes, throat, ears and heart and says 'I aint gonna have that no more.' I stomp away and take out my Swiss Army knife with the cross on it, because I suspect I'm being followed by French muggers and thugs. I cut my own finger and bleed all over the place. (14)

Kerouac's own paranoia leads him into this scenario where a combination of high pathos and low comedy ensues. It turns out not to be so simple to have a clear-cut financial transaction with the French, let alone negotiate the whore-houses of Europe. The text ends with a similar bitter and confused sneer: "So here we are in Paris. All's over. From now on I am finished with any and all forms of Paris life" (113). Still, he came for a 'satori' (Buddhist enlightenment), and have one he will, even if he has to have it in the taxi towards the airport. The encounter with "The Satori taxidriver of page one" (116) ends with this exchange where the cabbie says: "But, work, yes, yowsah, this and that, or as you say Monsieur thissa and thatta, in any case, thanks, be of good heart, I'm going" (116). This mock epiphany or 'satori' is finally what Paris had to give Kerouac. Thus we see an emptying out of even the representation of the language spoken by the Europeans in this text. The American is depicted as seriously, but confusedly questing for origin and originality, but frustrated in this search by the very strangeness of the original language of Europe, of Paris. The response is that inimitable mix of denial and claimed immanence that Hassan referred to in our theoretical preamble, although this late Kerouac effort can no longer maintain a convincing case for immanence, despite all the surface similarities between the cabbie's talk (and driving skills) and that of Dean Moriarty.

The literary topography of the 'Blank Generation' writers is remarkably free of images of Europe. Their USA is very much a world of its own, and it is only in McInerney's *Ransom* that the setting is relegated to a locality outside the States. In Bret Easton Ellis' *The Rules of Attraction* we do, however, have a sort of memoir of a trip to Europe, almost vomited up by a minor character, named Victor, in an apparently interminable, affectless monologue (Ellis, 1987: 24–27). This instance prefigures depictions of "Eurothrash" in the '90s novels and songs we shall examine later. To Victor it matters little what he sees or does, or with whom, let alone who does what to him, whether it be molestation by an old man, or attack by dogs. This character is confused about geography and languages as well as the whereabouts of friends and acquaintances, whom he may be "sort of in love with" (25). European localities are dismissed in short, declarative sentences with very limited vocabulary: "Rome was big and hot and dirty" (26) or "That's all I did in Crete, was walk" (27). In short Europe is not really represented as a locus, as much as images of the prejudices of the character who goes there, and who is conclusively represented as American.

Caveney states, in summation, about Ellis' use of place and of his representations of otherness, specifically in his first novel:

> *Less Than Zero* features no Europeans, and only Clay is allowed to present himself with the distance of the outsider. The novel's location is as fragmented as its narrative, set in parties, clubs, sushi bars and cafés. These settings are linked by car journeys rather than any real sense of place; a spatial blankness which, as Elizabeth Young points out, mirrors the characters' ethical emptiness. (Young & Caveney, 1992: 124)

This, of course, begs the question of what a "real sense of place" might be, since the best we can expect are texts about place, as we established in the introductory remarks to this chapter. None the less, the observation that Ellis uses representations of place to signal symptomatics of his characters' emptiness is astute.

Of the 'X' generational novels, by far the most fertile ground for European representations is found in Douglas Coupland's second novel *Shampoo Planet*. The strategy of this novel is to transfer the generational focus of *Generation X* from the generation born from 1961–1965, to the somewhat younger siblings of these cohorts. The protagonists of *Shampoo Planet* are the group that was featured as 'global teens' or the 'poverty jet-set' ("Poverty Jet-set: A group of people given to chronic traveling at the expense of long-term job stability or a permanent residence" (Coupland, 1991: 6)) in *Generation X*.

The main character is named Tyler, a name he shares with Andy, the narrator of *Generation X*'s younger brother. Tyler has been to Europe, much to the puzzlement of his surroundings ("'Europe? I don't get it,' said Harmony. 'We have a perfectly good Europe here at EPCOT in Florida. It's not good enough or something?'" (Coupland, 1993: 96)), where he has had a summer affair with Stephanie, a French girl, who has now decided to visit Tyler in America. The problem is that Tyler has a girl friend, the all-American girl, Anna-Louise, who does not know anything about Tyler's fling in France.

Thus the scene is set for a romantic comedy. What concerns us here are scenes set in Europe, told in flashback by Tyler, and scenes where the Europeans enter into intercultural encounters with the American protagonists in Washington.

First we shall investigate Tyler's incomprehensible longing for a European experience. He himself relates it to a dream of Europe holding a complex set of keys to understanding himself and his own country:

> I had my reasons. I remember peddling my fake watches and wondering what sort of land would make the real watches. And I wanted to see what sort of world my ancestors found so intolerable they needed to leave. And I'd heard reports Europe was the total place for partying. (96)

The elements in this triptych of reasons are telling and familiar. The desire for first-hand experience is common for all three and an important part of a cultural symptomatic of second-handness often experienced by characters in postmodern American fiction. The quest for the land of the real watches, can be seen as a specific symptom of this curiosity for the original, here specifically the cradle of not only precision technology (something Tyler almost reveres), but also the cradle of brand name technology. The desire to see the wellsprings of the ancestral gene pool is a reversal of the quest for originality, since the ancestors were forced to pack up and leave, and therefore their origin must be couched in unpleasantness. Still Tyler has another project later in the novel, concerning finding his biological father, an unreformed hippie, so the drive back toward your genetic *Ursprung* is not accidental as a motive for going to Europe. Thirdly, the desire for Europe as a sexual and (im)moral haven is what remains for the post-'X'ers of the Bohemian desire of previous generations of expats. However, there is yet another motive behind Tyler's migration:

> In general I remember thinking how modern and snappy Europe appeared in photos: lively tinkling geometric buildings sprouting like crystals from the tedious stone drabness below. Europe seemed like a place where the future was advancing more rapidly than in Lancaster, and I love the future, so that was *that*. Funward ho. (96)

Thus, Europe is being figured here as growing out of its age and "tedious stone drabness", striving towards the future, towards modernity. Being enamored with the future is the one specific trait of Tyler's that sets him apart from the future terrified and apocalyptically paranoid characters of

Generation X. Perhaps it is not surprising then, that Tyler is about to be disappointed in both his own time, his potential future, and Europe:

> But after three weeks of Eurailing, Europe's patina of modernity was dulling considerably. Europe tries to be so modern, but the effort always sort of, well ... *flops*. Germany, to the country's credit, is higher-tech than the inside of a CD player, but their platform toilets are like a torture device straight out of the Inquisition. France has never heard of Sunday shopping. And in Belgium I saw a nuclear cooling tower with *moss* growing on its convex northern slope. Modern? (96)

These amusing cultural symptomatics, which mean that Tyler loses his illusions about Europe, indicate the values Tyler associates with modernity: creature comforts, shopping opportunities and the maintenance of outward appearances. Europe's true state of evolution is thus revealed as a mere "patina of modernity", an interesting oxymoron in itself. Deeper than even that is the sneaking *post festum* awareness that is pressing itself upon Tyler after he comes 'home' that Europe is infested by American corporate interests, whose omnipresent logos he afterwards discovers in all his snapshots. Thus the future is not what it is cracked up to be, and maybe it is really all the Americans' fault anyway.

The disillusionment that spreads in Tyler over the state of Europe, comes to a head in transit from Denmark to France, where Tyler observes about a Belgian landscape, marred by a nuclear plant: "I had never seen a landscape in which human beings seemed so irrelevant" (99). Europe seems filled by "graves of dead Europeans of old". It seems a clear case of History Poisoning, as described at length in *Generation X*. Fortunately there is redemption on the way, figured thus: "Right then I knew I wanted to return home, but as fate would operate, before I was able to create new plans, I arrived in Paris" (100).

This over-determined entry into Paris can only lead to trouble, as we already know it will. This figuring of Paris as a form of "moveable feast" à la Hemingway is borne out in the following. Tyler heads for the *Pére-Lachaise* cemetery on a mission for his sister to steal a flower from Jim Morrison's grave. This banal quest for a relic of another generation's culture hero is, however, only incidental to Tyler's experience in the graveyard. He has his own private epiphany at the grave of another exile; not of an American cultural icon, but rather that of Oscar Wilde, the Irish wit and aesthete, where Tyler performs the following rite:

> I stripped myself of my shirt and leaned against the stone, suntanning, bagging what diminishing rays there were to be had from the clouded sun. I sniffled with hay fever; I turned my head around and licked the dusty stone. I surprise even myself on occasion. (103)

What penetrates Tyler during this rite and what he takes in through his lick remain open questions (the tongue kissing of the marble edifice representing the celebrated homosexual, Wilde, of course indicates the same type of ambiguity surrounding a Coupland protagonist as the one we encounter in a main character in *Generation X* - Dag(mar), who is "a lesbian trapped in a man's body"), but the communion with the European exile rather than the American one is surely significant in itself. Tyler leaves the cemetery primed for conquest:

> Our browned exposed limbs popping out of our khakis and T-shirts and our puppy-dog naïveté were our true passports from the New World that afternoon as we entered the real world - our passports and our armour as we entered the jaded, elegant hysteria of Paris. (105)

These positions of liminality and transition operate with some standard ascriptions, for instance that the visitor to Europe bears innocence with him or her, is a version of a rugged individualist with "browned limbs", and comes bearing something 'New' with him or her. (The quote tonally echoes Kerouac's narrator in *On the Road*: "Somewhere along the line I knew there'd be girls, visions, everything; somewhere along the line the pearl would be handed to me" (Kerouac 1957: 11)). Further the 'Old World' Paris is figured as inscrutable, classy and - interestingly – hysterical. No wonder one has to be armored against it (and preferably pass for Canadian, rather than American).

Paris changes Tyler's life, and that first night it figures as a free space for him offering him liquor, sexual encounters and apparently unlimited freedom to do what he wishes, including redefining his future. Then he meets Stephanie, who semiotically has all these significations transferred to her person, and Tyler falls in love:

> I saw these lips smile and poke out the window saying "'allo" to me but I was then also momentarily transfixed by the glinting bistro lights reflected on the onyx skin of Stephanie's car. Yes [...] they looked just like the stars. I think there is a Paris inside us all. (107)

Thus the lips of Stephanie melt into the lights of the bistro, and the paint of her car melts into a "skin", and the bistro lights melt into the cosmic light of the stars. In that moment Paris is one big throbbing cosmic body, both outside Tyler's own body and "inside" it. Paris is, thus, indeed a moveable feast, which Tyler seals by kissing its/her/Stephanie's lips.

Of course, there is Hell to pay, which Tyler realizes long after the separation from Stephanie and Paris, when she decides to return to his life as so much inadequately recycled Eurotrash. In Coupland's book this is the figure of choice for both Europeans visiting America and Americans visiting Europe, and also for what they might find there. The term 'Eurotrash' seems to be a bricolage from airline ticketing language, where 'Euroclass' is what you fly if you can afford it, whereas 'Eurotrash' then must be the opposite. A form of rhyming slang. The term is symptomatic of a change in the attitudes to things European, exemplified by the one that Tyler undergoes in the course of the novel, and also of a broader change in American ways of figuring Europe's older cultural tradition. As far as I can trace this sensibility, that Europe may be old, but at the same time it is decaying, it was first expressed by Bob Dylan in his song "When I Paint My Masterpiece" which depicts an American in Europe running through very much the same gamut of fear and loathing as Tyler. The key line of the song is "The streets of Rome are filled with rubble", which in a typical Dylanesque ambiguity, both encompasses a critique of cultural tourism à la the one Tyler is later performing, and a critique of the oldness and decay which Europe is trying to pass off as culture to the traveling American observer/cultural agent.

"Eurotrash" made its debut in print in Ellis' *American Psycho* (Ellis 1991: 41), but finds by far its fullest literary use in *Shampoo Planet*. It is also a neologism used in other pop-cultural products, my favorite of which is the rock band Cracker's song "Eurotrash Girl" (1993), a third similar travelogue of an American in Europe, bumming around, selling his plasma, and looking for that elusive all-black wardrobed "Eurotrash Girl" ("Well I've been up to Paris, and I slept in a park. And I'll search the world over, for my angel in black, I'll search the world over – for a Eurotrash girl"). In Coupland's novel there are several occurrences of "Euro-compounds" such as the already quoted "Eurailing", "Europals", "Euronuggets", "Euroweeks", etc., etc., all sharing the element of "Euro-ness" fused to well-known nouns. But the most recurrent and significant one is clearly "Eurotrash", as in "[W]e would [...] watch the sun set over Paris from the rooftop of the Pompidou, afterward descending to the Eurotrash-clogged piazza below to taunt the mimes and watch the digital clock that counts down the seconds to year 2000" (110). The motion described by the quote of someone descending to watch the possible apocalyptic countdown to the millennium is indicative of Tyler's ascent once he meets Stephanie. He is elevated from ordinary touristhood, and plucked out of the Eurotrash. The opposite motion is to be played out in the second half of the novel.

Needless to say, Anna-Louise finds out about Tyler and Stephanie and Tyler is thrown out of his hometown's security and dragged along on Stephanie's ambitious trek to Los Angeles to become a celebrity. The intercultural clash between the two love interests in Tyler's life is of course figured largely as a clash of European snobbery and class consciousness versus American provincialism tempered with ruthless honesty. Anna-Louise: "I wore my nicest dress over for dinner last night to meet these Eurotramps, and you know what she asked me? She asked me what I wear when I want to dress up. What a cow" (120). Tyler begins to figure his own personality development as a descent into a spiral of lies and deceit, and links it with his sojourn in Europe: "Why am I becoming this human being I am? I wasn't like that before I visited Europe. Is Dan [his step-father] what I am slated to become? Him? Scary" (126). Thus Europe is the scene of the fall for Tyler in this figuration.

When Stephanie finally leaves him in Los Angeles he hits rock bottom, becoming a street person, before finding redemption through a novel idea of his ("making wax-crayon rubbings of the brass celebrity stars inlaid on the sidewalks of Hollywood Boulevard" (254)). This saves him long enough to get further redeemed by apparently realizing his childhood dream of entering yuppiedom through a job offer from a multinational corporation. The redemption is figured thus in the novel:

> I cry because the future has once again found its sparkle and has grown a million times larger. And I cry because I am ashamed of how badly I have treated the people I love [...] back before I had a future and someone who cared for me from above. It is like today the sky opened up and only now am I allowed to enter. (274)

Not incidentally this motion through overconfidence, through betrayal and punishment back to Heaven's gate is also inscribed in the peculiar paratext to *Shampoo Planet*, which consists of two sets of homemade periodical systems giving the tables of the elements of a 1990s accelerated culture. In the last of the two systems the first element is "1 H - Heaven" and the last in the layout is "103 Rx - Redemption", although of course there are 106 elements as in the real periodical system. The final three read "Me - U - Lg" or 2Me - You - Light", also indicative of a narrative development at the end of the book, where "the cool clear light of the moon" (298) illuminates the floor of Anna-Louise's apartment. Tyler and her are getting back together again, *"the world is alive"* (299) are the last words whispered by Tyler to her. There is again a me and you.

   Tyler has thus been cured of his Euro-fascination, and found redemption in his hometown. It seems that in contradiction of Thomas Wolfe you *can* go home again in this regressive fiction. The final showdown between Stephanie as Euro-representative and Tyler is a heated argument, where Tyler lashes out at Stephanie as an index of Europe: "Why don't you take your strange class hatred and phobias and lug them back to your cramped, futureless little country?" (243) Here Tyler stereotypes France and Europe as such in terms of size (America is a BIG country) and lack of true democracy ("class hatred"), but most significantly in terms of who has a future and who has not. He elaborates in an apology:

> It's just that all of your history in Europe is so seductive. [...] History tricks you into not valuing what you have now. History's dead, but right now is *alive*. History is jealous of right now – jealous of that life. (243)

This is the crucial operation separating Europe from Tyler's future-secured America. Note how Stephanie as index of Europe, and the one actually doing the seduction of Tyler so successfully, becomes aligned with Europe, which thereby is gendered in this construct. Of course she also betrays him, as history did, as Europe did. Only through his self-reliance does he regain the bright glittering future he was destined for. I hope he remembers to wear sunglasses, as pop group Timbuk 3 advises in the brilliantly titled yuppie satire, *My Future's So Bright I Gotta Wear Shades*.

Conclusion

We have seen some of the images of Europe played out in generational novels of the last 70 years. There is a clear motion in the instances we have investigated. This investigation of specific images of place has highlighted the generational difference discourse, as it plays itself out with Europe being identified with 'oldness' and America and its representatives as carriers of 'newness', thus extroverting the generational agon of the characters into an intercontinental cultural battle waged over progress and progressivism. Hemingway's twenties text saw Europe as locus of a duality of freedom and entrapment, both figured within sexual as well as intellectual parameters. Europe was dangerous, wounding, but alluring. In the fifties and sixties the allure of otherness was still ascribable to Europe, but the reality of the continent with its languages and mores was unintelligible, for Kerouac at least. American solipsism and isolation was on the uptake. The glittering yuppie characters of the '80s saw no reason to go to a tired old continent, when after all, the best manufacturers of brand name merchandize were already busy migrating the opposite way, from Europe to America. When the '90s inaugurated a new sensibility and a rediscovery of the *Bildungsreise* via Eurail, we surprisingly saw stereotyped images of Europe as a femme fatale metaphor resurface and play themselves out in Coupland's text as a complete reworking of *Pilgrim's Progress*, with the American hero finally coming home, liberating himself of history and its trash, finding himself, and thereby re-invigorating the whole world.

References:

Barth, John (1984) *The Friday Book: Essays and Other Nonfiction*. Baltimore and London: Johns Hopkins University Press

Carmichael, Th. (1991) "Buffalo/Baltimore, Athens/Dallas: John Barth, Don DeLillo and the cities of Postmodernism". *The Canadian Review of American Studies*. Fall 1991. Vol. 22. No. 2

Coupland, Douglas (1991) *Generation X*. St. Martin's Press, New York

Coupland, Douglas (1993) *Shampoo Planet*. London: Simon & Schuster

Cracker (1993) "Eurotrash Girl". On *Kerosene Hat*. Virgin Records CD

Dylan, Bob (1971) "When I Paint My Masterpiece". On *Bob Dylan's Greatest Hits. Vol. 2*. Sony Music CD

Ellis, Bret Easton (1985) *Less Than Zero*. London: Picador

Ellis, Bret Easton (1987) *The Rules of Attraction*. London: Penguin

Ellis, Bret Easton (1991) *American Psycho*. London: Picador

Hemingway, Ernest (1926) *The Sun Also Rises*. New York: Scribner Paperback Fiction

Hemingway, Ernest (1964) *A Moveable Feast*. New York: Bantam Books

Kennedy, J. Gerald (1993) *Imagining Paris: Exile, Writing, and American Identity*. New Haven & London: Yale University Press
Kerouac, Jack (1957) *On The Road*. London: Penguin
Kerouac, Jack (1966) *Satori in Paris*. London: Quartet Books
McInerney, Jay (1985) *Ransom*. New York: Vintage Books
Timbuk 3 (1990) "Future's So Bright, I Gotta Wear Shades". On *Greetings from Timbuk 3*. MCA CD
Young, Elizabeth & Caveney, Graham (1992) *Shopping In Space: Essays on American "Blank Generation" Fiction*. London & New York: Serpent's Tail

The Idea of Europe in Selected American World History Textbooks

Dovile Budryte and Charles Perrin

The goal of this essay is to analyze the treatment of Europe within the mode of historical discourse known as world history. Although there is no one universally accepted definition of world history it is increasingly understood as a field that, instead of merely recounting the stories of political entities known as "nations" or "civilizations", encompasses the stories of "past connections in the human community" (Manning, 2003: 15). The concept of "civilization" (traditionally the main unit within the study of world history) has come under scrutiny as well. In a recent book Felipe Fernández-Armesto defines civilization, not as a state or political-religious tradition, but as "a style of life" (Manning, 2003: 99). In addition to changes in how world history and civilization are defined the writing of world history has also changed, with the "triumphant symphony of European moral supremacy" being replaced by "a querulous cacophony of regional diversity and global interdependence" (von Glahn, 2003: 56).

To make some sense of this "querulous cacophony" several attempts at classification have been made. For example, Patrick Manning has argued that numerous publications in world history since 1990 fit into four categories: area-study approaches, thematic studies, conceptual studies at the global level, and studies that attempt to establish linkages between world history and European and American history (2003). Area-study approaches tend to embrace case study methodology, paying attention to the historical connections between regions. Thematic approaches focus on politics, economy, society, religion, ecology, and other aspects of world history. Conceptual studies explore the waves of globalization and the structure of global politics by paying attention to theory.

Approaches falling within the fourth category try to establish a relationship between the West (i.e., Europe and North America) and the rest. Until recently, there was a strong tendency to connect European and American history to world history by telling the story of the global past through a Western prism. Manning describes such a tendency as "Eurocentrism" – the idea that "history outside 'the West' was the story of Westerners staying away from home, or the history of Western impact on other areas of the world" (2003: 101). Although frowned upon in academic circles, this approach continues to be very popular in history textbooks. At the same time, according to Manning, few studies have managed to connect European and American history to world history successfully (2003).

If Manning is right, then the Eurocentric bias in the writing and teaching of world is unlikely to disappear any time soon. Richard von Glahn, a prominent scholar of Chinese history, also suggests that the Eurocentric bias in the writing of world history has persisted. Pre-modern China in world history discourse, for example, is sometimes still portrayed as a stagnant society and an "oriental despotism".

Von Glahn identifies five basic orientations in world history: the stimulus-diffusion approach, European exceptionalism, the European hegemony model, counter-hegemony, and the regional networks approach. He emphasizes that most world history writing does not fit neatly into any one of these categories and in fact tends to combine several of them. The stimulus-diffusion approach uses an anthropological model of stimulus and diffusion to explain the interactions of various civilizations. It has drawn attention to a wide variety of agents of historical change: long-distance trade and travel; the diffusion of technology; transfers of plants, animals, and diseases; imperial expansion; and missionary activity. Von Glahn believes that one of the most important contributions of the stimulus-diffusion approach has been "to push back the horizons of an integrated global history well before the expansion of Europe launched by the Iberian sailors in the fifteenth century" (von Glahn, 2003: 58).

European exceptionalism is the belief that Europe had some quality deeply rooted in its heritage – environment (temperate climate), society (feudal class structure), demography (nuclear families with low birth rates), knowledge (rationality and a belief in progress), or government (a competitive multi-state system) – that explains its dominance after 1500. One of the leading proponents of this approach is E.L. Jones, author of *The European Miracle*. In his search for the origins of European dominance Jones goes all the way back to the medieval period when Europe's distinctive pattern of kinship, demography, and property, along with a competitive multi-state system, emerged. These qualities conferred certain advantages on Europeans which, according to Jones, they were later able to exploit in the modern period. The advantage of a competitive multi-state system, for example, is that it eroded political constraints on innovation and encouraged the diffusion of technology and methods of organization.

The European hegemony approach attributes the rise of Europe not to cultural or economic factors intrinsic to Europe, but to the formation of a world-system by which powerful European nations imposed an international division of labor on weaker societies, thereby enabling them to extract a greater portion of global wealth. The chief proponents of this approach are Immanuel Wallerstein and Fernand Braudel.

The counter-hegemony approach reduces Europe to a marginal province within the world system. According to several scholars, such as Janet Abu-Lughod and Andre Gunder Frank, during the thirteenth century the world system was Eurasian, and it was shattered by the break up of the Mongol empire and the ruinous effects of the Black Death.

Finally, the regional networks approach suggests that parallel phenomena took place in Eurasia in 1500–1800. These phenomena included the growth of regionally dominant cities and the development of urban commercial classes. These trends did not have any single point of origin. In fact, they are indicative of "horizontally integrative continuities" (von Glahn, 2003: 64).

The increase in the popularity of non-Eurocentric approaches to world history reflects a change in America's identity in relation to Europe. Since the end of the Cold War, the United States has been rethinking its status and role in the world. This process is reflected in world history discourse, which, as expressed in world history textbooks, has the power of creating historical consciousness and contributing to the reconstruction of American national identity. Currently, world history is a required course at most American universities. Therefore, it is reasonable to suggest that world history discourse as expressed in the world history textbooks used in these courses is going to have at least some effect on the way that future Americans see themselves in relation to other parts of the world, including Europe.

Analyzing the ways in which Europe is treated in selected American world history textbooks may shed some light on whether (and why) American students are still being exposed to a Eurocentric view of the world.

The remainder of this essay analyzes two textbooks that are currently used in world history classes taught at the university level in the United States: *World Civilizations: Their History and Culture* (Philip Lee Ralph et al., 1997) and *Traditions & Encounters: A Global Perspective on the Past* (Bentley & Zeigler, 2003). Each case study is organized around the following questions: what is the unit of analysis within the textbook, how prominent is the "European" theme, how do the authors describe the development of European societies before 1500, how do they explain the rise of Europe after 1500, and how do the authors describe European interactions with other parts of the world?

Europe Viewed from North America

World Civilizations: Their History and Their Culture is described by its publisher as "a top choice at colleges and universities with over 400 adoptions in its eighth edition" (W.W. Norton & Company, 2005). According to the copyright page it has gone through nine editions since 1955 and even includes material from Edward M. Burns' *Western Civilizations*, first published in 1941. It is therefore not without justification that the authors of this textbook, whose living members currently hale from universities in North America, call it a "classic" (Philip Lee Ralph et al., 1997: 1; xiii).

The first volume starts with a description of the "earliest beginnings" of humankind and traces the steps, such as the emergence of villages and long-distance trade in western Asia during the period 6500 to 3500–3000 B.C.E., in the evolution toward "civilization". The authors use a geographical area study approach. Consequently, the chapters span the globe, covering the Mesopotamian civilization, ancient Egypt, the Hebrew and early Greek civilizations, ancient Indian civilization, ancient Chinese civilization, ancient Greece, the Roman civilization, the rise of Christianity, Islam, Byzantium, and the early medieval Western world. The textbook ends with a description of the early modern world focusing on the Renaissance and Reformation in early modern Europe.

In the preface, the authors explain the reasoning behind the broad scope of the book: "Our effort throughout this ninth edition has been to enhance the book's coverage of the non-Western world, to draw out comparisons and connections between civilizations where apt, in short, *to strengthen the global dimension of the book*" (Ralph et al., 1997: 1; xiii, our emphasis). For the ninth edition, sections on China, Africa, Japan, Latin America, South Asia, and the Middle East were "substantially revised" to include descriptions of "social and economic institutions, the status of women, literature and philosophy, science and technology", and, in the case of Africa, the impact of European imperialism. Substantial changes were also made to the chapters on Europe and North America.

The authors conceptualize civilizations as entities with more or less distinct borders and even "real" characteristics. Civilization "may be defined as a stage in human organization when governmental, social, and economic institutions have developed substantially to manage (however imperfectly) the problems of order, security and efficiency in a complex society" (Ralph et al., 1997: 1; 23). Therefore, the authors argue that "civilization" was created around 3200 B.C.E. in Mesopotamia because that area had cities with social classes and that is when the Mesopotamians began to keep records.

Throughout the first volume, the authors emphasize the achievements of every civilization. The Mesopotamians "had their unattractive qualities" but "were profound thinkers" (Ralph et al., 1997: 1; 27). The ancient Egyptians "had found a way to cooperate with nature and each other in order to live in peace and self-sufficiency for centuries at a stretch" (Ralph et al., 1997: 1; 68). The Greeks "were vastly more experimental and creative" than the Egyptians (Ralph et al., 1997: 1; 68). Thus, the text creates the illusion that each civilization consisted of unified groups of people who worked together and achieved a lot together.

The construction of an image of a "European" civilization begins after a survey of the Mesopotamian, Egyptian, and Hebrew civilizations. This construction is built on a primordial understanding of identity. The authors state that the Minoan and Mycenaean civilizations "were the earliest civilizations of Europe", adding that "in some respects the Minoans and the Mycenaeans seem to have looked forward to certain later European values and accomplishments" (Ralph et al., 1997: 1; 96–97). The "worldly and progressive outlook" of the Minoans and Mycenaeans, with their devotion to "comfort and opulence... their love of amusement, zest for life, and courage for experimentation" (Ralph et al., 1997: 1; 97), therefore prefigured the values of later Europeans.

In their analysis of the Minoan and Mycenaean civilizations, the authors compare these early Europeans with various "others" (that is, the ancient Assyrians, Babylonians and ancient Egyptians). The "non-Europeans" were more warlike than the early Europeans, especially the Minoans. The authors make the latter point in their consistently eloquent way: "whereas ancient Assyria, ancient Babylon, and even ancient Egypt all breathed their last as 'corpses in armor,' ancient Crete breathed its last amid joyous festivals celebrated in cities without walls" (Ralph et al., 1997: 1; 97).

This vision of early Europe is reminiscent of the dualistic approach to transatlantic relations recently developed by Robert Kagan. Even before the second Gulf War, Kagan saw Europe as entering a "post-historical paradise of peace and relative prosperity". To him, the "other" (that is, the United States) has remained "marred in history" and war. Kagan traces the "roots" of Europe, not to the Minoans, but to the European Enlightenment (Kagan, 2002).

The authors fully develop the "European" theme in the second part of the first volume. This part is called "The World of the Classical Era". The European focus also prevails in the last two parts of the textbook. Eleven out of fifteen chapters are devoted to the "European theme". The fourth part, entitled "The Early Modern World", is devoted entirely to the rise of Europe in the early sixteenth century. The image of Europe changes from "peaceful" and "joyous" to more warlike, as "intrepid mariners and conquistadors ended Europe's millennium of self-containment (during the Middle Ages) by venturing onto the high seas of the Atlantic and Indian ocean and by planting Europe's flag throughout the world" (Ralph et al., 1997: 1; 617). Territorial expansion coincides with the Commercial Revolution which "spurs the development of overseas colonies and trade" and encourages agricultural and industrial expansion (Ralph et al., 1997: 1; 617). Why did Europeans start venturing out to far away lands? The most important reason for the commercial revolution (which brings about the "rise" of Europe) was economic. They argue that overseas expansion in the fifteenth century was fueled by the "quest for Asiatic spices and other luxury goods". Religious reasons (specifically, a desire to find "lost Christians") mattered, but they were only secondary to the economic desires of the Europeans (Ralph et al., 1997: 1; 670). To help the readers understand what the authors have perceived as the major reason behind the expansion of Europe, they ask the readers to "imagine a civilization without refrigeration". With this image in mind, "one can easily understand why wealthy Europeans hankered after tangy spices to keep their food from putrifying and to relieve the monotony of salt" (Ralph et al., 1997: 1; 670). Like E.L. Jones, the authors suggest that climate and geography played a role in the rise of Europe, especially during the initial stage of overseas expansion.

The authors maintain that the start of the overseas expansion around 1500 C.E. immensely helped the spread of capitalism by "providing marvelous opportunities for people with ability and daring to make new fortunes" (Ralph et al., 1997: 1; 676). These new entrepreneurs helped to foster the economic growth of "Europe" during the sixteenth century. However, the encounters with "Europe" during the early modern period were deadly for the new world. For example, the authors point out that the population of Mexico declined by about 90% after one hundred years of Spanish rule. "For the original inhabitants the appearance of the white man was an unmitigated disaster" (Ralph et al., 1997: 1; 677). The period from the mid-sixteenth to the mid-seventeenth centuries was, in the words of the authors, a "century of pronounced crisis for European civilization" (Ralph et al., 1997: 1; 711). Europe was plagued by economic problems and religious wars. (What a contrast to the "peaceful" beginning of Europe during the Minoan period!)

Paradoxically, the textbook suggests that "European civilization" could regain stability by losing its "civilizational" cohesiveness and breaking apart into separate nation-states. Europe becomes stable only in the second volume of the textbook which focuses on the modern era since the sixteenth century. It is argued that religion, "the factor that had torn Europe apart" during the sixteenth century, was "increasingly" superseded by "newer 'interests' – commerce and international balance and stability" (Ralph et al., 1997: 2; 122). These newer interests led to the emergence of a nation-state system, in which national interests were pursued by diplomacy and sometimes war. France, Prussia, Britain, Russia, and Austria-Hungary (that is, separate nation-states, not one "Europe") become the main actors in the world scene.

European nation-states play a major role in the second volume. They develop absolutist monarchies (except Britain) and get engaged in the scientific revolution, the Industrial Revolution, nationalism, and liberalism. Industrialization brings the "West" (Western Europe) into the "world's center" (the title of the sixth part is "The West at the World's Center"). The non-Western, non-European civilizations are marginalized: major historical developments in India, East Asia, and Africa during the early-modern era are summarized in one chapter. (There are forty three chapters in the second volume of the textbook.) The experiences of China, Japan, and Africa "under the impact of the West" during the nineteenth century are also synthesized into one chapter. The non-Western parts of the world receive more attention in the third part, after the "emergence of world civilization" (that is, after World War II). Four out of seven chapters describe developments in the Middle East, Africa, South Asia, and Latin America.

In this "new" post-World War II "world civilization" Europe is one of several regions. The authors emphasize the creation of a European community and the "economic renaissance" that took place during the nineteen-fifties, which was brought about by the Marshall Plan and the creation of the European Economic Community (Ralph et al., 1997: 2; 658). These developments are described in the first two chapters of the concluding part of the textbook, and they are depicted in more detail than post-World War II developments in other geographical areas.

As this new "world civilization" is being created, Europe is "assembled" from separate nation-states into one civilization through an "economic renaissance". "Prosperity" becomes a distinctive feature of Europe, at least until the mid-nineteen-sixties and nineteen-seventies, when (due to economic problems and protest movements) European societies are described as becoming "fragmented in new and confusing ways" (Ralph et al., 1997: 2; 681). This fragmentation, brought about by social forces such as women's and peace movements, was "overshadowed" by the birth of a new, post-Communist Europe after the disintegration of the Soviet Union. The lack of prosperity and "brutish" life, exemplified by ethnic conflict in the former Yugoslavia, made Eastern Europe different from the prosperous West, at least during the post-Cold War era (Ralph et al., 1997: 2; 701).

In the last chapter, the authors do not dwell on the future of "one" Europe after the fall of Communism nor do they try to predict the future of the "world civilization" characterized by US dominance after World War II. They describe current global issues such as the environmental crisis brought about by the Industrial Revolution. Given the geographical approach to world history used in both volumes, the concluding ideas about the "common" global issues in a "common" world civilization are not entirely convincing. It is also not entirely clear which historical forces have created a common "world civilization" if the nation-state system created during the seventeenth century has remained more or less intact.

World Civilizations exemplifies the pros and cons of the area study approach to world history. On the one hand, moving from one geographical area to another (especially in the first volume) helps to create a sense of order and clarity in world history. Area studies are interesting and rich in detail. This is why the textbook has remained quite popular in world civilization classrooms in the United States. On the other hand, this approach does not lend itself well to the portrayal of on-going encounters and exchanges between different cultures and civilizations. As a matter of fact, the second volume creates an impression that (in the words of Patrick Manning) history outside the West was "the history of Western impact on other areas of the world". The second volume (more than the first one) focuses on Western Europe and its wars and revolutions, thus failing to establish a seamless connection between European history and non-European, non-Western entities.

Europe Viewed from Hawaii

Traditions & Encounters: A Global Perspective on the Past is described by its publisher as "a market leader" (McGraw-Hill, 2003), a claim that, judging by its popularity at one large American university, is certainly hard to refute.[1] Its authors, Jerry H. Bentley and Herbert F. Zeigler, are both professors of history at the University of Hawaii. In the preface they assert that "it [...] is impossible to understand the world's history by viewing it through the lenses of any particular society" and point out that the second edition of this textbook includes expanded treatments of several non-European societies (Bentley & Zeigler, 2003: xxxi; xxxiii). This suggests that the perspective on the past that Bentley and Zeigler offer will be one that is relatively free of Eurocentrism.

The chapters in *Traditions & Encounters* focus either on a world region or a specific theme in world history. In the pre-modern era chapters on world regions, such as "Early Societies in Southwest Asia and the Indo-European Migrations", predominate and the authors use "complex societies" as their unit of analysis. In the modern era chapters on specific themes, such as "The Building of Global Empires", predominate and there is no clear unit of analysis. Bentley and Zeigler define complex society as "a form of large-scale social organization" in which "many individuals... congregate in urban settlements, where they devote their time and energy to specialized tasks other than food production" (Bentley & Zeigler, 2003: 2). The authors' use of the term *complex society* instead of *civilization* is an attempt to overcome some of the problems inherent in using that value-laden term. By identifying some societies as civilized, does that suggest that other societies are

---

[1] The university at which *Traditions & Encounters* is quite popular is Georgia State University in Atlanta, Georgia.

uncivilized? Are "uncivilized" societies truly uncivilized? Bentley and Zeigler have certainly given these questions some thought and their solution to the problem is a radical one: no other world history textbook in the United States that is as widely used has shown a similar willingness to completely abandon the term *civilization*.

The term *European civilization* is therefore absent from the pages of this textbook. Instead, the authors speak of a distant, more unfamiliar "European society". And when, according to Bentley and Zeigler, did European society begin? In the chapters on Greece and Rome they point out the long-term influence that Greek philosophy, Roman law, and Christianity have had on the development of European society, but they do not actually identify Greece or Rome as European societies. The first complex society which Bentley and Zeigler identify as being unequivocally "European", is western Europe during the early middle ages, which they describe as "a violent and disorderly land […] [that] played little role in the development of a hemispheric economy during the era dominated by the Tang, Song, Abbasid, and Byzantine empires" (Bentley & Zeigler, 2003: 518). It should come as no surprise then that only two of the twenty-two chapters on the pre-modern era in *Traditions & Encounters* deal exclusively with western Europe. China, in contrast, is the subject of three chapters.

The first chapter on western Europe, "The Foundations of Christian Society in Western Europe", does not use any of the approaches identified by von Glahn. The second, "Western Europe During the High Middle Ages", does, but in a very limited way. In that chapter, medieval Europe is described as "a political mosaic of independent and competing regional states" that, although frequently at war with one another, "organized their territories efficiently, and […] laid the political foundations for the emergence of powerful national states in a later era" (Bentley & Zeigler, 2003: 519). Although the authors stop short of making an argument in favor of European exceptionalism it is clear from a later chapter that this is in fact what they have in mind. Also, at the end of the chapter, the Crusades are described as having "profoundly influenced European development" by enabling "a large-scale exchange of ideas, technologies, and trade goods" (Bentley & Zeigler, 2003: 542) – a brief, but clear example of the stimulus-diffusion approach in world history.

In the last chapter on the pre-modern era, "Reaching Out: Cross-cultural Interactions", Bentley and Zeigler completely embrace the stimulus-diffusion approach, describing how, between 1000 and 1500 C.E. "the peoples of the eastern hemisphere traveled, traded, communicated, and interacted more regularly and intensively than ever before" (Bentley & Zeigler, 2003: 574). Europeans figure prominently in this chapter, but they share the stage with the people of other societies. This is reflected in the maps, which, although simple, are quite thought-provoking. For example, one map shows the travels of *both* the Venetian Marco Polo and the Moroccan Ibn Battuta; another shows the voyages of *both* Chinese and European explorers in the fifteenth century. By juxtaposing the travels and voyages of Europeans with non-Europeans these maps put the accomplishments of pre-modern Europeans into proper global perspective.

In sharp contrast to the chapters on the pre-modern era, Europe figures quite prominently in the chapters on the modern era. Roughly half of the eighteen chapters on the modern era deal, in part or in whole, with Europe. In "Transoceanic Encounters and Global Connections", Bentley and Zeigler adopt the European hegemony approach, describing how the expansion of European influence "resulted in the establishment of global networks of transportation, communication, and exchange" and "brought about a decisive shift in the global balance of power" (Bentley & Zeigler, 2003: 608). They also continue with the stimulus-diffusion approach, describing the global diffusion of plants, food crops, animals, people, and diseases that took place after the European voyages of exploration in the fifteenth and sixteenth centuries.

Although Bentley and Zeigler clearly have reservations about introducing the idea of European exceptionalism in the chapters on pre-modern Europe, they have no such reservations in the chapters on the modern era. In "The Transformation of Europe", they describe how the existence of a competitive multi-state system in Europe provided the stimulus for technological innovation in the arms industry, observing that "in China, India, and Islamic lands, imperial states had little or no incentive to encourage similar technological innovation [...]" (Bentley & Zeigler, 2003: 652). They also describe how the Enlightenment, with its belief in reason and progress, "helped to bring about a thorough transformation of European society", (Bentley & Zeigler, 2003: 663) but do not explicitly link this with Europe's rise to global hegemony.

In "Revolutions and National States in the Atlantic World" the French revolution is grouped together with the American and Haitian revolutions, thus making it an Atlantic, not a European, revolution. Bentley and Zeigler return once again to the stimulus-diffusion approach in "The Building of

Global Empires", describing how "western European peoples... imposed their hegemony throughout the world" in the nineteenth century (Bentley & Zeigler, 2003: 934). It is in this chapter that the term *civilization* makes a rare appearance. The authors explain how Europeans worked to bring subject peoples "'civilization' in the form of political order and social stability" and how French imperialists "routinely invoked the *mission civilisatrice* ('civilizing mission') as justification for their expansion into Africa and Asia" (Bentley & Zeigler, 2003: 937–938).

In the chapters on the twentieth century Europe goes from global primacy to being a trading bloc with a shrinking population. "The Great War", which is the term that Bentley and Zeigler use to describe World War I, "undermined the preeminence and prestige of European society, signaling an end to Europe's global primacy" (Bentley & Zeigler, 2003: 973). Although the authors describe the Holocaust as a case of "genocide", other cases of genocide in the twentieth century (e.g., Armenia, Cambodia, and Rwanda) go unmentioned, thus giving the impression that genocide matters only if it occurs in Europe.[2] De Gaulle is described as a man "who dreamed of a Europe that could act as a third force in politics", and although he "failed to convince Europeans to leave the protective fold of the United States", his dream "persisted in a different guise" (Bentley & Zeigler, 2003: 1083). The European Union is important enough to receive a whole paragraph in a textbook that is 1,169 pages long and a helpful table shows how Europe is the only area of the world whose population is projected to decline over the next fifty years. This suggests that the authors do not see Europe as a "superpower" capable of challenging the power of the United States any time soon.

Throughout *Traditions & Encounters*, Europe is just an actor, one of many, which had its day in the sun during the modern era. In the post-modern world of world history constructed by Bentley and Zeigler, Europe is "only" a complex society, one of a great many in the world.

---

[2] As this article neared completion the authors received an advance copy of the third edition of *Traditions & Encounters* from the publisher. New to this edition is a series of brief essays called "Contexts & Connections", each of which takes a specific issue from an individual chapter and seeks to understand it within the larger historical context. The chapter on World War II includes an essay on genocide. This essay describes, not only the mass murder of Jews during World War II, but the genocides that took place in Armenia, Cambodia, and Rwanda as well, thus correcting the impression given in the second edition that genocide matters only if it occurs in Europe (Bentley & Zeigler, 2006: 1052).

Conclusion

Our textbook case studies suggest several insights and hypotheses. Both textbooks exemplify the influence of intellectual trends, such as "de-Europeanization" and constructivism. The authors of both textbooks make it clear to the readers that they are going to include regions other than Europe in their analysis. They also make it clear that their goal is to show cultural entities, whether "civilizations" or "complex societies", interacting with each other through trade and war. Bentley and Zeigler are more successful than Ralph et al. at portraying their units of analysis as constructs instead of relatively self-contained geographical areas inhabited by people who create extraordinary artifacts. They are also more successful at contextualizing "Europe" and showing its rise to power in comparison with other complex societies.

In *Traditions & Encounters* Bentley and Zeigler follow the trend toward de-Europeanization and post-modernism (e.g., analyzing "complex societies", not "civilizations") more closely than Ralph et al. in *World Civilizations*. It should come as no surprise, then, that *Traditions & Encounters* has become increasingly popular among professors at American universities. From a practitioner's point of view, those students with only a weak background in world history may find the numerous complex societies and cross-cultural contacts in this textbook to be a bit overwhelming. On the other hand, volume one of *World Civilizations*, which portrays each civilization as "naturally belonging" to one geographical area and traces the origins of Europe to ancient times, offers a somewhat simplified approach to the ancient world.

It may be possible to hypothesize that one of the negative unintended consequences of the primordial approach to civilizational identities, such as that used in volume one of *World Civilizations*, is the creation of a mythology about "ancient hatreds" that are abundant "out there" in the world. (Similar beliefs about "ancient hatreds" in the former Yugoslavia were very popular during the early and mid nineties in the United States.) If so, then history textbooks embracing such approaches may contribute to the strengthening of America's isolationism and its simplified view of world affairs.

At the same time, the influence of history teaching on national consciousness should not be over-stated. We realize and admit the limits of formal education. The worldviews and opinions of American students are shaped by myriads of other variables, such as the mass media, friends, family, church, sororities, study abroad, and so on. However, world history textbooks do play a role, even if it is a small and insignificant one, in the construction of identities. At the same time, they are a reflection of America's relations with the outside world. It is not a coincidence that world civilization courses in the United States have their origin in a course that was first taught to servicemen during World War I to help them understand why they were fighting. If history textbooks can indeed be viewed as the "mirrors" of a country's consciousness, then our analysis of two very popular textbooks suggests that, in the United States at least, world history is seen as a complex mosaic of societies and cultures instead of the rise and fall of great powers. Europe is one part of this mosaic, and not the centerpiece.

References

Bentley, J.H. & Zeigler, H.F. (2006) *Traditions & Encounters: A Global Perspective on the Past*. 3rd edn. McGraw-Hill

Bentley, J.H. & Zeigler, H.F. (2003) *Traditions & Encounters: A Global Perspective on the Past*. 2nd edn. McGraw-Hill

Von Glahn, R. (2003) "Imagining Pre-modern China". *The Song-Yuan-Ming Transition in Chinese History*. Paul Yakov Smith and Richard von Glahn (eds.) Cambridge: Harvard University Press

Kagan, R. (2002) "Power and Weakness". *Policy Review Online*. June 2002 [http://www.policyreview.org/JUN02/kagan.html]

Manning, (2003) *Navigating World History: Historians Create a Global Past*. New York: Palgrave Macmillan

McGraw-Hill, (2003) *Traditions & Encounters*. [http://highered.mcgraw-hill.com/sites/0072424354/]

Ralph, P.L. et al. (1997) *World Civilizations: Their History and Their Culture*. 2 vols. 9th edn, W.W. Norton & Company

W.W. Norton & Company (2005) *World Civilizations Overview*. [http://www.wwnorton.com/college/titles/history/worldciv9]

Passage-way to Culture and Writing – Literature of Transit: Codrescu, Federman, Hoffman, and Simic

CAMELIA ELIAS

One is both using language and being used by language.
– Charles Simic

The aim of this paper is to introduce the genre one might call the literature of transit. Fiction writers and poets such as Andrei Codrescu, Raymond Federman, Eva Hoffman, and Charles Simic, who, while unable to account for notions of identity formations within a cultural realm that belongs to one particular place, still have made a transatlantic passage crucial to their lives and writing, strategically combine facts of personal history with the facts of living 'fictitiously'.

While every transit or exile is an individual experience, there are always some shared experiences when it comes to the questions that the exiles concern themselves with. In a recent collection of essays, *Letters of Transit*, which gathers voices such as Hoffman and Simic's, André Aciman formulates some of their essential concerns: to what extent can one ever "rebuild a home?" "what kinds of shifts must take place for a person to acquire, let alone accept, a new identity, a new language?" (Aciman, 1999: 14) Here I would suggest that these questions are as much pragmatic questions as they are existential. In other words, they are strategic questions whose answers must address, on the one hand, the specificity of each confrontation with the rebuilding of a language, identity, and even class, and on the other hand, the universal applicability of the confrontation in a larger context.

In my contention, one of the main characteristics of the literature of transit is its ability to turn writing into a sort of religion which observes and subverts the customs of new territories. While this goes for all four writers, Codrescu makes his allegiances specific: "My religion is Creolisation, Hybridization,

Miscegenation, Immigration, Genre-Busting, Trespassing, Border-Crossing, Identity-Shifting, Mask-Making, and Syncretism" (Vianu, 2001: http). When Federman declares that "history is bankrupt", he is suggesting that history, like money, is a liability in the hands of investors who can lose it, gain it again, invest in it, sell it, buy it, conceal it, reveal it, make it available. One must therefore write history and memoirs from a potential point of view. Simic's literary goal is to invent a new type of writing: "My aspiration is to create a kind of nongenre made up of fiction, autobiography, the essay, poetry, and of course, the joke!" (Simic, 1994: 106) Hoffman's literature of transit charts literary experience as a "geography of emotions", thus exploring the implications of what it means to write from the position of being "here now".

One of the more interesting aspects of these authors' autobiographies and memoirs is that their writings combine the concrete awareness of having crossed the Atlantic with a more abstract understanding of in-between-ness. Unlike African-Americans for whom crossing the Atlantic is (collectively) remembered as a traumatic experience, Europeans have a different perception: the Atlantic represents both a neutral space and anticipation. This is the experience of the immigrant who crosses the Atlantic already knowing that the new place is a place with fewer constraints. Exile poses a different set of questions insofar as it is marked by coercion. The immigrant writers discussed here crossed the Atlantic, yet the space separating their original homes from Canada and respectively the United States is brought on board. This was not a privilege African-Americans were allowed to enjoy. Allowing oneself to be in-between cultures is ultimately rendered as a transit experience. Immigrant writing is thus a concern with how to represent the state of in-between-ness both literally and metaphorically. A good example is the authors' relationship to language: they have all remained bilingual and insist on emphasizing their 'double' linguistic nature. On the other hand, they are extremely apt in English and have developed a highly sophisticated style of writing. On a more general scale, these authors' writings have had a strong impact on the way we think not only of second language acquisition, but also of strategies for integration which use language as a primary step towards acculturation.

This paper will also undertake to look at what functions such transatlantic passages have for the idea of belonging, insofar as strategies for "being here now" in the works discussed emphasize a double settling.

Strategic Belonging

Some critics have already pointed out that at least in terms of the reception of the literature produced by exile or immigrant authors there is a problem with the specificity of the term exile and its universal appeal. Michael Bernstein goes against publishing houses that promote books on exile experience by suggesting that in spite of the described individual experience – which the publishers are very eager to sell en masse – the exile feeling is somehow universal and something we supposedly all share. Catchphrases such as "the private is political", Bernstein shows, are nowhere near the truth or the message that these books might put forth. Thus squaring off against critics such as Eva Figes, who has it in *The New York Times* in her review essay of Eva Hoffman's autobiography that the book "is not just about emigrants and refugees. It is about us all", Bernstein makes the pertinent point:

> But that is just what *Lost in Translation* is not about. Instead, and in strict accord with the paradoxical law of literary imagination, which holds that what is most personal and distinct will touch readers most deeply, it is the very narrowness and exclusivity of Hoffman's self-absorbed curiosity that gives her writing its distinctive tone (Bernstein, 1996: 182–183).

Hoffman herself is a self-conscious writer and her *Lost in Translation* (1989) offers invaluable insights into the way language operates for the alienated individual. One of the main points she makes is that if one does learn a new language, and acquire a new identity, the degree of successfulness has little to do with what one learns in (language) schools. It is through developing a certain strategy of belonging that any effort at integration is made possible.

This insight parallels Andrei Codrescu's ideas developed in works such as the three-part autobiography *An Involuntary Genius in America's Shoes (And What Happened Afterwards)* (2001) and numerous other essays which Codrescu delivers with faithful regularity on National Public Radio's "All Things Considered". What is being considered is that while in transit, even when one has lived, worked and written in and about America, one is always imbued with a sense of waiting, not for things to happen, but for expectation itself. All immigrants have expectations regarding the final place of destination, yet when these expectations are being interrupted or cut off by some other place of transit, the emerging memories are altered. Before Hoffman became an American she was a Polish teenager growing up in Canada in the 60s. Canada has always been seen by Hoffman as a place of transit. She ended up there both against her will and against her expectations, as the latter were oriented towards Israel, the place where most of her family friends went. Codrescu's adventures in America are filtered through his experiences with leaving Romania for Israel, yet the interposition of a transit period in Italy and France made him change his mind: he ended up in New York instead. His departure was a result of a governmental agreement between communist Romania and Israel which stipulated in the 60s that every Romanian Jew was permitted to emigrate in exchange for 2000 dollars which the state of Israel was responsible for paying. That Codrescu never made it to Israel may be interpreted as a rejection of the idea that one's life is mere merchandise, though as he self-ironically remarks in various interviews, he still owes the state of Israel a certain amount of money.

Charles Simic's memoir *A Fly in the Soup* (2002) explores belonging through assuming the position of one who develops elaborate strategies of detachment and disengagement from authorities that make it clear that "no one likes the refugees" (Simic, 2002: 3). One of Simic's major observations is that "Immigration, exile, being uprooted and made a pariah may be yet the most effective way devised to impress on an individual the arbitrary nature of his or her own existence" (4). Thus the Cartesian dictum, *cogito, ergo sum*, is here reversed: thinking is not enough to establish the fact that we exist. The underlying statement that writers such as Simic make is that we need others' recognition of our beliefs and capabilities. We need the Other, even if the Other occupies the dominant position.

Now, what these books have in common is the way in which they develop a pragmatic sense which links a desire for belonging with adopting a detached position in that relation. One belongs, but not directly. One crosses the Atlantic but no so easily the culture borders. In their introduction to the collection of essays *The Postnational Self*, the editors make the following observations in connection with how we perceive belonging: "'home' and 'belonging', thus conceived, are affectively, rather than cognitively, defined concepts; the indicative, seemingly neutral, and very simple statement 'home *is* where we belong' really means 'home is where we *feel* we belong'" (Hedetoft and Hjort, 2002: vii). The problem with the difference between cognition and affection is furthermore complicated by the co-existence of two incompatible thoughts within the very concept: "'belonging' separates into two constituent parts: 'being' in one place, and 'longing' for another"[1] (vii). This paradox is certainly much explored in Hoffman's *Lost in Translation*, but less so in Codrescu, Simic, and Federman's works. For the latter three the nostalgia inherent in the notion of belonging is reversed so that it implies a mode of being in one place and longing for the same place simultaneously. In this sense, while I do not intend to suggest that these authors' works are scholarly treatises on integration, in their concern with belonging beyond one's place, as it were, they equal some of the most outstanding academic research in fields dealing with culture, language acquisition, integration politics, and the politics of recognition.[2] My interest, however, lies with exploring the idea that what mediates between the personal and the public, between belonging directly and not so directly is first of all a question of strategic neutrality.

Here I want to suggest that this neutrality parallels in a way the vast neutrality of the Atlantic and its seemingly lacking borders. By neutrality I mean a position of detachment that is necessary in respect to distinguishing between the multifarious choices available to one in a new society. Eva Hoffman's concern in *Lost in Translation* and her desire to "claim" an "ordinary place" for herself by adopting such a detached position illustrates the point. She is made to feel naïve by a friend who tells her that such places do not exist anymore. Hoffman learns, however, not only that the language she speaks is as artificial as is the language that the natives speak (both literally and metaphorically), but that she should be suspicious of any such pronouncements which have it that in America "you are who you think you are" and that identity is subject to re-invention (Hoffman, 1989: 160). Hoffman is thus thrown into confusion, as she "can't figure out how this is done", and she begins to pose questions whose thrust revolves around a rhetoric of detachment and neutrality: "You just say what you are and everyone believes you? That seems like a confidence trick to me, and not one I think I can pull off. Still, somehow, invent myself I must. But how do I choose from identity options available all around me? I feel, once again [...] faint from excess, paralyzed by choice" (160). The implication of Hoff-

---

[1] The issue of "belonging" is also dealt with from a less pacifistic (domestic) perspective by the contributors to *The Postnational Self: Belonging and Identity* as the authors examine notions of citizenship and cultural hybridization, migration and other forms of mobility, displacements and ethnic cleansing, and the nature of national belonging.

[2] See for example, Charles Taylor's *Multiculturalism and the Politics of Recognition* (1992) and *Sources of the Self: The Making of the Modern Identity* (1992), and Vikki Bell's *Performativity and Belonging* (1999).

man's inability to be in synch with American slogans for her understanding of the American culture is that she cannot learn what an "ordinary place" is without first assigning the place a good deal of neutrality.

What I furthermore mean by neutral place here is the idea of a space which opens itself up to contribution. If one's presence in a country which is not one's own is generally ignored, or seen in opposition to the cultural and mental values of that place, contribution is not possible. If however one is allowed a position of neutrality in relation to those values, a process of true learning is initiated and one is able to contribute. Neutrality does not mean *not* getting involved. Quite the contrary, one is involved as soon as one discovers that one belongs neither here nor there. One is involved in a process of neutralizing one's sense of belonging in relation to a well defined space of integration. This is perhaps what it means to belong ultimately beyond one's place.

One of the ways in which emigrant writers imagine themselves belonging involves a process of recreating for themselves a space where cultural and geographical displacement incorporates strategies for belonging to the new society. Yet the ways to deal with belonging are not marked by signposts indicating which path to go. One must create for oneself a neutral space where linguistic and cultural re-creation can be staged independently of the place as such. Asserting neutrality is the only condition for the possibility to fashion one's sense of belonging in an interesting, not a dictated way. One of the lessons of multiculturalism shows that it is not enough to live by the rules of the old proverb which emphasises the basic assumptions for survival: when in Rome do as the Romans. Rather, when in Rome, do as the Romans do at the height of their interestingness, when they assert their own ambitions in relation to the politics of recognition that rule in their country. Immigrant writers' contribution to culture is not only to affirm a potential, but actualize it between success and excess.

Now, one of the consequences of transatlantic crossings in this regard is that crossing in all its senses creates a platform for nonconformity. I argue that the four writers' experience of the state of being in-between lands and cultures, never giving up the Atlantic, as it were, makes room for the emergence of a poetics of nonconformity. This poetics of nonconformity is furthermore a consequence of their strategies of belonging which uses neutrality and detachment as first rules. What these writers observe in their works from the outset is the difference between crossing borders and crossing waters.

Transatlantic Nonconformity

Literally being some place while mentally being some other place is often represented in the use of narrative frames. Codrescu, for instance, makes a number of candid statements as to the emergence of a certain narratorial authorship against the background of the more conventional autobiographical genre. His personal narrative, which uses fiction as a support for memory, clashes with conventional narrative rules and establishes in precisely that event a poetics of nonconformity. As he informs us in the preface to his *An Involuntary Genius*: "I am not all that interested in 'myself' – I am only curious to see what kind of person is going to emerge from a certain arrangement of personal stories – which are in themselves not 'facts' but earlier arrangements – for certain practical uses" (Codrescu, 2001: 14). The effect of this narratorial self-framing is not only to set up the first person narrator, but also the reader's expectations. 'Blow some conventional borders' thus becomes imperative and the reader approaches the work from the author's activist perspective.

Writing from the position of both difference and transition is intertwined with the idea of border, both with its connotations of something tangible that can be overcome, and something less definable.[3] The border is the epitome of self-exploration in the sense that one passes judgement on the act of transition from a position of potentiality which opens itself to actualization. All these writers are extremely self-aware of the fact that their transatlantic crossing involves a degree of nonconformity. In his book Codrescu problematizes in parentheses – (quite literally, as the subtitle indicates: (*And What Happened Afterwards*)) – the notion that border-crossing almost always begins as an involuntary act which leads to a constant state of being amused at one's own displacement. When Codrescu declares that he likes to "stay amused", as "it has the word muse in it", he emphasizes the implication of what it means to be in transit while crossing (Vianu 2001: http). One changes masks. The changes of masks and with them the writer and activist behind them constitutes for Codrescu a commitment to engaging in bending rules of conventions.

A useful definition of 'borderland' is provided by Gloria Anzaldua "a borderland is a vague and undetermined place created by the emotional residue of an unnatural boundary [...] People who inhabit both realities [...] are forced to live in the interface between the two" (in Grossberg, 1996: 92).

If the poetics of nonconformity to some extent relies on the deployment of what is in vogue at a certain time[4], insofar as it puts itself forth as an avant-garde, some rules of conventions regarding the degree of non-conventionality are already in the making. Codrescu's writings, developed in the late 60s, border on and go against the conventions surrounding nonconformity. These writings, which also found full expression in later editorial works such as the volumes of essays and poems collecting the 'non-conformists' under the title *Exquisite Corpse*, define the poetics of nonconformity in its own right by enforcing a way of seeing things while looking at something else. Strongly influenced by writers such as Allen Ginsberg, yet following his own transitions, Codrescu not only creates mini platforms for nonconformity in his essays, but also associates the very notion of nonconformity with registering the absurdities of society. (Absurdities of all kind are Codrescu's specialty and nowhere are they better represented than in the short commentary pieces that he delivers for NPR's "All Things Considered".)

Charles Simic, on the other hand, is a writer whose experiences as a refugee from Yugoslavia, coming to the United States in the 50s through France, enforce a way of seeing, unlike Codrescu, facets of the same thing while looking at something else. For Simic, both in his memoirs from 2002, tellingly titled *A Fly in the Soup*, as well as his poetry and essays with titles such as *The World Doesn't End* (1989) and *The Unemployed Fortune-Teller* (1994), the concept of border is associated with registering the subtleties of society while making use of the fragment and the prose poem. The fragment is an impropriety of the proper while the prose poem, which in itself "is a fraud", cancels out the borders of both poetry and prose (Simic, 1998: http). Simic's transatlantic nonconformity is expressed through epigrams: the longer the crossing, the shorter the writing. Epigrams and aphorisms enable the writer not only to cross borders, but also trespass other domains, here in terms of genre and culture.

For both these writers, the border has a certain immediacy in the sense that they make use of images, characters, events, plots, little narratives, and descriptions that exemplify the border as that which creates a sharp distinction between being here now, the "nowness" of the situation, marked

---

[4] Here I am thinking of Codrescu's second part of his autobiography – *In America's Shoes* – in which he brings valuable insights into and descriptions of the avant-garde literary scene in America from the 60s and onwards. New York and San Francisco are the primary sites.

by causality, and being somewhere else, often the past, marked by temporality. Thus, the border creates a tension between causality and temporality. The border is a place of both potentiality and possibility. The border suggests belonging beyond one's place.

At the other pole, though not very far removed from Codrescu and Simic's concerns, Eva Hoffman's own "triangulations" between the past, present, and the future, follow the compass that establishes with a fairly high degree of precision and certitude the point where one finds herself.[5] In geometry one can only triangulate by surveying the earth's surface "broadly". For Hoffman, the awareness of being a transatlantic writer comes with assuming the position of a surveyor who takes remarkably much ground in sight. But *Lost in Translation* is also an example of the kind of writing which brings nonconformity to its edge. Hoffman is not interested in dismissing already existing rules, but in surveying their potential to also be bent. There is a lot of reflection on landscape and geography in the book, which indicates that the author is engaged in mapping experiences. We thus have a geography of place, a geography of emotion, and a geography of convention. Each corresponds to a state of mind described in the book's three parts: *Paradise*, *Exile*, and *The New World*. This symmetry furthermore reflects three very different representations of the self so that the book's literal representations of place correspond to a metaphorical geography of place, representations of language correspond to mapping a geography of emotion, and representations of writing correspond to mapping a geography of convention.

Federman's writings are similar to Hoffman's in regard to 'calculations'. The writer is obsessed with experimenting with form and symmetry. The autobiographical account of how Federman escaped the Nazi camps in *The Voice in the Closet* (1979) follows a very strict and constrained format. The writing on the page is very carefully designed to emulate the form of a square, which is a representation of a closet, and the paragraphs and lines contain the same numbers of lines and words within their space. Thus, measuring, cutting, adding, and subtracting are cutting-edge methods for Federman, and this style enforces his personal credo that all writing is fiction. In his essays, some of which form the influential collection *Critifiction* (1993), as well as in his fiction, works such as *The Twofold Vibration* (1982), he expresses his intention to not conform by making language itself the interface between place and experience. As he puts it: "language is democratic, it

---

[5] The triangle is also a geometrical device used to measure exact positions.

belongs to everyone [...] what one does with it is a matter of personal choice, and personal responsibility" (Federman, 1982: 24).

Thus, coming to a new place, crossing the Atlantic to come to America, and giving one's own existence a sense of meaning through observing the new culture and habits, creates a tension that prompts some paradoxical questions. In the following I want to develop more fully the implications of some of these questions and the fact that what passes as nonconformity in these four writers' works is the double perspective they put on everything they explore. That writers often offer an account of their experiences or fiction through a double perspective is no news, yet what is interesting here is that this double perspective gets double crossed, so to speak, insofar as what these writers offer is an insight into transit(ory) states and their self-deconstruction. The questions which I think recur within the literature of transit are the following:

- How can one tell a story about true events?
- How can one translate one's existence into a story?
- Can the story told constitute one's life as such?
- Is memory itself a story?
- Can lying in writing constitute a true story?
- Can humor reconcile the difference between invented stories and remembered stories?
- Can crossings be the masks that borders wear?

Andrei Codrescu and the Exquisite Crossing

To this date Codrescu has published 4 volumes of autobiography. Two of them form *An Involuntary Genius in America's Shoes (And What Happens Afterwards)*[6]. The stories presented here follow a traditional chronology in exposing the narrator's life as it unfolds itself in three stages: from the life and times in communist Romania, via a transit period in Italy and France, to becoming an established poet in the United States. What unites the three parts is the overall theme of escaping and of challenging conventions. As the work was written in three installments and had parts of it published

---

[6] The other works have appeared under the titles: *The Disappearance of the Outside: a Manifesto for Escape* (1990) and *The Hole in the Flag: a Romanian Exile's Story of Return and Revolution* (1991).

earlier, Codrescu decided that a preface was required in order to situate the events in context. However, this preface, "Adding to My Life", does not follow any conventional rules, and before one knows it, the reader is presented with 5 mini stories all designed to (indirectly) explain the art of writing an autobiography. As Codrescu takes issue with the notion of autobiography he calls his writing in this genre a result of accidents. Each of these stories ponders a question which involves, respectively: the audience, genre, memory, narrative, and narrative alterations.

On the question of the targeted audience, we read that the book is written supposedly for the author's mother. The explanation we are given is that since mothers are authors until one becomes an author himself, it is only fair, then, to write for the mother. However, as soon as that possibility is presented it is immediately dismissed on the ground that one invariably also writes for oneself, hence the story becomes "the price of admission to everything". The claim is that money is people's substitute for a personal story, the implication thus being that since money circulates in public, and one's own persona circulates in public through a book, whatever private there may about one's public self is exchangeable. This idea points to questions of prestige, recognition, and most of all belonging. As Codrescu puts it: "money is one's way out of autobiography into the collective myth" (Codrescu, 2001: 7). Thus having an audience is a way of engaging in the politics of recognition, and for an immigrant, getting recognition becomes the first aim.

Codrescu then goes on to tackle the question of genre. The preface, with all its meta-dimensions as indicated by the idea of "adding", adds a new layer to the difference between an autobiography and a novel. The mother's question as to why he had to "call" the book an autobiography instead of a novel is embedded within a comic incident which shifts the focus from the mother's initial lamentations as to having the family affairs made public to accepting the story, as even the mother has to admit that it is a good one. For the sake of illustrating the point, I quote a longer passage which contains Codrescu's explanation:

> Just before the book came out I asked my mother about a certain incident I had labored hard to render accurately. It was about the time she left me with my grandmother, the Baroness, in Alba Iulia. I was five, and the Baroness kept chickens. There were chickens everywhere in the formerly grand manse she now had the top floor in, and both my mother and I were sternly warned to watch where we walked because there were eggs everywhere. In fact there were eggs in my bedroll when I went to sleep, and I woke up the next day,

holding in my hands two miraculously unbroken eggs. It seemed to me that over the years this story had become something of a legend among out kin. But my mother, when I asked her about it, said that the Baroness kept little pigs! That, furthermore, I was only three when I went to live with her, and that I was only there for one month. I remembered living there for a year. PIGS! I wasn't about to change anything so dear to me, so I let it slide. A year after the book came out, I was visiting my mother in Washington, DC, and she said that she felt sorry that she'd had to leave me with my crazy grandmother and her chickens when I was five years old. BUT MOTHER, I said. PIGS! WHATEVER HAPPENED TO THE PIGS! What pigs? She was annoyed. Denied ever having said anything about pigs. It had been chickens all along. (6)

What this paragraph suggests is that stories, whether true or false, have both private and public consequences. Changing your mother's "memory cassette", as Codrescu puts it, has to do with the way facts are rendered even when they do not rest on proof. Thus, the question of memory becomes a question of narrative, and narrative becomes a question of narrative alteration as if to suggest that every story is a transit story between different potentialities. Here we can make the following assumptions: if the story is rendered truly, then it must be individual. If the story is rendered falsely, then it must be collective. That is, from the point of view of the individual the story will always be false where the audience is concerned (even when the audience includes the one who told the story in the first place, here the mother). If the story is however rendered neutrally, and Codrescu went with this possibility, the story gains significance and becomes relevant at least for certain groups. This neutrality, transiting away, as it were, both from truth and reality, ultimately poses the question of all fiction which admits that it is autobiographical. Does it matter that perhaps it was not chickens?

This question frees Codrescu from being 'himself' and functions as a gateway into a number of different personae waiting to be taken over. The preface ends with an emphasis on different icons, cultural and literary, private, and personal: from the famous Romanian gymnast Nadia Comaneci, through Whitman and Rimbaud, to the absurdist Romanian playwright Eugene Ionesco, from Andy Warhol and Dracula to editors, scholars and critics, Codrescu gathers a multitude of voices which all can be said to have produced and still produce a discourse on transit. There is a clear crossing on Codrescu's part from being an auto-biographer to being a pseudo-biographer. He thus finds himself justifying precisely the border which separates genres: "Of all kinds of literature, autobiographies, no matter how humorous, are the least funny. After all, how much genuine irony can an autobiographer muster?" (11)

Autobiography is fiction in transit. Part two of Codrescu's book therefore takes issue with what it means to cross over into another culture. *In America's Shoes* shows that one is still in transit, not in America as such, but in her shoes. That is yet another story, and it happens afterwards (as the last four pages which form the last part inform us). What enables Codrescu to move past belonging to a certain place is the shift between the uses of personal pronouns every time there is a transition. *An Involuntary Genius* is told in the third person singular, *In America's Shoes* is told in the first person singular and *What Happened Afterwards* is told in the first person plural. This shift from the individual to the collective suggests that one's realities (filtered through reinstating a subjective narrative voice which is rendered neutral in the first person) are one's fictions. As Codrescu concludes with a couple of 'truisms': "The job of language, sensibly employed, is to defend reality against the telling" (352). "The reader closes the book, satisfied that life, no matter how wild, can be put in a book and it is, therefore, predictable" (355).

Raymond Federman and the Closet Crossing

For Federman, the genre of autobiography forms the poetics of nonconformity par excellence. One writes autobiography in a double fold: you write what you remember but you have to make a selection. As soon as selection is involved, subjectivity is lost. For Federman therefore all writing is fiction. In his essay, "Federman on Federman: Lie or Die (Fiction as Autobiography/Autobiography as Fiction)", we find various postulations which seem to situate Federman the autobiographer between fiction and criticism. Insofar as autobiography uses language as a medium – and language is unreliable – autobiography by definition is a distortion of life. As far as Federman is concerned fiction informs life. Only fiction is real insofar as life comes in "different" versions. Hence life is fictional. Fiction comes in different versions, hence it is true. One of the 'selected' themes in Federman's autobiographical/fictional oeuvre is the story of escape from Auschwitz where his entire family ended up. He was saved by his mother who had enough spirit to push him into a closet just as the Germans were at the door ready to pick them up. He stayed in the closet three days. In 1947 at the age of 19 he immigrated to America and the other story, yet embedded with the Holocaust story, that Federman tells from then on is the story of how he became a writer. Yet Federman's narrator, and there are always several voices speaking simultaneously, often both in French and in English, is a writer who always writes the same story, namely the escape from the Nazis. Federman's autobiography is thus construed as a meta-narrative frame: a writer writing on how to become a writer who is already a writer of writing stories including autobiography. The point that Federman tries to make is that a writer in transit (here taken both literally and metaphorically) necessarily must produce a discourse which annihilates the borders between genres: one can be suspicious of autobiography, and yet trust a life story. As he puts it:

> What is interesting in the relationship between fiction and autobiography is the mechanism by which a writer transforms elements of his life into stories. What is fascinating is the process which makes it possible for a life to become fiction, or vice versa for fiction to make it possible for a writer to have a biography – real of imagined. (Federman, 1993: 100)

This clearly stems from Federman's own experiences with being a refugee in America, a state which ultimately contributed to his exercising the art of making variations on the same story. One may be still in transit culturally and linguistically, but one is not without possibilities. Having to tell the same story over and over again enables the writer to precisely distinguish between what Federman calls "remembered events" and "invented events". The space between autobiography and fiction, the in-between-ness of what is remembered and what is invented, is marked by a question of trust. What the reader is trusted to witness is the author's crossing. His coming out of the closet. Where Federman proves to be against the norm is in his yoking together of fiction and autobiography as the subtitle of his essay also indicates. Furthermore, the parenthesis around the subtitle makes it also clear that what we are dealing with here is the old dichotomy of container/contained. It is perhaps for this reason that in the essay, following an epigraph from Mallarmé which reads very conveniently that "All that is written is fictive", Federman marks the transient nature of being a writer with shifts between narratorial voice and authority. Thus he creates a discourse in the first person which is intended to overwrite the 'saved for later' third person narrative. Here is an example:

> If I were a critic (which I was once upon a time) and were asked to discuss (in spoken or written form) Federman's fiction, I would not discuss what Federman has written in his books (those curious books which seem to defy any classification and yet call themselves novels with effrontery) but what he has left unwritten. I mean unwritten not only in terms of substance and content, but also in terms of form and language. His books are full of holes, full of gaps, full of missing elements, to use an oxymoron. And his language too is full of holes, full of missing parts. His books are, in fact, always left unfinished. Federman writes unfinished stories made of unfinished sentences but which pretend to be finished stories made of finished sentences. (85)

Autobiography is fiction that looks forwards to its own future. Finding Federman in the gaps and in the holes, in what is presented as the in-between zone of existence, is an endeavor which finds its correlative in the act of lying and dying. These two alternatives to how existence or death is to be rendered on paper are the only means of reinstating authorial subjectivity. Subjectivity for Federman is transit, and transit translates as translation and self-translation. Thus 'trans' (Atlantic or otherwise) is a language in parenthesis.

Eva Hoffman and the Lost Crossing

Unlike Federman who 'finds' himself in translation, who then also loses himself on purpose in all the discourses that double cross his endeavor as a writer, Eva Hoffman portrays her experiences of being a writer in transit by being lost not in translation but in memory. For Hoffman, translating one's identity into an identity which is very much marked by the profession of being a writer is a conscious act of dealing with the idea of transit. More specifically transit is a notion that mediates various crossings between language as identity and identity as language. Hoffman's double take here is similar to Federman's in the sense that the space between the two, language and identity, is strategically thought of as forming a paradox. Whether in writing or language, or identity or culture of the self, the paradox of being somewhere while not yet arriving, or being somewhere physically while being somewhere else mentally represents a dilemma: as a confused immigrant whose perceptions of one's crossing the Atlantic into a world which seems surreal, can one take one's existence literally? If Hoffman talks of translation at all in her book, she talks about it as dependent on making existence a matter of the literary. She seems to suggest that the literariness of one's existence is lost on remembrance yet gained on words. Here there is a reversal, one does not write what one remembers, or from experience, but one remembers what one writes, and then experiences.

Remembering in words is crucial for Hoffman, insofar as her concern with the style of writing ultimately shapes the style of living, or living as style. For instance, having arrived in Canada at the age of 13, the first thing that the narrator pays attention to is style. The style of teenagers who, unlike their Polish counterparts, use a lot of make up and other artificial devices that enable them to pass as something else, is something the narrator can never quite understand. To the narrator the make up is a camouflage for not taking one's existence literally, and the example with girls confessing to each other everything between heaven and earth is an illustration of how some people's existence is not only rendered metaphoric by themselves but also taken for granted. What Hoffman registers is the Canadians' desire to conform to a certain set of norms, and she begins to wonder how that is made compatible with the Canadians' being proud of their freedom. Thus being in Canada (constrained by norm, yet 'free' to speak) as against being in Poland (free to be different, yet not free to speak) is rendered as being in transit without knowing what one is looking for. If, however, the narrator realizes that she does not know what she is looking for, she also observes that this ignorance characterizes Canadians as well. Their artificial houses and artificial lawns, artificial teenage lifestyle and artificial talk of independence suggests to the narrator that she in fact finds herself belonging to a place beyond the actual place she is at. Yet this is the only place that allows her to engage in deconstructing artificiality through language. Placing herself at odds with the Canadian life-style, and making an analogy between real and fictional existence, between real desire and invented desire Hoffman writes:

> Like so many children who read a lot, I begin to declare rather early that I want to be a writer. But this is the only way of articulating a different desire, a desire that I can't understand. What I really want is to be transported into a space in which everything is as distinct, complete and intelligible as in the stories I read. And, like most children, I am a literalist through and through. I want reality to imitate books – and books to capture the essence of reality. I love words insofar as they correspond to the world, insofar as they give it to me in a heightened form. The more words I have, the more distinct, precise my perceptions become – and such lucidity is a form of joy. (Hoffman, 1989: 28–29)

Now, although Hoffman talks about the desires a child gives expression to, the overall narrative tone in the book is imbued with the same desire for the literal manifestations of things. The stories Hoffman talks about are also family stories which are full of secrets, fears of war and destruction, aspirations and ambitions. The narrator feels lost in the task of translating her parents' stories into her own story. While she realizes that these stories are necessary and must be written, she also makes the point that it is impossible to get things right. As she puts it, when it comes to describing events that do not include her: "I don't understand what I remember" (24). Again she feels in transit in the family stories: within them, yet neither part of them, nor outside of them. However, as the story of the Holocaust runs parallel with Hoffman's own story, it neither takes off on its own, nor is it kept untold. As Mieke Bal has observed in her book *Acts of Memory: Cultural Recalls in the Present*, traumatic events, even those events that do not involve us or touch us directly resist incorporation into narratives (Bal, 1999: viii–ix). Hoffman thus translates her parents' discourse into an act of personal memory.

Thus against the background of struggling with language and narrative, the narrator's self emerges as "invisible". "I don't really exist" (108) she says, yet existence is made contingent on location. Hence, "being 'an immigrant' [...] is considered a sort of location in itself" (133). The only option out of that kind of place is to set one's aspirations higher. As the narrator later decides that she now wants to be a New York intellectual, she consequently crosses another border. Succeeding in her endeavor to be assimilated, and very specifically at that, Hoffman hammers a point home: the passage from being an exile to being assimilated necessarily goes through several periods of transit. These periods need to be translated into both lost and gained crossings insofar as they constitute a discursive approach to identification with a community. As Stuart Hall put it in his *Questions of Cultural Identity*: "the discursive approach sees identification as a construction, a process never completed – always 'in process'. It is not determined in the sense that it can always be 'won' or 'lost', sustained or abandoned [...] there is always 'too much' or 'too little' – an over-determination or a lack, but never a proper fit, a totality" (Hall, 1996: 2).

Hoffman's literature of transit thus opens up for both a construction and production of identity. Being caught between stories, "between the kinds of story we tell ourselves about ourselves" (268) is being lost in our endeavor to belong. Yet belonging is a crossing with a double significance: it imagines and re-imagines the self.

Charles Simic and the Fortune Crossing

As Eva Hoffman closes her personal account in *Lost in Translation* with the observation that circumstance guides the story: "In one story circumstance plays the part of fate, in the other character" (268), Simic refers to the same, yet the opposite, when he expresses his desire to write a book in which circumstance plays the part of imagination. One passage in *The Unemployed Fortune-Teller* illustrates the point:

> I would like to write a book that would be a meditation on all kinds of windows. Store windows, monastic windows, windows struck by sunlight on a street of dark windows, windows in which clouds are reflected, imaginary windows, hotel windows, prisons… windows one peeks out or peeks in. Windows that have the quality of religious art, etc. (Simic, 1994: 106)

What characterizes Simic's poetry and essays is the exploration of the proximity between writer and reader. The style in both genres is close to the tone in a memoir: one makes personal observations in passing when passing. Peeking out of the window if one is open. The aim is to come as close to the reader, his intelligence, and his imagination. 'Peeking' is a way of experimenting with economy in language: how to write as little as possible, using short forms, short sentences, and yet say as much as possible. His memoir, *A Fly in the Soup,* begins with the following statements: "mine is an old, and familiar story by now. So many people have been displaced in this century, their numbers so large, their collective and individual destinies so varied, it's impossible for me or anyone else, if we are honest, to claim any special status as victim" (1). This disclaimer, the rejection to be identified as a victim is mirrored in the epigraph from Raymond Chandler: "Don't tell me the plot… I'm only a bit-player". It is as if Simic wants his story suspended between telling and events. This kind of suspension combines transactional writing, which comes in the form of reporting, informing, proposing, and expressive writing, which is characterized by reflections, explorations, speculations, meanderings, discovering. These two types of writing are exploited by Simic's ability to write essays, and his memoir, recording his experiences with fleeing from Yugoslavia and being an immigrant in America in the 50s and 60s after a year-long stay in France, shows that identity is both determined by belonging to a group and derived at the same time. Especially the period in France is marked by the realization that one belongs to a group which is different from other social classes.

Simic's concern with identity demonstrates that the self is never secure, nor can it form its own narrative. At best there are scenes or moments to return to which arrange themselves and are representative of what is enduring. Yet the arrangement of these scenes in a chronological order runs counter to what Simic calls "the logic of imagination" (28). In order to be, one has to imagine. Only from the position of imagining (belonging, identity, or the place of language) can one locate difference within difference itself. Being bilingual represents this best. As Simic puts it: "To be bilingual is to realize that the name and the thing are not bound intrinsically. It is possible to find oneself in a dark hole between languages. I experience this now when I speak Serbian, which I no longer speak fluently. I go expecting to find a word, knowing that there was a word there once, and find instead a hole and a silence" (Simic, 1984: 112). What Simic identifies here is precisely a difference within difference, and this double difference opens the space for imagining.

Although Simic calls his work a memoir, it is also an autobiography to the extent that his voice expresses concerns that go beyond the first person singular. One of the interesting features of the book is in its considerations of both history and culture. Once the Atlantic is crossed, one of the first things that being in America enables him to do is begin to register a shift in discursive practices from 'the personal is personal' (still the situation in Yugoslavia at the time) and 'the personal is political' (the American way in the 60s) to 'the personal is both political and personal' (Simic's own conclusion from a transit perspective). Simic's considerations are very much linked with the observations he makes about the literary scenes of Chicago, where he mostly reads a lot, and New York, where he mostly writes a lot. Chicago lacking the intellectual drive of New York is rendered as an extension of being in transit: while learning takes place belonging does not. Once in New York Simic (and this goes for the other three authors as well) develops a sense of belonging which seems to "atlanticize"[7] the place. As was the case with the other three authors, Simic's work conflates in-between-ness with strategies for belonging which begin in a state of neutrality. His own

---

[7] I borrow the term "atlanticized" from Lene Yding Pedersen whose essay on O'Connor in this volume makes apt observations on how spaces can be seen to undergo an atlanticizing process.

discursive strategy is not just to say that the personal is political, in fact he has something very specific to say against that, but to advocate a position not of substitution but of gathering: the personal discourse and its material/historical location.

It is for this reason that Simic's book, after having recorded the best way of dealing with those who do not "like the refugees", ends with a full fledged poetic manifesto of nonconformity reflecting the writer's primary concern: the writing of poetry which places itself at odds with culture, history, gender, and class. However, Simic's poetics is not about stating how things should be, but suggesting that some things are already as they are. For instance:

> The secret wish of poetry is to stop time [...] the poet is driven by a desire to tell the truth [...] Truth matters. Getting it right matters. The realists advise: open your eyes and look. People of imagination warn: close your eyes to see better. There's truth with eyes open, and there's truth with eyes closed, and they often do not recognize each other in the street [...] The problem of identity is ever present, as is the nagging suspicion that one's existence lacks meaning. The working premise nevertheless is that each self, even in its most private concerns, is representative, that the "aesthetic problem", as John Ashbery has said, is a "microcosm of all human problems," that the poem is a place where the "I" of the poet, by the kind of visionary alchemy, becomes a mirror for all of us [...] What we love in it [poetry] is its democracy of values, its recklessness, its individualism, and its freedom. There's nothing more American and more hopeful than its poetry. (160–162)

Poetry thus expressed – either through autobiography or the memoir – becomes a testimony against oppression and consequently reinstates the speaking subject in a dominant position. But how can a dominant position be made poetical? How can it cross its own boundaries? Here Simic seems to suggest that by making recourse to a multitude of voices, the problem with difference can be, if not solved, then mediated. These voices which form the last pages of a *Fly in the Soup* are set in dialogue with the narrator:

> *Only idiots want something neat, something categorical – and I never talk unless I know!*
>
> *Aha! You're mixing poetry and philosophy. Wittgenstein wouldn't give you the time of day!*

> *"Everyone looks very busy to me," says Jasper Johns, and that's my problem too […]*
>
> *Who said, "Whatever can be thought must be fictitious"?*
>
> *You got me there! How about a bagel Hegel?*
>
> *Still and all… and above all! Let's not forget "above all".*
>
> *Here's what Nietzsche said to the ceiling: "The rank of the philosopher is determined by the rank of his laughter." But he couldn't really laugh.*
>
> *I know because I'm a connoisseur of paradox. All the good-looking oxymorons are in love with me and come to visit me in my bed at night.* (179–180; author's emphasis)

What is revealed is a high degree of self-consciousness combined with an attempt at understanding the paradox (or fortune) of difference. The writer makes himself an element of fiction in the thought which thinks poetry. And such is the nature of border-crossing too.

Concluding Transubstantiations

Writers such as Codrescu, Federman, Hoffman and Simic, writing from the perspective of being in transit, often tend to argue their case emphasizing the double character of their identity. For instance, it is not just Simic the Yugoslav in America or France that we become familiar with but Simic the Yugoslav and the American and the French. We see this double perspective at work when Simic characterizes his family or the condition of the immigrant. As he puts it: "We are all composite characters, made up of halfdozen different people, thanks to being kicked around from country to country" (120). Being in transit, crossing borders, re-imagining belonging to a neutral space emphasizes for these writers the desire to construe identity from the margins inwards and embrace dualities. What is ultimately said is that we are both ourselves *and* other people. Both here *and* some place else. Identity is socially constructed *and* individual. We are both philosophers *and* poets.

The border, then, with its potential to call forth crossing, is a literary device which discloses the subtleties of poetic expression within a realm where displacement can be played with and upon, and where crossing, like breaking, releases new energy.

References

Bernstein, Michael André (1996) "Exile, Cunning and Loquaciousness". *Salmagundi*. Saratoga Springs: Summer. Issue 111.

Bal, Mieke (1999) "Introduction". *Acts of Memory: Cultural Recall in the Present*. Eds. Mieke Bal, Jonathan Crewe, and Leo Spitzer. Hanover, NH: University Press of New England

Casteel, Sarah Philips (2001) "Eva Hoffman's Double Emigration: Canada as the Site of Exile in Lost in Translation". *Biography*. Winter, 24, 1.

Codrescu, Andrei (2001) *An Involuntary Genius in America's Shoes (And What Happened Afterwards)*. Santa Rosa: Black Sparrow Press.

Hedetoft, Ulf and Hjort, Mette, eds. (2002) *The Postnational Self: Belonging and Identity*. Minneapolis: University of Minnesota Press

Federman, Raymond (1979) *The Voice in the Closet*. Madison, Wisconsin: Coda Press.

—. (1982) *The Twofold Vibration*. København: The Green Integer

—. (1993) *Critifiction*. Albany: SUNY

Hoffman, Eva (1989) *Lost in Translation*. London: Vintage

Simic, Charles (2002) *A Fly in the Soup*. Ann Arbor: The University of Michigan Press

—. (1994) *The Unemployed Fortune-Teller*. Ann Arbor: The University of Michigan Press

Hall, Stuart (1996) *Questions of Cultural Identity*. London: Sage

Grossberg, Lawrence (1996) "Identity and Cultural Studies: Is that all There Is?" *Questions of Cultural Identity*. Ed. Stuart Hall. London: Sage

Spalding, J.M (1998) "Interview with Charles Simic". *The Courtland Review*. Issue 4. August [http://www.cortlandreview.com/issuefour/interview-4.htm]

Taylor, Charles (1992) *Multiculturalism and the Politics of Recognition*. New Haven: Princeton University Press

—. (1992) *Sources of the Self: The Making of the Modern Identity*. Cambridge: Cambridge University Press

Vianu, Lidia (2001) "Desperado Literature". Interview with Andrei Codrescu. [http://lidiavianu.scriptmania.com/andrei_codrescu.htm]

Atlanticized: Joseph O'Connor's Irish America

Lene Yding Pedersen

In the mid 1990s I spent one semester in the English Department at University College Galway. I was there through a European student exchange program, and that year UCG also had European exchange students from The Netherlands, Norway, Sweden, Spain, Germany, England, and Austria, to mention just the nationalities of those exchange students that I knew. In other words, several students had crossed the Irish Sea to study in Galway. However, the largest group of visiting students came not from across the Irish Sea, but from across the Atlantic: American students. In lecture halls, university clubs and societies, as well as bars in the city they could be seen and heard. They had crossed the Atlantic to take part of their education in Ireland, some of them doubtlessly also to track down the national heritage of their great-grandparents, who had crossed the Atlantic from Ireland some 150 years earlier to come to America (or to get away from Ireland). At the same time as they upheld the national and cultural heritage of their Irish ancestors, the American students of course also brought with them something 'American', or sometimes 'Irish American', to Ireland. These visiting American students exemplify the cross-Atlantic exchange of people, histories, traditions, and culture between Ireland and America, which is part of Irish history as well as contemporary Ireland.

It has been suggested in contemporary theory and criticism of Irish culture and history that Ireland 'Atlanticized' itself over the past centuries and in particular in the 1840s, when Irish emigrants in large numbers left a famine-ridden Ireland for America. In *The End of Hidden Ireland: Rebellion, Famine, and Emigration* (1995) Robert James Scally suggests that the emigrants onboard the ships bound for America became Irish in this moment of leaving Ireland, and that they lost Ireland in the very moment of their becoming Irish, and he ends his book with these words:

> Peering from the stern rather than the bow of the emigrant ship, that backward glace at the incongruous palms and gaily painted houses along the shore near Skibbereen was not only their last sight of Ireland but the first sight of themselves. (Scally, 1995: 236)

In "Found Drowned: The Irish Atlantic" Ian Baucom points out Scally's emphasis on the Famine narrative as a narrative of migration from place to space:

> The accelerated experience of 'modernisation' that saw a million peasants turned into wage laborers, often within a matter of weeks, was above all else an experience of exchanging a hyperlocalized territory of identity and belonging for the deterritorializing flow-dynamic of the Atlantic world system, that the Famine emigrants migrated less from Ireland to the Americas than from the knowledge of belonging to a place to the confusion of occupying the placeless space of the Atlantic economy. (Baucom, 2000: 136)

Building on Scully's argument, Ian Baucom speaks of an 'Atlantic self' that came into being at that time in history.

Apart from reading the Atlantic as an image of the move from place to space and the effect such a move had on notions of identity and subjectivity for the Irish emigrants, Baucom also emphasizes what he calls Ireland's "transoceanic dissemination" (142). In his reading of the American Wakes of the 1840s he sees something that marks "the moment in which Ireland takes its place within a transatlantic world, the moment in which Irishness comes to encompass not a lost place but a circulating, cross-Atlantic economy of memories, letters, songs, bodies, images and desires" (143). (On this point Baucom differs from Scully.) In other words, he emphasizes the importance of the Atlantic as a channel for "a circulating economy" not only of people but of narratives, and that this economy is what establishes a collective Irish identity as a community of belonging. It is not that the immigrants replaced stable notions of localized identity and the place of the nation with the placelessness of the extra-national: "they were marking, with no little degree of agony, their entry into an Irish place of belonging unbounded by the borders of the nation, a place of belonging that was less insular than circular, less rooted than routed, less national than Atlantic" (141).

In this essay I will take a closer look at the idea of a cross-Atlantic economy and the notion of an Atlanticized self in two books by contemporary Irish writer Joseph O'Connor. I wish to show both how O'Connor thematizes the idea of Atlanticized places, spaces and identities and how, and to what extent, he is himself an 'Atlanticized' writer. In many of O'Connor's novels and plays the Atlantic, and the fact that it can be crossed, is central to plot and characters. Here I will limit myself to a discussion of O'Connor's 2002 novel *Star of the Sea* and his 1996 travel book *Sweet Liberty: Travels in Irish America*. *Star of the Sea* tells the story of a "coffin ship's" journey from Ireland to America in 1847, and in *Sweet Liberty* O'Connor travels to America to visit his 'Irish America', which includes visiting the nine *Dublins* in the US, in search of connections between names, locations, people and history, and between Ireland and America, past and present.

As my introduction has already implied, it is almost impossible to speak of the importance of the cross- or trans-Atlantic in relation to Irish culture and history without dealing with the notion of 'the Famine' (definite article, capital F). *Star of the Sea* thematizes some important issues related to 'Famine writing' in particular and 'history' and its representations in general, which I will point out in my discussion of the novel. And it is likewise impossible to speak of the Atlantic without speaking of America. Just like the Atlantic in Baucom's reading of Irish history, 'America' is in O'Connor's writing both a literal place and an imagined space. In my reading of *Sweet Liberty* I hope to illustrate how these two notions of 'America' interact, and that they are not as easily distinguishable as they might appear.

Star of the Sea

The textuality of the past

In *Writing the Irish Famine* (1995) Christopher Morash emphasizes the elusiveness of the Famine. One of the 'problems' with the Famine as a historical event is that it is not framed at both ends by written texts – in other words, there is "no ceremonial beginning, no ceremonial ending" (Morash, 1995: 3). From his new historicist point of view, Morash points to the "absence of a stable, empirical reality" and instead claims that:

> Like all part events the Famine is primarily a retrospective, textual creation. The starvation, the emigration, and the disease epidemics of the late 1840s have become 'the Famine' because it was possible to inscribe those disparate, but interrelated events in a relatively cohesive narrative. For those of us born after the event, the representation has become the reality. (3)

In his book Morash deals with representations of the Famine in 19th century literature, and he emphasizes that what a writer like Canon Sheelan (born in 1852) 'remembers' is not the Famine itself but "a semiotic system of representations which had replaced the Famine", that is, textual traces. He then points out what he sees as the *danger* that "the dream of such access [to an empirical historical reality] will re-emerge in the literary text" (4), which is a quite concrete 'textual trace'. But we must remember that literary texts work by means of representational conventions, as all kinds of texts do, and Morash explains this in the light of an "intertextual archive" with reference to Roland Barthes, who sees the quotations of which a text is made as "anonymous, untraceable, and nevertheless already read"(Barthes quoted in Morash, 5).[1]

"If," as Morash notes, "history is textual, textuality is also historical" (4). This means that obviously representational conventions have changed from the 19th century to the 20th and 21st centuries, and this affects the way texts represent or create the Famine. Baucom considers some of the conventions in recent histories of the Famine and notes that they organize themselves around the figure of the incomplete, and that they attempt to "complete the record" by means of "a transposable set of images" (Baucom, 2000: 131). Baucom notes that it is often the exact same set of anecdotes, songs and events that are dealt with in different contemporary histories of the Famine. Furthermore, the images that appear in contemporary histories of the Famine are "not narratives of deaths but afterimages of the dead". And since histories of the Famine try to complete the incomplete, Baucom sees them as trying to somehow complete the dead. But why do that? "Why are the dead returned to view? Why must their perpetually unburied bodies be exhumed and exhumed and reexhumed?" (132) Baucom suggests that the answer has to do with the placelessness of the dead, most of whom got inadequate burials (in the Atlantic, cabins, fields, lime pits): "the dead must be disinterred, before the labor of remembering and mourning and reburying the Famine can be 'complete'" (133).

Star of the Sea is a literary representation of the Famine but it also self-reflexively points to the way in which such representations work. It writes

---

[1] To see what Morash means consider Jonathan Culler's definition of intertextuality in The Pursuit of Signs: "Intertextuality thus becomes less a name for a work's relation to particular prior texts than a designation of its participation in the discursive space of a culture: the relationship between a text and the various languages or signifying practices of a culture and its relation to those texts which articulate for it the possibilities of that culture" (Culler, 2001: 114).

itself into representational conventions of Famine representations and draws on both the histories of the Famine (such as Cormac Ó Gráda's) and the transposable set of images that Baucom speaks of. Furthermore it self-reflexively makes use of the conventions of the novel as a genre by employing the literary form of a Victorian novel. The novel thematizes the 1840s in both its content and form – from a 2002 perspective, of course.

Star of the Sea is framed as a book written by the fictive American journalist G. Grantley Dixon of the *New York Times*, *An American Abroad: Notes of London and Ireland in 1847*, large parts of which are based on the accounts of 26 days at sea in 1847 made by captain of the ship, Josias Tuke Lockwood, and G.G. Dixon's own notes and memories of the journey as well as the interviews he has made with a series of the characters in the story in and after 1847. Inserted into this story are passages from real-life letters from Irish emigrants, illustrations originally published in *Harper's Weekly*, *Judy* magazine, *Illustrated London News*, *Pictorial Times*, and *Punch* magazine, as well as quotes from contemporary politicians and writers (among them Charles Dickens), Irish songs and ballads, and statistics. Furthermore there is in each chapter a 'stand first text' written by G.G. Dixon's fictive publisher Mr. Newby. In G.G. Dixon's account we get the stories of four main characters: David Merridith, Pius Mulvey, Mary Duane, and G.G. Dixon. G.G. Dixon's book is itself framed by four epigraphs, each of which is a quote by a historical figure, and each of which represents an interpretation of the Famine. Thus we see that it is indeed the textuality of the past that is foregrounded: sometimes the material is historical, sometimes fictional, but always textual. There are layers and layers of texts, interpretations, and storytellers, which indicates that there is no direct access to the past.

The Commemorative One-Hundredth Edition of G.G. Dixon's *An American Abroad: Notes of London and Ireland in 1847*, which we find in O'Conner's novel, relies on its author's work to gather different kinds of material on the basis of which he can compose his story and complete it. G.G. Dixon's story includes essays, newspaper articles, notes, journals, science books, interviews, and notes. Dixon works both as a writer and a historian. As a historian G.G. Dixon tries to get all the details right: almost all the texts are dated, except for the real-life letters. (In all this dating, it is noteworthy that none of the real-life letters are dated. They may have become part of the collective memory of the Famine and the transposable set of famine texts that they no longer need to be specified: if so, they belong to the 'intertextual Famine archive', an archive that is literally cross-Atlantic.)

The use of dates points to 'the historian's way of working' and thematizes an attempt to connect the texts to certain verifiable points in history and thereby create a sense of empirical reality, though we are repeatedly reminded that all texts work by means of conventions, and that they therefore connect with other texts rather than empirical reality.

This edition has "Many New Inclusions" and an epilogue dated New York City, Easter Saturday, 1916 – that is, 69 years after the journey across the Atlantic. Easter Saturday, 1916, is an 'iconic' date in Irish history, which I shall say more about later. Thus, on the one hand the past is presented as texts and interpretations; on the other hand as factual historical events situated at a time line. And it is the interplay between these two conceptions of the past that is dealt with in the novel.

Composing the (Story of the) Past

The novel repeatedly faces its reader with the idea that "it is not in the material but the way it is composed", and the idea of 'composing' is emphasized at different levels. When Pius Mulvey starts composing songs, he soon finds out that it takes both experience and skills but not at all the ability to convey 'facts' or to present something 'new'. The first thing Mulvey notes about his first two lines is that he has heard them before, and he realizes that:

> The facts of what had happened on that wintry day were hard to meld into the lines of the ballad; if you could ever say clearly what the facts actually were. So he changed them a little to fit the rhyme scheme. It didn't really matter. Nobody would ever know the facts anyway; if they somehow found them out, they wouldn't find them worth singing. The main thing in balladry was to make a singable song. The facts did not matter: *that was the secret*. (102)

So Mulvey composes his ballad according to the conventions of the artistic genre, or "the principle[s] of the architecture of balladry" (100), such that each line moved the story forward; (like all good stories) it had choice at its heart; and "The last verse took the most time to compose. In a song like this it was a matter of custom to put something about Ireland into the climax. Mulvey didn't give a sparrow's fart for Ireland and he suspected many of his audience would give even less, but people liked a bit of a shout at a hooley. To leave it out would be not to finish the job; like building a cabin with no roof" (103). This stress on Mulvey's composing underlines that artistic 'composing' has more to do with conventions and expectations than it has to do with representing 'facts'. Furthermore it suggests that the concern with 'Ireland' in these songs (some of which we find in the novel) may also be a matter of convention rather than any political opinion held by the composer of the song. At the same time he notes that people who appear in these songs will live on in them (Mulvey considers including a farmer from Rosaveel named John Furey: "Mulvey had only met him twice, and had certainly never scratched or scarped alongside him, but his name had the requisite trio of syllables", but in the end he decides for "my brother" instead and "the fleeting candidature for immortality of John Furey from Rosaveel was thereby cancelled for ever" (101).

Mulvey's song became a great success in Ireland. Later on when Mulvey has moved to London, he changes the song so that it fits his new situation: now it was about East-End swell duds (188), and instead of the Irish, he now uses London slang. "Not a jot did it bother him to alter the ensemble" (188). One night Mulvey meets Charles Dickens who asks him about the origins of the song, as he is greatly interested in "anything authentic" concerning the culture of the working man. Mulvey tells a lying story about how he got the song from an aged pickpocket, a Jew who ran a school for young thieves and runaways, "It was indeed very old and extremely authentic" (190). So, here is an explanation as to how Dickens got the plot for *Oliver Twist*. Just as the theme of immortality in artistic representations was introduced in relation to John Furey and Mulvey's ballad, we hear that when Dickens asks for the name of the Jew, Mulvey tells him the name of the parish priest of Derryclare (the most evil old Jew-hater he had ever met), Fagan (190–191). In Mulvey's own words, he had used the opportunity "to magic the old bastard into what he most detested" (191) and into what he will live on as. Mulvey's song and its function in the novel shows the problems in talking about 'the authentic' as well as the notion that artistic representations should be able to convey 'facts' about certain situations.

The song Mulvey composes in O'Connor's novel is a version of a 19th century song "Arthur McBride", which – as the Sources and Acknowledgements say – has been recorded by Paul Brady (1976) and Bob Dylan (1992).[2] And of course there is a novel by Dickens about an old Jew named not Fagan but Fagin. But by intermingling these historical documents with the story of his novel, O'Connor problematizes as well as warns his readers

---

[2] A version of the song is available on the internet at http://www.chivalry.com/cantaria/lyrics/arthur-mcbride.html

that any artistic representation (Mulvey's ballad, Dickens' novel, as well as his own novel) is a *composition,* and that such compositions follow conventions rather than facts, and that they can be altered as can their origins (as thematized in the way O'Connor has Mulvey compose a version of Arthur McBride and the way we get a version of the origin of Dickens' novel). It is a warning that a composer can compose whatever he likes on the basis of the material within the framework of conventions (the melodies, the rhetorical figures, the conventions of the genre, etc), and that the search for 'authentic representations' will inevitably fail. At the same time it is an ironic comment to those historians who make the mistake Morash speaks of and read 19th century Irish songs and ballads as 'true representations' of an empirical reality. (In a review article in *The Independent* O'Connor comments on the Irish ballad and its form and says, "All this would be fine, except there are historians who examined these ballads as authentic social documents, when of course they're works of art designed with a specific purpose" (*The Independent Online Edition* published 04 January 2003).) While Mulvey's composing of his song in this way problematizes the conventions of history writing, it stays firmly within the conventions of the novel: in the plot and Mulvey's character we find all the motivation and explanation for the song and why he composed it and changed it the way he did that we could possibly hope for. In other words, the narrative conventions seem to outweigh the historical ones.

In the epilogue G.G. Dixon comments on his own composition, and he repeats the mantra that "[e]verything is in the way the material is composed" (397). It is clear that there are conventions that G.G. Dixon knows and follows when he tells his story. He has to focus on a limited number of characters, and he knows that the readers will want to know to what extent they are 'real people' (if he can verify their existence) and how each of their stories ended in America. G.G. Dixon then points to his situation as a writer when telling his story:

> I would like to think I am objective in what I have put down but of course that is not so and could never have been. I was there. I was involved. I knew some of the people. One I loved; another I despised. I use the word carefully: I did despise him. So easy to despise in the cause of love. Others again I was simply indifferent to, and such indifference is also a part of the tale. And of course I have selected what has been seen of the Captain's words in order to frame and tell the story. A different author would have made a different selection. Everything is in the way the material is composed. (397)

In the epilogue there is also a comment on Mary Duane which relates to the idea of immortalizing people (like John Furey and Fagan). In relation to Mary Duane, G.G. Dixon speaks of her *suffering* composition, "I would like to have been able to say more in the present account, to do more than record the few known facts of her existence in terms of the existences of the men who hurt her. But I am simply not in a position to do so. Some things I have invented but I could not invent Mary Duane; at least not more than I have already done. She suffered more than enough composition" (399). So composition is not only a way of gaining immortality, but also something a character can suffer. Perhaps what G.G. Dixon says is that in his story Mary Duane never becomes 'herself' but exists only a someone else's composition (as literalized in Merridith's drawings of her). Mary Duane is the only character whose story does not get a proper ending (in the sense of narrative conventions). From that point of view she becomes the one thing that transgresses the conventions of G.G. Dixon's genre and the architecture of the novel. Perhaps she is the image of the indefinable and elusiveness of the Famine, which means that she reflects the conventions of representing the Famine after all. O'Connor has emphasized that one of the things he likes about 19th century fiction is that it tended to try to answer all the questions. But even though G.G. Dixon's epilogue goes a long way to do that, it is as if Mary Duane escapes this convention of the form. The figure of the incomplete is still there at the periphery.

To claim that Mary Duane 'suffers' composition says something about the whole issue of writing historical novels and of the purpose of history writing as such. In the epilogue G.G. Dixon wonders whether it was right or not to tell the story – whether it was right to invent events and characters *for the story to be interesting enough to be published*. (In the novel we hear repeatedly of G.G. Dixon's wishes to become a fiction writer, and how he cannot get his fiction published.) He seems to be suggesting that by telling the stories of these characters, they are 'immortalized' in the novel, but that also means that they will never stop suffering. As the discussion of Mulvey's song illustrates, composing presupposes not only 'the material', skills, and the knowledge of conventions, but also motivation and purpose. We know *why* Mulvey composed the song the way he did, and we also know why (or at least partly why) G.G. Dixon composed his story the way he did. The composer has a responsibility for the way he presents his story and the reasons for presenting it, and as I will point out later, G.G. Dixon is much more involved in the story than he first appears. It becomes obvious that the historian's composition of the story relies on his own action in it, as well as his motivation. In the novel we hear that "history is a useless art" (said by Merridith) but G.G. Dixon nonetheless makes some use of it (and so does O'Connor in his novel).

O'Connor bases his novel on different kinds of material: he appears to have done a lot a historical research for his novel as also indicated by the section "Sources and Acknowledgements". He lists background sources of historical research (among them Mary Daly's *The Famine in Ireland* (1986) and Cormac Ó Gráda's *The Great Irish Famine* (1989)). By including contemporary histories of the Famine, O'Connor acknowledges the fact emphasized by Morash that events of the past are most of all a textual construct, and that these constructs change over the years. O'Connor lists eye-witness accounts of the famine and shipboard experiences, real-life letters, publications from the 1840s, and songs and ballads – he has in other words consulted the 'intertextual Famine archive'. As will be discussed in more detail below, the genre of the Victorian novel and Emily Brontë's novel *Wuthering Heights* also echo throughout the novel as does the reception in contemporary theory and criticism of *Wuthering Heights*. Thus O'Connor's material for the novel consists of 'primary sources' in the form of texts produced in the 1840s, historical representations of the 1840s in the form of contemporary historians' accounts, and literary representations of the 1840s in the form of the echoes of *Wuthering Heights* and Charles Dickens in particular.

Obviously, the phrase that "it is not in the material but the way it is composed" describes O'Connor's work as well as that of the characters in his novel. At first sight the 'historical texts' seem separated from the fictive story (they appear at the beginning of chapters almost as epigraphs), commenting on the story or some theme or element in it, but the distinction between history and fiction is blurred in O'Connor's novel. Considering the fact that this novel was written in 2002, this is hardly surprising, yet it is important to notice for the understanding of how the novel 'works' as a novel, and how it brings forward its thematization of the representation of history in general and the Famine in particular. This does not mean that the novel claims that "everything is fiction" or that "there is no reality": O'Connor's novel points to the textuality of history and to the way in which historical representations rely on the ways in which they are composed, and that there may be different kinds of motives behind such composing.

The Frame Structure of the Novel and Echoes of *Wuthering Heights*

If we take a look at the form and structure of *Star of the Sea*, we see that it is a reworking of literary conventions of the Victorian novel in all its complexity. As O'Connor reminds us in an interview, the novel of the 1840s was still a relatively new literary form with a lot of energy and a license to make mistakes:

> But when you read the Dickens books of the era and the Brontës – it's an exaggeration to say that it has the same kind of energy as punk did, but there was something about having a licence to make mistakes. They just didn't care. There was a sense that the novel could take on anything, no subject too big to defeat the novel. Thus current vogue, the slim, terse, well-made novel where the entire plot is, the hero takes a sip of a glass of water and Spring comes and it's 90 pages of beautiful, elegant perfect, rather kind of deathly prose… I love Dickens for his faults as well. I just love the bravery and the scope and the ambition of it all. (identitytheory.com interview, posted June 26, 2003)

In another interview O'Connor has said that he wanted the novel to be "one of those big, noisy books you can get lost in" (*The Independent Online Edition*. Published on January 4, 2003). As such the form of the novel (and its 410 pages) is a way of pointing to and making use of the understanding that if history is textual, textuality is also historical.

In O'Connor's novel, G.G. Dixon is given the manuscript for *Wuthering Heights* by his publisher, and as such *Wuthering Heights* is part of the textual representation of 1847 that is constructed in the novel. Yet there are also obvious parallels between *Star of the Sea* and *Wuthering Heights*, and these parallels in different ways function in relation to the thematization in *Star of the Sea* of the past in general and the Famine in particular and its emphasis on textuality and composition. There are parallels between *Star of the Sea* and *Wuthering Heights* in terms of form, characters, and themes. The frame structure of *Star of the Sea* with its many layers and storytellers, which I have outlined above, reflects that of *Wuthering Heights* (the Captain of Star of the Sea is even named Lockwood). There are significant similarities between Pius Mulvey and Heathcliff, and the themes of property, kinship, inheritance, law, and economic exchange which may be said to structure the plot of *Wuthering Heights* is also emphasized in O'Connor's novel (there are other thematic parallels as well which I shall not get into here). Apart from these parallels, *Star of the Sea* also integrates some of the reception of *Wuthering Heights* in contemporary criticism.

If we take a closer look at the frame structure of O'Connor's novel, we see the similarities between G.G. Dixon and Lockwood: like Lockwood G.G. Dixon comes from 'the outside' (America) to experience violent events in Ireland and London. And like Lockwood he is at the same time entangled in the stories he tells: he is in love with Laura Merridith (and ends up marrying her in New York), and he despises David Merridith ('in theory' because G.G. Dixon is a socialist and Lord Merridith a landowner, as 'in practice' because Lord Merridith is married to Laura Merridith). As in *Wuthering Heights* the frame structure, at points, dissolves. In the end of the novel we hear that G.G. Dixon married Laura Merridith after David Merridith was murdered on the ship, and we realize that G.G. Dixon was much more directly involved in this murder than expected: for 69 years he has kept the secret that he murdered Merridith (for love, for hate, for Merridith's children, or perhaps for the story). This is again a warning that representations (historical as well as literary) work by means of conventions and that storytellers may have different motives for telling their stories.

There are also similarities between Pius Mulvey and Heathcliff in the way they are constructed as ambiguous and contradictory characters, and some of these parallels concern the characters' ability to survive by making the most of any situation they find themselves in. Within the setup of O'Connor's novel as G.G. Dixon's book, much of the 'background' stories set in Ireland and London rely on Mulvey's story. At a critical point in the story (G.G. Dixon has just recognized Mulvey as the killer from Newgate), G.G. Dixon makes a deal with Mulvey: a story for a life (334). Within the economic logic of the story, Mulvey is able to trade in his story for his life (if G.G. Dixon gets Mulvey's story, he promises not to tell anybody who Mulvey really is). Apart from functioning as a way of describing the characters of G.G. Dixon and Mulvey and their motives for acting the way they do, this important event also points to the way *Star Of The Sea* relies on the same 'economic logic' as *Wuthering Heights* does. In both novels goods, land, properties, names, inheritance, and people are bought and sold or in other ways exchanged (at specifiable rates). In *Star Of The Sea* this logic of exchange comes to cover also lives and (hi)stories, which also rely on deals that are made for various reasons and motives – including those of the historian's representative, G.G. Dixon.

Why these echoes of *Wuthering Heights* in terms of narrative structure, characters, and underlying thematic logic? As suggested in relation to G.G.

Dixon's status as a historian, the frame structure may be seen as a way of 'authenticating' the story. At the same time, and perhaps even more importantly, the frame story takes away the focus from the teleological logic (which the cross-Atlantic journey itself indicates) and sets up a more confused one, which the echoes of *Wuthering Heights* only stress further. By writing Brontë's character Heathcliff into an Irish context, O'Connor also literalizes a connection between Brontë's novel and Ireland – a connection explored by, for instance, Terry Eagleton in *Heathcliff and the Great Hunger* (1995), a book also listed in the 'Sources and Acknowledgements'. This means that O'Connor situates his novel within a particular literary and theoretical historical context. Eagleton is a left-wing critic and his reading of *Wuthering Heights* draws attention to exactly those issues of materiality in that novel (see also Eagleton's essay "Myths of Power in 'Wuthering Heights'" from *Myths of Power: A Marxist Study of the Brontës* (1976)). In his own reconstruction of 'Heathcliff in Ireland' O'Connor in a sense reads Brontë's novel from Eagleton's theoretical perspective. This means that certain theoretical and/or political points about history and the workings of society in the 19th century are made in O'Connor's novel through its echoes of *Wuthering Heights* and its critical reception.

The American Abroad

By having G.G. Dixon as the author of *An American Abroad* O'Connor has chosen the viewpoint of an American of events that happened in 1847 Ireland, that is, he has presented Ireland as seen from an American's point of view. Furthermore he has transferred G.G. Dixon's point of view to 1916 (where the frame story of the epilogue takes place). At the same time we must remember that the novel *Star of the Sea* is written by an Irish writer in 2002. There is the time of events, the time of narrating, and the time of the novel. What we have, then, is a mixture of three historical points in time (1847, 1916, 2002), and two geographical locations (New York and Ireland). Between the geographical locations lies the Atlantic, which *Star of the Sea* crosses in G.G. Dixon's story, and between 1847 and 1916 are certain connections suggested by G.G. Dixon in the epilogue. G.G. Dixon is therefore both part of the story and distanced from it.

G.G. Dixon is set up as an apparent contrast to David Merridith: G.G. Dixon is from the 'new' world, Merridith is the son of an English Lord. G.G.

Dixon is a socialist, Merridith is an Aristocrat. G.G. Dixon is a journalist, Merridith is interested in the fine arts, etc. However, in the course of the novel these binary oppositions are deconstructed as for instance when we hear that G.G. Dixon grew up on a plantation and his family used to be slave owners (and later again when we hear that G.G. Dixon and Laura Merridith were not permitted to foster or adopt a child because G.G. Dixon's father was quarter-Choctaw), and G.G. Dixon's moral is not so much higher than Merridith's when he makes the deal with Mulvey. If we include Pius Mulvey as another contrast (to both Merridith and G.G. Dixon) we find that, again, apparent contrasts are undermined. (In the epilogue GGD reflects that "In a different world they [Merridith and Mulvey] might not have been enemies; at a different time, perhaps even friends" (397)). The only contrast that stands is the difference between those who were born rich and those who were born poor, and between those who have power and those who have not. The construction of these characters and their similarities and differences seem to suggest that things are a little more complex than they seem. While it seems correct to say that O'Connor's novel is peopled with Irish icons, as a reviewer of the novel has pointed out (*Guardian Unlimited*. Published January 25, 2003), these icons are not left untouched. This means that – apart from telling his story through quite complex characters – O'Connor also questions their underlying iconicity. In the course of the novel it gets more and more difficult to maintain the differences between sufferers and exploiters, between those with high morals and those without. (The exceptions to this are Captain Lockwood and Mary Duane.) In the novel G.G. Dixon literally replaces Merridith when he marries Laura Merridith and David Merridith's two sons change their family name form Merridith to Dixon. In other words, G.G. Dixon is part of the logic of exchange in the novel.

G.G. Dixon is not only characterized through his relations, similarities and differences from the other (male) main characters, he is also characterized through his status as the narrator of the story. G.G. Dixon is a journalist and a travel writer, as also the title of his book indicates. According to Helen Carr, travel writing in the 19th century was usually produced by missionaries, explorers, scientists, or orientalists, and the aim was the purveying of privileged knowledge (Carr, 2002: 74). The purveying of privileged knowledge seems to be G.G. Dixon's aim in so far as the purpose of his writing is to give an account of the social conditions of London and Ireland in 1847 to the American readers of the New York Times. This is in itself a noble enough motive; G.G. Dixon is a socialist and his political commitment shines through his journalistic writing. But we also learn about his sexual relationship with Laura Merridith (which may also explain his eagerness to go to Ireland and London), and we repeatedly hear about his ambitions to become a fiction writer. Besides writing about the social conditions of London and Ireland for his American readers, G.G. Dixon also uses his travel writing as an alternative form of novel writing (since he cannot get his fiction published anywhere). Apart from his socialist wish to make the world a better place for the underprivileged, G.G. Dixon is therefore also driven by his own vain ambitions to become a fiction writer, as well as by love or sexual desire.

G.G. Dixon tells the story 69 years after the journey across the Atlantic. This means that he is given the advantage of being able to look back at 1947 and consider the events of the story as well as his own role in them from a temporal distance. This becomes evident in the epilogue, where G.G. Dixon is allowed some comments of a more general character on the themes in the novel. We learn that there have been several editions already and that changes have been made from one edition to the next, and that in this edition there are "many new inclusions". G.G. Dixon is dying as he writes the epilogue and decides to include the "never published in previous editions" accounts in chapter xxxiii (325), which tells of the bargain with Mulvey as well as David Merridith's family relation to Mary Duane (she was an illegal child of David Merridith's father's and so biologically his half-sister). We also learn in the epilogue that it was G.G. Dixon, who murdered David Merridith, and not Pius Mulvey.

The epilogue is important for O'Connor's use of the Victorian novel as a frame for his own: it is place where all loose ends can be tied up and where things can come to their proper ends (the story told, his crimes confessed, G.G. Dixon can die in peace). The epilogue is also the place where the stories of Star of the Sea's journey across the Atlantic are put into perspective: as already mentioned Easter Saturday 1916 is an iconic date in Irish history, as it marks the Easter Rising against British Rule. This ties historical events of 1847 to historical events of 1916, and suggests that it is the same mechanism in people and society that leads to violence, murder and suffering, "all the way back to Cain" as G.G. Dixon phrases it. In the epilogue G.G. Dixon emphasizes a notion of society as structured around power and as divided between those who have power (regardless of nationality) and those who do not. In a stylistically very pompous paragraph G.G. Dixon puts it this way:

And the poor of both islands [Ireland and England] died in their multitudes while the Yahweh of retributions vomited down his hymns. The flags flutter and the pulpits resound. At Ypres. In Dublin. At Gallipoli. In Belfast. The trumpets spew and the poor die. Yet they walk, the dead, and will always walk; not as ghosts, but as press-ganged soldiers, conscripted into a battle that is not of their making; their sufferings metaphorised, their very existence translated, their bones stewed into the sludge of propaganda. They do not even have names. They are simply: The Dead. You can make them mean anything you want them to mean. (388)

Now, in a 2002 novel a writer may need the frame of a Victorian novel and the character of a G.G. Dixon to make such a statement, and this is what O'Connor does. When asked if he considers himself a political writer, O'Connor says that he does not consider himself a political writer "in a narrow way", but that he thinks that there should, occasionally, be novels that "illuminate a little bit of how the world works" and that he sees "writing a novel as a secret way of writing about politics and the world" (*Socialist Review* interview. Published May 2004). Perhaps G.G. Dixon's most important function is to allow O'Connor to do so in this novel. Despite his far from perfect character G.G. Dixon and his points of view (political and moral) are given a privileged position in the novel.

1847, 1916, 2002

The story takes place in 1847, which was the year that saw Marx's *Poverty of Philosophy*, Verdi's *Macbeth*, Boole's *Calculus of Deductive Reasoning*, Emily Brontë's *Wuthering Heights*, Charlotte's Brontë's *Jane Eyre*, Ralph Emerson's *Poems*, and Engel's *Principles of Communism* (386), and all these historical texts are listed in the epilogue. The point of listing these names is a double one: on the one hand it illustrates some of the 'modes of thinking' at that time; on the other hand it shows how 'history' remembers 1847. Right after the listing of these names O'Connor has G.G. Dixon reflect, "Quarter of a million starved in that year's nowhere-land: nameless in the latitudes of hunger" (386). As already mentioned, we hear Merridith speak of history as a useless art (386), and even though O'Connor's novel is saturated with history, it still takes the form of a novel (that takes the form of a journalist's recounting in a fictionalized and historicized kind of travel writing). This novel includes a fictional voicing of a few of those quarter of a million who died in 1847, and who are not heard in 'history'. At the same time it connects (thematically and temporally) events happening at the same time (in 1847) and between 1847 and 1916. By that it engages with the problematics of 'writing the Irish famine'.

By setting the story in 1847 and the epilogue in 1916, O'Connor writes his novel into the semiotic web of history. These years are not just coincidental points in history conceived of as consisting of events and facts along a time line, but signs that have themselves acquired meaning and significance over time. O'Connor's novel explicitly relates itself to such historical signs and systems. By inserting the real life letters in the novel, O'Connor both reinforces the 'intertextual Famine archive' and indicates a way of dealing with history as textual: these are not the writings of a Marx or Engels, but the writings of historically 'anonymous' people. In general there seems to be an attempt in the novel to give a name to the historically nameless, and a sense of place to the placeless (in the beginning of the novel we get the names, ages and towns of those who die onboard *Star of the Sea*, but in the course of the novel even Lockwood refers to them only as "the dead"). What we get, then, is a mixture of 1847 philosophical 'modes of thinking', the naming of the nameless, and – through the illustrations and other historical texts – different textual representations of the historical elements of the Famine.

Even though O'Connor claims to have chosen the form of the Victorian novel because it implies closure and completion, the figure of the incomplete is still present in his novel. All we get is (of course) an incomplete representation of a historical event (the Famine) through some fictional characters (Merridith, Mulvey, Mary Duane, and G.G. Dixon) at a point in history (1847) represented in a representation (a novel) by a writer (O'Connor) at another point in history (2002).

Sweet Liberty

O'Connor's 1996 book *Sweet Liberty: Travels in Irish America* deals with a crossing of the Atlantic in the 1990s – some 150 years after the story of *Star of the Sea* takes place. If *Star of the Sea* deals with the need to represent the past and with problems of authenticity implied in doing so, *Sweet Liberty* may be seen as dealing with the question of representation and authenticity, but in a contemporary context. In *Sweet Liberty* there is not the same temporal distance to the events described as in *Star of the Sea*. However, it remains uncertain whether the present is more 'authentic' than the past, and/or less textual, and whether we have access to the present in a more direct way than to the past. If one wishes to represent contemporary America, of course one can cross the Atlantic and actually go there (which is what O'Connor does in this book), but – just like the Atlantic in Baucom's reading of Irish history – 'America' is both a geographical place and a kind of mental space, and it is in between these different conceptions of 'America' that we find the issues of representation and authenticity thematized in *Sweet Liberty*. *Sweet Liberty* does not raise these questions through its narrative structure as *Star of the Sea* does – in terms of narrative structure and narration it is a far simpler book – but through the way it represents America as both a literal place and a mental space.

Sweet Liberty is an example of travel writing. Instead of presenting the traveling through a constructed character like G.G. Dixon in a Victorian novel set-up, O'Connor here does the traveling across the Atlantic 'in his own person'. This means that there are other conventions to be followed, even if the basic narrative situation is the same: like G.G. Dixon's story in *Star of the Sea*, this book deals with a writer who has crossed the Atlantic in order to write about what is on the other side of it. Whereas G.G. Dixon came from America to write about Ireland, O'Connor in this book travels from Ireland to write about America, or Irish America to be more precise. If we look at the characteristics of contemporary travel writing, we see that the genre has changed quite a bit since the 19th century, and that the aims of travel writing are no longer (just) the purveying of privileged knowledge, which we may see G.G. Dixon's book as an example of. In his overview of the travel writing genre from 1940-2000, Peter Hulme defines five "broad and overlapping strands that can be detected within travel writing of the last 25 years: 1. the comic, 2. the analytical, 3. the wilderness, 4. the spiritual, 5. the experimental" (Hulme, 2002: 93). O'Connor's book is not experimental and it is not concerned with the far off places Hulme mentions in relation to no. 3, but it combines features of the other three strands, in particular no 2 and 4. What characterizes no 2 is a mixture of personal reportage and socio-political analysis, and no. 4 is characterized by the inner journey merging with memoir, for instance when the writer's personal history is moulded into a cultural history.

The subtitle of *Sweet Liberty*, "travels in Irish America", indicates the characteristics of no 4 and no 2: the book is both about (Irish) America in the 1990s and about the author's "own imaginary America", and what importance that notion has had for him growing up in Ireland in the 1970s.

'America' is therefore not only a geographical 'place' but also a mental 'space' constructed on the Irish side of the Atlantic. In the book O'Connor visits his private American-Irish places (those that helped define his imaginary America) as well as nine American towns called Dublin (which he claims he included "purely for the hell of it" but which nonetheless call attention to the historical cross-Atlantic connections between Ireland and America as do the real-life letters in the beginning of each chapter, some of which are the same as those in *Star of the Sea*). *Sweet Liberty* therefore composes a picture of 1990s America (which characterizes the "analytical" kind of travel writing) as well a portrait of an 'Atlanticized' author (which makes it also a kind of "spiritual" travel writing), with a reference to the historical cross-Atlantic connections between Ireland and America.

Having just arrived in Boston, O'Connor tries to explain 'travel writing' to Eugene (a young Irishman who works in a hotel):

> I explained that I was writing a travel book about all the Dublins in the United States, and the various places in between them.
>
> 'A guidebook, is it?' Eugene said, his lips turning blue.
>
> 'Well, not really,' I said, blowing on my thumbnails. 'It's, you know, travel writing.'
>
> 'What's travel writing?' Eugene said.
>
> That was another astoundingly good question. I found myself wishing, for perhaps the first time in my life, that I was Paul Theroux. Eugene was giving me cause for some pretty serious self-analysis.
>
> 'It's where you just wander around a place,' I said, brilliantly, 'and you write down your impressions and what happens to you in a book.'
>
> 'You're fucking joking me?' said Eugene.
>
> 'No,' I tittered nervously.
>
> 'And would people buy a book like that?' he gasped, astonished.
>
> 'This is the theory,' I said.
>
> 'Sweet mother of holy fuck,' he said. 'I might write a fuckin book like that myself one day.' (O'Connor, 1996: 43)

Here O'Connor ironically thematizes the apparent uselessness of travel writing while also referring to another writer who has made himself famous exactly as a travel writer. This means that he acknowledges the genre he writes himself into, but that he also distances himself a little from it by means of irony.

Real America/Ireland

In the introduction O'Connor recounts how in the late 1960s and early 1970s his father would take him to Connamara in the summer. O'Connor is from Dublin, and he mentions how his parents (like many Irish people) felt that "the West was in some unquantifiable but equally undeniable sense the real Ireland" (6), and how they wanted O'Connor and his brother and sisters to have some notion of what it meant to be Irish. That sense of Ireland and Irishness was mediated through the American tourists staying at the Bridge House Hotel where the O'Connor family stayed in Spiddal. O'Connor recounts his fascination with these great-grandsons and -granddaughters of the poor Irish emigrants and their loud, exuberant and self-confident ways. These Americans would sing sentimental Irish ballads about places O'Connor had never seen in his life, and he was actually introduced to "the magic of rural Ireland by these American tourists and their sentimental songs". These "passionate Americans" would also sing patriotic rebel songs with tears in their eyes (much to the embarrassment of the Irish grown-ups). "But, at the time, I must confess that I loved the way the Americans went on. I loved their bravado, their shamelessness, the heady ease of their unthinking extremism. They were patriotic about Ireland and America in equal measure" (4). This means that 'real Ireland' was at least partly introduced to O'Connor through its Irish-American representations. At the same time as these Americans introduced O'Connor to 'the real Ireland', they also helped form O'Connor's private America, as did the names of American cities on the banners of those Americans "who had come all the way over to Ireland to march and celebrate our freedom with us' on St. Patrick's Days in Dublin". The place names on their banners became almost magical to O'Connor.

Just as O'Connor's father wanted to show him the 'real Ireland' when they went to Connamara, O'Connor was repeatedly told that "New York was not the real America" (17) when he first went to America in 1991. And *Sweet Liberty* is O'Connor's attempt to make this "journey into the heart of the real America". So, there is an idea of a 'real' America just as there is an idea of a 'real' Ireland in O'Connor's universe. However, it is important to notice that those 'real' places are imagined spaces as well, as we see when

O'Connnor emphasizes that he was actually introduced to the West of Ireland through sentimental songs of American tourists. Likewise, O'Connor's 'own imaginary America' is a mediated space (through music, film, literature, history and personal memories). The ideas of both a 'real Ireland' and a 'real America' are questioned in O'Connor's book, but even with the disbelief in ideas of the real, there is still in O'Connor's book a search for authenticity as well as a critique of the lack of or lost sense of reality in 1990s America (this is one of the ways in which O'Connor's book is "analytical" in Hulme's sense of the word).

Hyperreal America/Ireland

O'Connor's book is a search for the 'real' America – both O'Connor's own mental America and the actual place America. The book comes across as an attempt to literalize his own private America: having these images of America, he goes to see what they are 'really' like. What he finds, however, is that that 'real America' is a lot less real than one would think, and that 'the authentic' is hard to find: O'Connor is repeatedly surprised by the anonymity and lack of authenticity in places like hotels, restaurants, and train stations, and he is likewise surprised by the anonymity of people working there. In the last chapter of Part 1, "The Greenfields of Amerikay", O'Connor reflects on the mall and sees it as the ultimate symbol of contemporary American society (as well as America's immigrant past). "These are places removed from history, geography, context [...] It tells you that you are everywhere, and nowhere. It tells you that you can create yourself" (247). However, O'Connor points out the problem that the mall – as emphasized by some contemporary critics – has replaced the real urban reality, and that you can more or less live your entire life in it. "The mall has replaced the school, the church and the dancehall in the new architecture of social cohesiveness. [...] A whole country full of people in love with a dream, rather than a reality. But an American dream, I suppose. An American dream, after all" (248). The mall epitomizes the sense of an American hyperreality that O'Connor conveys in the book. At first sight this reads like a critique of 1990s *American* society, but the chapter includes a little episode from Dublin, Ohio, where O'Connor recounts how he walked into the Old Dublin. The main street was a sort of hyperreal representation of all things Irish, and O'Connor talks to the owner of a gift shop selling

Aran sweaters and tartan kilts and complains that "[t]his isn't the real Ireland". The shop owner replies:

> 'I go to Ireland twice a year,' he said. 'I've been doing that for twenty years. Twice a year, regular. The wife and me, we have to go, for the business, you know. We go on buying trips. And you go to any city in Ireland now, it's got places like this and stores like mine all over. I mean all over. I never saw the phoney Irish thing anywhere in the world till I went to Galway last summer. Jesus, even the nuns were wearing Aran.'
>
> Outside on the street, the shamrock-painted police car swept past once again. 'This is the real Ireland all right,' he grinned. 'Maybe you just don't like what you see.' (250)

Here O'Connor sees 'the real Ireland' through its American representations, but because of the shop owner's description of what he sees when he goes to Ireland, the story does not only function as a comment on the 'vulgar' American version of 'the real Ireland', which we see other places in the book, but also as a critique of Ireland, and the way it represents itself. Just as there are American dreams of the American dream and hyperreal places like Las Vegas, Ireland represents itself through certain 'dreams' and imaginations of itself. O'Connor seems to reject this idea of both the mall as the symbol of American society and Dublin, Ohio as the symbol of Ireland, and instead insists on something 'real' or 'authentic'. But maybe – as the shop owner puts it – it is just because he does not like what he sees. Perhaps this is as real as both America and Ireland can get. The Dublin, Ohio story actually parallels the story about the American tourists and the West of Ireland that O'Connor recounts in the "Introduction", but here he is much more critical concerning the mediation and construction of 'the real Ireland' by Americans. But there is no *essential* difference between the way the American tourists of his childhood memories constructed Ireland and the way in which Dublin, Ohio and this shop keeper – as well as their counterparts in the 'real Ireland' (geographically speaking) – construct Ireland.

In the above story, the hyperreal becomes something that threatens 'the *real* real', and O'Connor insists on there being such a real real. At the same time, however, O'Connor acknowledges that his 'own private America' is an imaginary America, and when he travels to find the 'real America', he is not simply 'testing' his own private America against some kind of factual reality to see if it matches that; he is also constructing that America in the light of – and by the means of – his own private America.

O'Connor's Irish America

When O'Connor describes his flight across the Atlantic from London to Boston, he does it in terms of American popular culture: *The Sound of Music* (Hollywood musical 1965), *Airplane!* (American film 1980), Madonna (American popular performer, songwriter, producer, and actress, born 1958), and Ripley (American cartoonist (1893-1949), founder of "Believe it or not!"), to mention some of those references. These cultural references are all part of O'Connor's framework of reference and they are all used as comparisons in O'Connor's description of the flight. (everything is *like* these things). The in-flight movie was a prototype American action film (O'Connor ironically suggests that it might possibly have been titled *Bludgeon II* or *Stab III*), and even though O'Connor refers to it as "a criminal waste of good celluloid" as it displays stereotypical American action heroes and wickedly sniggering Arabs, the very next paragraph displays O'Connor's own images of American inner cities being influenced by films like that. Thus, O'Connor's Irish America is influenced by American popular culture – in particular film and music.

This way of describing what he sees in terms of (mostly) American popular culture characterizes the book as such. And it is not only when he describes things American: the house he and his family stayed in in Connamara is likened to the kind of house you would see in *The Quiet Man* (American 1952 movie about a disgraced American boxer who retires to Ireland.) and at another point he describes the atmosphere in an Irish pub in terms of an American movie. These are examples of the Irish America that O'Connor brings with him to America. Apart from American films and TV series, O'Connor has a great knowledge of what he calls the "native musics of America" (blues, gospel, country and western, jazz, and rock and roll) as well as contemporary American literature (such as Raymond Carver and Dylan Thomas) and drama (such as Eugene O'Neill and Arthur Miller). In the book there are also references to various history books, and O'Connor is quite well-informed on contemporary American politics. In the beginning of the book, we hear that O'Connor has bought a statistical book about America in London. Thus, O'Connor's America is composed of his experience with and knowledge of American culture in terms of literature, film and music, his reading of historical accounts of "the area of Irish immigration, settlement, internal migration, social customs and culture in the United States" (365), and the statistic materials he reads in the book he bought in London prior to the trip to America. It is with this 'private America' that O'Connor arrives in 'the real America'.

When he arrives in Boston, O'Connor recounts images of Irish America as it manifests itself in the America he has just flown into. Apart from the Irish flag in the airport (which for a second makes him afraid that the plane has been accidentally flown back to Ireland) and the icons and images of Ireland in the streets of Boston, the first two persons he talks to are Irish-Americans (the immigration officer and the taxi driver), whose great-grand parents had immigrated from Ireland. O'Connor sets up some differences and similarities between the mid nineteenth century and the 1990s in terms of immigration by remarking that the poor Irish immigrants of the 1840s and 1850s were not exactly received with open arms in Boston; today their great-grand children are immigration officers. O'Connor is welcomed warmly, whereas "visitors who were black or brown in aspect seemed to be questioned for a much longer time than visitors who were white, tanned or pink" (30).

In his hotel he meets another Irishman, Eugene, who had come to Boston with his brother five years earlier to get a job (which means that things have not changed completely since the 19th century), and with whom O'Connor goes to an Irish bar, where Irish rebel songs are sung, where everybody (except O'Connor) joins in the singing of "A Nation Once Again", and where *An Phoblacht* is sold. In other words, the Irish America he first meets consists of sentimental notions of Ireland (represented by shamrocks, harps, and the Irish language); politically nationalistic attitudes; and the fact that Irish people still cross the Atlantic to come to America to work because of the unemployment rate in Ireland (93). In the bar Eugene and his brother are in a sense the Irish as distinguished from the Irish-American, and they find the idea of buying *An Phoblacht* quite laughable and the rebel songs as "only songs. They don't mean shit" (49). Nevertheless Eugene's brother agrees to sing the Irish republican song, *The West's Asleep*, which to the audience must have looked as if Eugene's brother was in line with the more nationalistic mood of the place. (Rather than expressing his nationalistic devotion, Eugene only sang the song because he had been promised a blow job by his girlfriend if he sang (50) – this episode reminds one of the way we get Mulvey's motivation for his song in *Star of the Sea*).

Real Representations

It is possible that that the Irish songs "don't mean shit", but when O'Connor recounts a young black woman singing an Irish ballad in a Californian accent in an Irish bar in San Francisco, this ballad acquires some meaning in O'Connor Irish America:

> I had heard the song many times before, but I had never heard it sung by a black woman in California. The way she sang it, and the fact of her singing it at all, brought a new level of meaning to the song which was both humbling and moving. (363)

This recontextualization of the song exemplifies the way things and songs and idea and identities can be Atlanticized. No longer tied to its geographical origin (if it ever were) the song has been not just decontextualized but recontextualized. The song becomes about emigrant longing that is not tied to national boundaries and which is not particularly 'Irish' in the traditional sense of the term, but more in the way Baucom defines Irishness. With the emphasis on music throughout the book, O'Connor may be seen as presenting music as the 'best' representation of Irish America. At the same time it is a kind of deconstruction of the Irish ballad to have it sung – even the Irish words in it – in a Californian accent and by a black woman.

Even with O'Connor's deconstruction of the Irish songs we hear Eugene's brother and the black Californian woman sing; music as such is quite central to his America. In the course of the book O'Connor experiences the "native musics of America". It is obvious that he sees music as tied up with the notion of 'the real America', and he finds what he is looking for in Memphis one hot morning in a bar:

> The music was hot. The beer was cold. I took another big mouthful of food. This was the real America, I thought, as the music and the applause drifted in from the street. This was living.

> Oh ashes to ashes and dust to dust
> Lord, the Whiskey don't get you then the women must.
> Oh tell me how long, how long must I wait?
> You're playin' in my orchard, now don't you see
> If you don't like my peaches stop shakin' my tree.
> Oh tell me honey, how long, how long must wait… (302)

Despite O'Connor's fascination with music as "the living poetry of America" (108), he is a little troubled by the way music works in relation to

American notions of Ireland: throughout the book O'Connor is haunted by the 1991 film *The Commitments* based on Irish novelist Roddy Doyle's novel about a band and their Dublin working-class life. In an Irish bar in New York O'Connor comments, "It was a pleasant irony that Ireland's greatest living band is actually made up of fictional characters", and when he tries to get some information about the history of the civil rights movement in America from the young woman who runs the National Parks Department office in Atlanta, all she wants to discuss is *The Commitments*. She claims to have been to Ireland but cannot remember anything about it. (Was it North? Was it South?) Yet she liked the film. From this point of view the 'Ireland' that O'Connor finds in America is as shaped by representations and pop culture as his own private Irish America. The band in *The Commitments* is inauthentic (because it consists of fictive characters), yet these inauthentically Irish representations help shape the notion of 'Ireland' for some of the people O'Connor meets in America. O'Connor seems a little concerned that Ireland has been 'reduced' to such pop cultural representations, yet he acknowledges that this is so. When he talks to two teenage boys outside a high school in Dublin, Maryland, he fails to explain to them the notion of Ireland in terms of geography, but instead mentions U2 (who they know of). Apart from showing the crossing of popular culture like music and film, these examples of American images of Ireland also function as a kind of reflection on the way he constructs his Irish America in the book, and perhaps as a warning not to take the idea of the 'real America' as he finds it in Memphis too seriously.

Icons – authentic or not

Apart from his great interest in the musics of America, O'Connor also examines some of the icons by which America has been represented / has represented itself: Martin Luther King, Elvis Presley, John F Kennedy, and Billy the Kid. O'Connor sets up some oppositions in his dealing with these icons of America: when visiting Atlanta, the hard to find Martin Luther King museum is contrasted with the hyperreal Coca Cola museum (marked on all city maps), and O'Connor therefore criticizes the way America presents itself, and the way it does not pay enough attention to things he sees as really important (such as human rights). Whereas the Coca Cola museum is presented as totally lacking in authenticity, O'Connor finds Martin Luther King's voice alive and present in the Baptist service he goes to in Atlanta.

Later we hear of Elvis Presley and all the contradictions about him. O'Connor sees Elvis as the voice of the 20th century – not a particular American voice, but a voice beyond nationality. (Elvis is contrasted to Nixon as the best and the worst.) O'Connor insists that Elvis was authentic (304), even though he has become a myth, and even though it is sometimes hard to remember that he was human after all (291). O'Connor wishes to find out if Elvis Presley had Irish blood, and he speaks to a kind shop assistant in a music store, who assures him that "'The thing about Elvis,' Bert said, 'we get 'em all here in Tennesee, from all over the world. Man, we get Chinese fellers and Russians and all. We get Orstralians and Jews and Hindu folks and you name it. And they all love Elvis. Don't matter where they're from. So I guess the king belongs to everybody, huh? So you can say Elvis was Irish if you want to'" (286). This attempt to 'make' Elvis Irish is backed up by some music history explaining the connections between gospel, rock and Irish music as laid out by Bert (288). What is more important than this, however, is the other sense in which Elvis is part of O'Connor's Irish America: O'Connor recounts how his mother had told him that Elvis was a real part of the working-class suburbs of Dublin where O'Connor's mother and all the other teenage girls would dress up and go to the cinema to scream at the Elvis films (297).

O'Connor spends a good many pages deconstructing the myth about John F Kennedy and presenting him in the words of the historian Richard Walton as "the most dangerous cold worrier that we have had since the end of Word War II" (313). After his death John F Kennedy has retrospectively come to epitomize "the fantasy of itself which America constructed in the sixties" (311), and it is this fantasy – together with the Kennedys as the personified culmination of the immigrant-American dream – that O'Connor, with the help of other historians, challenges, and he ends his challenge with the words that "the tragic truth is, Jack Kennedy was not Jack Kennedy either. The sooner Irish America comes to terms with that, the sooner it will come to terms with itself" (316). It is a little hard to see why Martin Luther King and Elvis should be more 'authentic' than JFK, except for the reason that O'Connor simply sympathizes more with their points of view and iconic status than with John F Kennedy's.

O'Connor reads Billy the Kid through Argentinean author Jorge Luis Borges' rewriting of the Kid's story, which is "all the more intriguing for being at least partially invented" (324). Here Billy the Kid was born in New York to poor Irish parents, and he got inspired from vaudeville melodramas of cowboy life, which, Borges suggests, were to profound effect on him (325). O'Connor's way of reading the Billy the Kid myth again relies on notions of the imaginary: if Billy the Kid had lived a hundred years later, he would have been inspired by the same cowboy movies O'Connor grew up with. By reading the Kid through Borges, O'Connor again emphasizes how myths are shaped and shape themselves through the ways they are imagined.

Concluding Remarks

In this discussion of *Sweet Liberty* I have emphasized O'Connor's treatment of 'America' both as a literal place and a mental space, paying more attention to the latter than the first. In doing that I have focused on the cross-Atlantic exchange of popular culture like film and music, and I have discussed O'Connor's presentation of American icons (and thereby left out many other issues taken up in O'Connor's book). In general O'Connor presents America (and by extension Ireland) as a hyperreal place, *but* he also presents glimpses of authenticity (in the form of some of the 'real people' he meets and above all in his experiences of music). The end of the book (the black woman singing an Irish ballad in a Californian accent in an Irish bar in California) reads like an allegorical comment on the whole notion of what is 'the real America' and what is 'the real Ireland': here people, place, song, language, past and present have merged into a moment of (be)longing. And this may the 'Atlanticized self' based on, in Baucom's words, "a circulating, cross-Atlantic economy of memories, letters, songs, bodies, images and desires".

Star of the Sea and *Sweet Liberty* deal with the issues of the Famine and America – issues that are tied up with the function of the cross-Atlantic in Irish culture and history. Both books emphasize the ways representations (of past events and geographical places/mental spaces) are constructed or *composed*, and they both acknowledge their own status as such compositions. Especially in *Star of the Sea* O'Connor deals with issues of form and conventions and the idea that textual representations relate to other textual representations. And both books emphasize the idea of a cross-Atlantic economy of memories, letters, songs, bodies, images and desires (through

Star of the Sea's narrative structure and O'Connor's Irish America in *Sweet Liberty*), and O'Connor presents himself as an 'Atlanticized' writer especially in *Sweet Liberty* through the way in which he establishes his Irish America.

If history is a useless art and if travel writing is at least potentially useless, why write books like *Star of the Sea* and *Sweet Liberty*? O'Connor in different ways distances himself from 'history' and 'travel writing', yet what he does deal with in these two books is exactly history and travel writing. O'Connor is critical and/or ironical towards notions of 'real America' and 'real Ireland', yet he continuously searches for such things. O'Connor emphasizes 'the composition' over 'the material', yet his books rely on historical accounts and statistics. In these two books it is as if the only way of dealing with the Famine and Irish America is through self-reflexive meta-discourses, and yet the books are representations of the Famine and Irish America respectively and the function of the Atlantic and the cross-Atlantic in relation to these issues. These underlying paradoxes affect O'Connor's books as well as the way he represents himself as an 'Atlanticized' writer: the (cross- and trans) Atlantic has a place in the semiotics systems of Irish culture and history which in O'Connor's representations of it is both a literal, imagined and allegorical place.

References

"Another country" (2003) *Guardian Unlimited*. Published January 25
    [http://books.guardian.co.uk/review/story/0,2084,880838,00.html]
"Arthur McBride"
    [http://www.chivalry.com/cantaria/lyrics/arthur-mcbride.html]
Baucom, Ian (2000) "Found Drowned: The Irish Atlantic". John Kucich and Dianne F. Sadoff (eds.). *Victorian Afterlife: Postmodern Culture Rewrites the Nineteenth Century*. Minneapolis/London: University of Minnesota Press
Carr, Helen (2002) "Modernism and travel (1880-1940)". Peter Hulme and Tim Youngs (eds). *The Cambridge Companion to Travel Writing*. Cambridge: Cambridge University Press
Culler, Jonathan (2001) *The Pursuit of Signs: Semiotics, Literature, Deconstruction*. Florence, KY, USA: Routledge
"Fame and the Famine" (2004) *Socialist Review*. Issue 285 May
    [http://pubs.socialistreviewindex.org.uk/sr285/croft.htm]

Hulme, Peter (2002) "Traveling to Write (1940-2000)". Peter Hulme and Tim Youngs (eds). *The Cambridge Companion to Travel Writing.* Cambridge: Cambridge University Press

"Joseph O'Connor". (2003) Posted June 26. *Identitytheory.com – a literary website, sort of.*
[http://www.identitytheory.com/interviews/birnbaum113.html]

"Joseph O'Connor: Some Irish made vast fortunes out of the Famine" (2003) *The Independent Online Edition* published January 04
[http://enjoyment.independent.co.uk/books/interviews/story.jsp?-story=365979]

Morash, Christopher (1995) *Writing the Irish Famine.* Oxford: Clarendon Press

O'Connor, Joseph (2003) *Star of the Sea.* London: Vintage: (first published in Great Britain in 2002 by Secker & Warburg)

O'Connor, Joseph (1996) *Sweet Liberty: Travels in Irish America.* London: Picador

Scally, Robert James (1995) *The End of Hidden Ireland: Rebellion, Famine, and Emigration.* Oxford: Oxford University Press.

Continuity Breach: The British Revision of the American Superhero

STEEN CHRISTIANSEN

In the early 1980s American superhero comics were reaching an all-time low in terms of both sales and quality. This down-period was particularly harsh on DC Comics[1]; the former so popular Superman and Batman series were a mere shadow of themselves, no longer the frontrunners they had been. Although the censorship of the Comics Code had been removed long ago, the waning of interest could not be helped despite an initially popular run of the TV-series of *Batman* starring Adam West in the 60s or the attempted cartoon show. While the direct market provided hope, since it allowed a lower break-even point, it still needed innovative, fresh works to draw new readers in.

Interestingly, most of the writers who took on this challenge to innovate superhero comics were British. Three writers in particular stand out who exemplify what might be called the British way; Alan Moore, Neil Gaiman and Grant Morrison. While minor stars in their homeland, it was with their American-published work that they became stars of the comics industry. There was also revision made by American writers, particularly Frank Miller, but it was the British writers who paved the way for what comics could be, despite being published by the major houses. What is particular about the British writers is that they very often break the conventions established, challenge them through metafictional parody and genre

---

[1] DC Comics, originally Detective Comics, Inc, is the publisher of Superman, Batman, Wonder Woman, Green Lantern and many other superheroes. They were the first publishers of superhero comics with Superman in *Action Comics #1* in 1938 and Batman in *Detective Comics #33* in 1939. As opposed to Marvel Comics (see footnote 2), DC has generally been regarded as aiming at a more grown-up audience than Marvel's insistence on a teenage audience.

contamination, choosing what might be considered more literary techniques in their writing.

This paper will investigate the impact the British writers had on such an all-American genre as superhero comics. The investigation will be twofold, the first part dealing with the textual strategies employed by the British writers, at times compared with their early British work and at times compared to the more general aspects of the genre. As such, this first reading will be a genre-semiotic reading pointing to the intertextual relations, while also employing parts of Harold Bloom's anxiety of influence poetics, in order to clarify the types of revision made. Here I will also discuss how these writers employed the medium of comicbooks, specifically how they depended on an extension of the visual techniques usually employed. The second part will look at the cultural production which sprang up around these new works by innovative writers. Reception of the texts will be the main focus, along with the paratextual presentation to show how comics as a medium achieved a greater degree of acceptance in contemporary culture. As exemplary works I have chosen Alan Moore's *Watchmen* to showcase the textual strategies and media-specific awareness, and Neil Gaiman's *Sandman* to examine reception and cultural production. Moore's work is one of the standard works used in comics analysis, but this emphasizes its extremely canonic status and therefore relevance for this paper. Gaiman's *Sandman* is much less discussed, probably because it falls uneasily between superheroes, horror and fantasy. It remains the comicbook which has had the largest cultural impact and the broadest. I will also briefly examine Frank Miller's *The Dark Knight Returns* since it represents probably the most important American comicbook at the same time the British writers made their excursion into the US during the mid to late 1980s. Miller's revision of the superhero is quite different from the British and shows an entirely different approach to the genre.

It is essential to establish one of the guiding principles of the superhero genre in order to appreciate what exactly happened during the 80s. The one which is generally unspoken but vital for the continued existence of the various series: the concept of what Tony Bennett calls "shifting signifiers", (Bennett, 1990) in essence parallel to Umberto Eco's idea of the comicbook as an oneiric climate (Eco, 1979/1984: 114). Despite variations in different stories, times and formats, the characters remain the same. If we take Batman as an example, it is the same Batman whether we see the original Bob Kane creation, the camp TV-version of Adam West in the 60s, the grim Frank

Miller version in *The Dark Knight Returns* of the 80s and so forth. Obviously there are differences between these versions of Batman but they all orient themselves, however differently, towards the same myth and the readers accept that different writers and artists have differing views of the character. Superhero characters, then, have a peculiar status, as they constantly change due to different renderings of them, but on the other hand they never change, remaining at the core the same basic character. Time stands still in some ways and yet moves forward in others, as Mila Bongco points out:

> [...] the most popular comicbooks often provide the feeling of an eternal present tense; characters do not age with their 'celebrity life' while the background and settings which are ambiguous and fantastic may rarely be equated with any particular time period. (Bongco, 2000: 81)

This is only partially true; however, as for instance 9/11 was implemented into the storyline of most of Marvel Comics'[2] New York-based comics, such as *Spider-Man*. This was clearly an exception to the norm, though, and generally superhero comics take place in this oneiric climate. This unchanging nature is probably the most obvious discrepancy new readers encounter. It seems peculiar that with such an acceptance of a non-time within the textual world that superhero readers place such an emphasis on the continuity of the characters and the general timeline of the setting.

Continuity is the term for the special intertextual status which superhero comics have created over time, such as origin stories, first encounters, loves, deaths and so forth of the different characters, and any evolution in powers (or devolution). This continuity is extremely complex and the subject of many reader discussions taking place in the community-constituting 'Letters' columns present in practically all superhero comics. Fans question, discuss and criticize quite directly the events in previous issues, trying to figure out where these events all match up with each other. Richard Reynolds points out three types of continuity:

Serial continuity which is similar to that of soaps and other TV series, where every single episode helps create a back-story which must be preserved in order to remain consistent. This is the timeline which must be obeyed when creating new stories, since the serial continuity represents the

---

[2] Marvel Comics is the publisher of Spider-Man, Xmen, Fantastic Four and many other superheroes. While starting in 1939, they mostly came into their own in the late 1950s, early 1960s with Stan Lee writing many of their now classic lines of Fantastic Four, Spider-Man and so forth.

history of the character, and as such this is the diachronic element to the comicbook setting, representing the characters' development over time.

The synchronic part of superhero comics is *hierarchical continuity* which is a form of pecking order in terms of the powers of heroes and villains. If hero A defeats villain B and villain B subsequently defeats hero C, then hero A must logically be more powerful than hero C. This type of continuity thus represents the state of affairs at any given moment and can thus be countered by serial continuity, which may show how a certain character increases or decreases in power.

The combination of serial continuity and hierarchical continuity merge to create *structural continuity* which is the entire content of a given universe, such as either DC's or Marvel's. It furthermore contains all those elements, or gaps, which must logically exist and can be added in later stories. Although we do not know the name of Peter Parker's grandfather, we realize that he must have had one and that he could be the subject of a *Spider-Man* story (Reynolds, 1992: 38–43).

Structural continuity represents what Gerard Genette would term the architext, which is dependent upon earlier texts, though in the case of superhero comics there are two issues which must be addressed. The first can be considered part of any given popular genre, which is that of the sheer number of given genre texts; so large as to be impossible to read in their entirety. Because of this, the architext remains 'virtual' or indefinite since no single person has read all the necessary texts. Despite this paradoxical status of the timeline, it is considered of utmost importance to readers, and heated discussions may easily arise over the validity of a particular event. Again, the 'Letters' column exists to provide a place to discuss the most relevant elements of a given character's continuity, but whereas most other genres leave some room to ignore the less significant texts, comic fans have a tendency to incorporate every single installment into the continuity. Continuity, then, represents one of the strongest aspects of the reading protocol for superhero comics.

The clearest sign of the presence of a superhero is of course the costume. While most superhero costumes are often quite flashy, they also tend to provide a form of insight into the psychology of the character; one could say that the costume functions as an indexical sign of the personality of the superhero. More than that, the most popular superheroes also have very iconic signs associated with them, such as Batman's bat-signal, Superman's emblematic 'S' and Spider-Man's mask. While the costumes certainly seem ridiculous to readers outside the reading community, they are a vital element in the genre and often carry great significance. Not only do they make the superhero stand out in the crowd (useful in the early period of superhero comics, as printing was often poor and unclear), but they also point out the dual nature of the superhero's identity; most superheroes shift personality when in costume, whether from Peter Parker's nerdy science geek to Spider-Man's flippant wit, or Bruce Wayne's suave to Batman's grim determination. Also, the costumes are quite often sexually coded, though this is generally implicit and evident most clearly in that of the female superheroes, where their costumes often draw on a pornographic subtext of spiked heels, chains, whips and generally revealing costumes (Reynolds, 1992: 34). This subtext is left blank, no one ever remarks on the revealing costumes or the impracticality of spiked heels when fighting for world-freedom, and so it is left to the reader to fill in based on his competences. There has been a development in this area, from the joking, offhanded remarks in *The Sensational She-Hulk* (1985) to swimsuit issues and centerfolds of the female superheroes, particularly evident in the Image Comics of the 1990s. It is no accident that superhero costumes are so tight, since this allows for bodily fixation and fetishism. With the male, muscular bodies, and the female, pin-up-styled bodies, there is definitely a strong eroticism working in many of the texts.

If we turn to the narrative structure, we find that the basic plot is extremely simple, order is destroyed by villain(s) creating a disorder which the superhero must restore to order through violence. The end, however, is quite perfunctory and irrelevant as a whole to the main part of the story: the fight(s). There is usually little detail in the closure, since everyone knows that this order will be disrupted in the next issue. So, while most superhero comics are clearly hegemonic in their intent, quite often creating an ideologically closed text, encouraging readers to accept the text's very specific preferred readings, it is also evident that the end and thus the hegemonic reestablishing effect is not the primary interest of most superhero comics and certainly not what the readers read for. Here the plot is in many ways indifferent since the end is pre-programmed, so to speak, and while the programmatic closure might be reassuring, it is not the reason for reading the texts.

Law and justice, then, holds a peculiar place in superhero comics, for although law and order are apparently upheld by the righteous heroes, it is significant that the heroes always go above and beyond the letter of the law and the law enforcers, such as police and criminal courts since many villains go free afterward. Indeed, superhero comics by their very nature reveal a deep suspicion of society's ability to defend itself. As Reynolds states: "The set of values they traditionally defend is summed up by the Superman tag of 'Truth, Justice, and the American way'" (Reynolds, 1992: 74). The high moral values of superheroes implicitly critiques the (American, though not only) society for not being sufficiently moral itself. This dependency on supermen and women have often been argued to be a fascist feature of superhero narratives, not only showcasing the old American myth of the frontier where vigilantes are needed to protect society, but also to represent the view that most people lack the ability to defend themselves and that their superiors should instead do it for them. Society so depends on those superior beings, those mightier than the common people, to control and direct itself.

Evil is clearly present in superhero comics, as practically all the villains are evil to an extreme degree. These villains clearly reflect superhero comics' origins as coming from many writers of pulp magazines, where cardboard characters were the norm. Evil is generally seen as an absolute, something even mythic in origin and existence. Despite the fact that superheroes' moral values provide a way to critique society, evil is rarely seen as the springing from society or having a sociological root. The evil villains are not justified through society's lacking concern for its citizens or similar explanations. Instead, evil remains, although personified by the villains, utterly inexplicable and mysterious. As such the comics argue that while some people are evil, this evil has no specific point of origin or cause. Clearly, this is one of the reasons why superhero comics have been seen as simplistic entertainment for children.

However, the growing use of psychology during the 60s, particularly in the Marvel Universe, paved the way for deeper investigations of why people turn to evil. The Green Goblin's paranoia after a chemical accident and his son's subsequent madness upon learning that his father is the Green Goblin, which in turn transforms the innocent Harry into the successor the Hobgoblin, is evidence of justifying evil through psychological trauma. Dr. Doom's transformation is also explained through the scarring of his face and despite his evil intentions the nation he himself governs as a tyrant (Latveria) is generally represented as a pleasant community with few of the social problems present in contemporary US. Despite these exceptions, most villains remain simplistically evil. This is particularly true in the DC comics which have a longer, and hence stronger, continuity to obey. As a result, new writers could not easily alter these origins of villains or even heroes.

Simplicity is generally seen as the clearest marker of superhero comics: simplistic morals, simplistic narratives, simplistic characters. However, the comicbook is a multimodal medium and a number of techniques create what is a polysemic text, encouraging multiple interpretations, even oppositional to any specific artistic intention. This is a very important aspect of comicbooks, but more important is the fact that the polysemic nature of the comicbook medium was recognized in the 1980s by a number of writers and artists. Whereas previous comicbooks had emphasized the unification of words, images and narrative into the basic hegemonic structure which had arisen from the Comics Code and the general conservatism of both DC and Marvel, the rise of the new comics challenged the basic conventions and attitudes of earlier works. While the largest challenge rose from British writers, there is one American writer who rose to fame during this period and it will be useful to examine his work before turning to the British, in order to clarify the differences between the American revision and the British.

Frank Miller was given the opportunity to write a Batman story based on the fame he had acquired writing *Daredevil* at Marvel. This story became *The Dark Knight Returns* published in 1986. Significantly, Miller challenges the continuity of the Batman character in two ways: the first is an attempt to create a synthesis of the entire history of Batman, pulling everything into a coherent continuity and scrapping the pieces which are regarded as unwanted. The origin story is revisited and Batman's history made whole and realistic. The second challenge to continuity is to make Batman old; now Bruce Wayne has become middle-aged which breaks the basic assumption that superheroes do not age, only the environment may age. Such a challenge to the most ingrained protocol did not go unchallenged; hefty discussions arose among fans of whether this story should be regarded as part of the Batman continuity (Reynolds, 1992: 40). This type of explicit canon-formation is quite unique to the comics community, but also reveals the unusual nature of Miller's text; revising the continuity of a major character is not something accepted lightly by readers.

Geoff Klock correctly argues that "*The Dark Knight Returns* is one of the most important works in the tradition of superhero narratives because it is the first strong misreading of comic book history, specifically the history of Batman" (Klock, 2002: 28). Klock writes within a Bloomian anxiety of influence poetics[3] and so understands Miller's text to be a creative misprision of earlier Batman texts. Such an approach is helpful in this connection because there are so many references to the Batman myth, and the entire architext of all previous Batman texts. As Klock goes on to argue, Miller's text is a revision of the Batman architext, an attempt to view 'correctively' how Batman could exist.

Most of this revision is achieved by trying to show how a superhero would 'realistically' exist in our world; the peculiar aspects of Batman's identity are provided with an explanation which, due to superhero comics' particular structural continuity, retroactively fills the gaps previously left out. One example, which Klock also points to, is the explanation for the Bat-icon on Batman's chest which clearly acts as a target. In Miller's revision, this target becomes an armored plate which attracts attention so that he will not be shot in the head, which he cannot amour (Miller, 1986: 51). There is a certain wry humor in this passage, an ironic comment on the ludicrous design of Batman's costume, which Miller is not really at liberty to alter, since it would disrupt the contract which exists between text and reader; Batman's costume is part of his identity and to change the costume would mean to change the entire character. Instead, Miller must come up with a 'realistic' explanation for the icon/target.

However, the most significant alteration in the Batman universe is the clearly contemporary setting which Miller employs; there are direct references to President Reagan which also breaks the typical oneiric climate depending on the always 'our world only slightly different' definition. Not to say that the setting is particularly realistic, since it draws heavily on the Chandleresque/film noir style which Miller developed in *Daredevil*. New York is shown as filled with rainy, mean streets where criminals reign. Rather than dealing with these problems themselves, people instead ask where Batman disappeared, in the hope that he will come back and solve their problems. Here we find a serious indictment of people's attitude which is rather to complain and wish that others will solve their problems than do

---

[3] Harold Bloom's anxiety of influence is a historical version of intertextuality, where the influence of earlier, great writers is traced through the work of new writers. Bloom's basic argument is that writers may only create new works of literature by misreading earlier works, a creative act in Bloom's vocabulary. As such, new works of literature always have a certain relation to these earlier works, either refining the earlier works or resisting them. New literary works are therefore textual continuations of what has already been written.

anything about them themselves. We will return to this briefly, for now we need to look at what happens when Batman does return.

Violence is the clearest mark of Batman's return for unlike most versions of Batman, Miller's middle-aged obsessive psychopath has no compunctions about killing; be it major villains or minor henchmen. A very extreme departure from the typical version of Batman, and also one which the editor at the time, Dennis O'Neil, disagrees with: "That is why I have to edit the writers who have Batman kill somebody. I think this is not something he does" (O'Neil, 1991: 19). The fact that Miller's text was not 'corrected' to conform to Batman's canonic continuity shows Miller's popularity but also shows that there was an understanding from DC that this story did not fit completely within the typical continuity. However, the fact that Batman kills is a more unpleasant retroactive explanation than the Bat-icon, since such killing points to the fact that Batman has killed earlier. In a sense, what Miller does is simply to show what could not be showed before due to the Comics Code and cautious publishers. In the same way that the Bat-icon has always been an armored plate, so Batman has always killed people. This represents a major revision of the character and one that could only be made at that time due to the power individual talent had won as a side-effect of the direct-market (Boichel, 1991: 15).

Miller, in a sense, accuses the superhero comics for depending on a subtext of violence which they can deny because violence is never directly presented to the reader. Through the power of the gutter, the more grisly aspects are left out. As McCloud argues, what lies in the gutter can always be more effective than anything which can be drawn on a page, since it depends on the reader's participation in filling in the blanks of the narrative (McCloud, 1993: 68–69). This is exactly Miller's point, of course, that by leaving out much of the gory details the publishers can hypocritically both sell comics based on violence, while at the same time deny that their comics contain violence. Miller's corrective reading, then, specifies that superheroes are enmeshed in violence and that it is better to face this subtext than to suppress it.

Here Miller begins to indicate something extratextual, something which is part of the broad reception of superhero comics and not just *Batman*. It indicates an interest in using the text to comment metafictionally on the character of Batman and the genre in general. An aspect which is specifically located within the Batman architext is the ever-present question of homo-eroticism. This takes two forms, Batman's relationship with Robin and the relation to the Joker. Many have argued for the existence of a gay relationship between Batman and Robin, due to their secret life together. This accusation came first from Fredric Wertham's censorious book *Seduction of the Innocent* (1954), where he stated that Batman and Robin's relationship was "a wish dream of two homosexuals living together" (Wertham, 1954: 190). Miler's text changes Robin to a female character since the old, male Robin was dead. While some view this change as agreeing that there is a sexual relation between Batman and Robin (Miller, 1991: 37–38), only now heterosexual, the evidence of the text points rather to a father/child relationship, such as when Batman commends Robin's actions with the comment "Good soldier" (Miller, 1986: 138). Such a comment seems a general part of the older Batman's personality also evident in the ending of the text, where Bruce Wayne leads a group of youngsters.

The text seems intent on denying the homosexual reading of Batman, and instead transfers much of this homosexual discussion to the Joker. Since the Joker has always represented a distorted mirror version of Batman, to an even greater degree than other Bat-villains (Boichel, 1991: 8), it seems almost logical to transfer homosexual status to him. Indications of the Joker's gay sexuality is rampant and clear in the text, such as when the Joker refers to Batman as 'Darling' throughout the story, wears make-up rather than being disfigured by toxic chemicals, or when we learn that his psychosis is caused by Batman and by "sexual repression, of course" (Miller, 1986: 126). This explanation must also be regarded as a joke on the cliché that all mental illnesses are due to sexual repression, but even this double-coding does not take away from the fact that the Joker is portrayed as homosexual in an explicit way, rather than through the blank subtexts so indicative of superhero comics.

The Dark Knight Returns, then, makes explicit a number of usually blank subtexts, in order to read the text correctively. The reading attempts to bring a certain element of realism into the tradition of superheroes, revealing that violence and sexuality is part of this tradition and always has been. It is presented as normal, though at times disturbing. The status of the superhero, although problematized and made more complex than the typical simplistic superhero narrative, is never questioned. The need for a superhero is clear in Miller's text and although in an unusual manner, the conclusion of the story also vindicates Batman's return.

Alan Moore's *Watchmen*, which was published at the same time as Miller's *Dark Knight*, is very often compared precisely to Miller's work (Reynolds, 1991; Bongco, 2000; McCloud, 2000; and Klock, 2002 all draw an explicit line between the two texts), but the impulse, or what we might call the textual intention, seems very different. Indeed, Miller himself sees a rather large discrepancy between not just the comics themselves but also him and Moore as writers (Miller, 1991: 43) and I see it as quite clear that whereas Miller's text specifically attempts a corrective misreading, in Bloom's terms a tessera[4], Moore is far more intent on destroying the entire genre. In other words, Moore's misreading is a kenosis[5] of the entire superhero tradition. Whereas Miller wishes to craft a new tradition and continuity for the Batman-series, something he continued in *Batman: Year One*, Moore seemingly has no love for the superhero tradition and instead wishes to empty it out and defeat it.[6]

Alan Moore and Dave Gibbons created *Watchmen* in 1986, inspired by an earlier group of characters whose copyright DC Comics had recently purchased from Charlton Comics. Although Moore/Gibbons' characters are unique in their own right, they were heavily inspired by these earlier characters but the fact that they were bought by DC meant that anything could be done with them. So, Moore created an entirely new continuity and an entirely new universe, which was most definitely unusual at the time. All DC's comics implicitly took place within the same universe, and the same was the case over at Marvel Comics. The notion that characters would be added which did not take part in this same universe had not been done, perhaps only because the profit-making cross-over issues could not be made otherwise. However, with this new universe, Moore was free to create whatever history and background he wanted without being constrained by masses of earlier stories. Not that he had felt burdened by such things earlier, for when he took over *Swamp Thing* in 1983, his first American line of comic, he immediately created an entirely new origins story for the line where it was discovered that it was not Alec Holland who was Swamp Thing, which had been the original explanation for Swamp Thing's creation. This breach of continuity did not harm *Swamp Thing*. Instead it became very popular.

---

[4] Tessera, as Bloom describes it, is what the author's "imagination tells him would complete the otherwise 'truncated' precursor". The new writer thus completes what s/he perceives to be the project begun by an earlier writer.

[5] In a way opposed to tessera, kenosis is a disruptive device which attempts to destroy an earlier project rather than complete it. Instead of repeating or completing a particular tradition or project begun by earlier writers, kenosis attempts to discontinue this project and empty out the precursors.

[6] I use this line of argument from Klock, though I disagree with a number of his findings.

However, despite this being Moore's first American line it is not considered in detail here, since it is a horror, rather than a superhero, comicbook.

The similar approach in *Watchmen* is used significantly to create a setting where superheroes have existed for a long time, rather than deal with the origins of superheroes or the first important team of superheroes. Instead, rather than having the series deal with the group called *Watchmen* it focuses on events decades after the group's disbanding. In terms of narrative structure, the series also breaks with the infinite run which is the standard of superhero comics, where not even poor sales can kill off a character so badly that s/he could not return decades later. In this case, however, *Watchmen* is a limited run of twelve issues with a concluded story. Here is a parallel to Miller's work, in that his work is also concluded but since it is part of the Batman line, more stories will follow, and Miller has even written a sequel called *The Dark Knight Strikes Again*. Despite the popularity of *Watchmen* there has been no sequel or spin-offs with new lines starring only one of the characters. This is one of the first clues where *Watchmen* begins to resemble a typical novel rather than a standard comicbook. Of course, Alan Moore's refusal to work with DC Comics ever again after their self-imposed censorship of printing "Recommended for Mature Readers" on *Watchmen* (Bongco, 2000: 178), must also be seen to provide part of the explanation, but even this is indicative of a different approach to copyright, since at that time creators did not own their characters, the publishing house did. As a result, DC could get any writer to continue the series or write spin-offs. Instead, DC has kept away from *Watchmen* in essence regarding Moore as the author, providing him with an unusual status in the comics industry.

Despite creating this new continuity, there are still resemblances between the Watchmen characters and those of DC's. Rorschach resembles Batman as a violent vigilante, Ozymandias as a benevolent Lex Luthor, Silk Spectre is Wonder Woman and so forth. While there is not a perfect match for all the characters it is significant that the history of the Watchmen reads like a fictionalized version of superhero comics' history. With the ironic twist that masked heroes began after the publication of *Action Comics #1*, the first Superman story and hence the first superhero story ever, we see the first of many metafictional strategies in the text. Blending fact with fiction, Moore critically examines the history of superheroes through the history of the Watchmen's rise and fall. The history of the group becomes a parody of superhero comics history and so mounts a critique of the entire genre. Such an element of critique is already implicit in Bloom's concept of kenosis, where the emptying out of tradition carries an attempt to discontinue the tradition. Moore's work, then, is best understood as a critical response to a genre which has become stagnant.

Such a reading is not possible based only on the creation of a new continuity and the resemblance between some characters to the general DC roster. However, there are several cues which point to this critical reading. Instead of having the typical 'Letters' column, *Watchmen* introduces a new device: essays, articles, excerpts and similar documents from the narrative world providing further information on specific subjects. In the first three chapters we get excerpts from an autobiography called *Under the Hood* by Nite Owl, a Watchmen member. These excerpts tell of the rise of superheroes and present the only real detail, aside from a few flashbacks, of how masked heroes arose in the Watchmen world and the history of the Watchmen. It is significant that this history represents a parallel to the rise of superhero comics in our world. The explosive rise of costumed heroes is similar to the meteoric popularity of masked heroes in the late 30s, early 40s even to the extent that Will Eisner got his character The Spirit accepted simply by saying that he wore a mask. When the Watchmen group begins to lose its tight-knit unity it occurs at the same time that superhero comics sell worse, and where more 'realistic' genres such as war stories and westerns take over much of the market. Costumes come up as being slightly ridiculous and linked more to sexual perversity than serving any practical goal. Tellingly, the group disbands and most members become disillusioned, more interested in the money available from various merchandises based on their likenesses, such as action figures (Moore & Gibbons, 1986: 1–17).[7]

Moore's alternative history becomes more accusing the closer we get to the 80s, refusing to view the heroes in the typical romantic light. Accused during the McCarthy hearings, superheroes are suddenly unpopular. When Dr. Manhattan helps Nixon win the Vietnam War, Nixon gets a third term in office and believing that the US is practically invulnerable due to Dr. Manhattan's immense powers, he provokes the Soviet Union, bringing a nuclear war closer to occurring, indicated by the clock moving ever closer to midnight on every inner cover of the chapters, in reference to the Doomsday Clock of nuclear destruction.

The criticism which Moore levels at superheroes is quite strong. They could not save President Kennedy from being shot (4–16), but they can help

---

[7] This notation indicates Chapter 1, page 17, since there is no consecutive numbering in the text.

win the Vietnam War (4–20). Because they can prevent most of a nuclear assault from the Soviet Union, the US refuses to use diplomacy to solve crisis between US and USSR (4–31), despite the fact that it will cause many casualties in both Europe and the US. In the final analysis, superheroes have not made the world a better place to live in. Instead, they are portrayed as dangerous vigilantes, murderers, rapists, fascists, bigots, racists, and perverts. Ozymandias, the smartest man on Earth, prevents nuclear war only by destroying half of New York City. Superheroes, in the Watchmen world, cannot save the world, they can only destroy it. Moore's criticism clearly reveals how one should not trust those who watch over you. The epigraph "Quis custodiet ipsos custodes./Who watches the watchmen?" introduces the story and Moore's criticism takes every superhero convention and shows the implicit subtext.

By revealing the different subtexts which are generally left blank for the reader to fill according to personal competences, the text becomes a deconstruction of the genre. It is this interest in the format of superheroes and the revision of them which connects Moore and Miller, but the difference is Moore's suspicion of superheroes, or even heroes generally, as being the solution to any kind of problem. In questioning all the conventions and turning them upside down, Moore is not just questioning the genre of superheroes, but just as much the readers and the culture which consumes them. It is this aspect of *Watchmen* that I will turn to now.

As we know from Linda Hutcheon, "Postmodern parody is a kind of contesting revision or rereading of the past that both confirms and subverts the power of the representations of history" (Hutcheon, 1989/2002: 91). Moore's text places itself within this mode in the way it functions as a parody of the superhero history. Also, there is a connection between Bloom's concept of revision and Hutcheon's in the above quote; they both specify a transtextual relationship between one or more texts. While there are still differences in their approach, what is significant here is this dependency on previous texts which are transformed into something different. Hutcheon's approach, however, deals more with the cultural implications of new texts' revision of older ones. She argues that "Its [postmodern parody's] ironic reprise also offers an internalized sign of a certain self-consciousness about our culture's means of ideological legitimation" (Hutcheon, 1989/2002: 97).

This is exactly what Moore does when he inscribes superhero comics' history and architext into *Watchmen* and lays bare the subtexts of superheroes. What is questioned is not just the comics themselves as a genre, but just as much contemporary culture's need and desire for superheroes and the reasons for this need. As noted earlier, most comicbooks, especially superhero ones, provide hegemonic representations of contemporary society and do not challenge these representations. At most, they may provide a number of blank subtexts, to be decoded based on the reader's own competences and hence not explicitly part of the text proper. What Miller did was confront these blank subtexts and show the reality of what would be if one assumed that the superhero world was a real place. Moore goes further than that, presenting a text which shows what superheroes would be like if they existed in our world. This accusation against contemporary society is far more serious since it reveals that what is often considered to be an idealist hope is instead representative of unpleasant fascist urges, such as Nite Owl's admission that "Yes, we were crazy, we were kinky, we were Nazis, all those things people say" (2–30). This admission is unsettling because it not only says something about the superheroes, but also about the readers. The reader is confronted with this undesirable side to superhero comics, but the problem is that this indictment does not come from the outside as an attack on comicbooks which can be ignored or discredited because these attacks rarely understand comics in the first place. Instead, the attack comes from within.

Watchmen places itself firmly within the superhero genre and tradition; one cannot ignore the knowledge of this genre which is presented through the text. Part of the successful critique comes precisely from the fact that the Watchmen group is placed so clearly within the two most popular periods of superhero history; the Golden Age of the 40s, represented by the early Minutemen group, and the Silver Age represented by the early Watchmen period and most of the visual style of the entire comicbook. What is striking about *Watchmen* is the way it resembles the superhero comics of the 60s rather than the much sleeker style of the 1980s. Considering that it was published at the same time as *Dark Knight*, it looks antiquated by comparison. This resemblance to the 60s style is part of the parody which the text launches against the genre, using the tradition against itself in the typical double-coded parody.

Through this double-coded parody, the genre is both legitimized and subverted, while it seems clear to me that the parody aims at deconstructing the tradition and confronting the reader with the question of whether s/he agrees with the hegemony presented by the typical superhero narrative or not. By presenting these subtexts in a negative light, the text is an attempt at destabilizing the dominant ideology of the genre. However, while this may also have been Moore's intention, it is also clear that it was not how the text was understood by many, if not most, readers at the time. Such a reception shows the problem of using double-coded parody, since some readers evidently did not respond to or decode the destabilization of the genre, and instead took it as re-inscribing the dominant ideology, thus inadvertently equating this ideology with that of some readers' subjectivity; in other words, reaffirming their beliefs in superheroes and the dangers of implicit fascism. Moore himself regrets the fact that Rorschach became a popular character for all the wrong reasons:

> Undoubtedly, at the end of the day – whatever else *Watchmen* did – the most popular character in it was Rorschach. And I don't really think that he was a popular character because of his ironic portrayal of the worthlessness of the vigilante ideal. I think people were getting off on him because he was a tough, scary, frightening character that they identified with. (Moore, quoted in Reynolds, 1992: 117–118)

This reception is particularly interesting because of the way the text is understood by some as opposed to how it was meant. Not because aberrant decoding is unusual, far from it, but rather the way it occurs. Typically, one argues that a decoding which goes against the encoding of the text is either a negotiated reading or an oppositional reading. However, in this case we see that the readers who decode the text against what Moore certainly seems to argue in the above quote, are actually producing a dominant reading, or a hegemonic reading, on a text which has actually been encoded in a counter-hegemonic fashion. Due to the double-coded parody, some readers have read the text as a typical superhero comic and so completely missed the critique embedded in much of the narrative.

Such a decoding shows the different approach to superhero comics which Moore took, and the fact that practically none followed in his or Miller's footsteps shows the difficulty the genre has had absorbing the devices of parody and critique. As has often been mentioned, by both Moore and Miller, this hegemonic appropriation is how the superhero genre took what they saw as the newness of the texts and used that extensively in creating new comics. Unfortunately, what seemed to be innovative for the new creators, however, was violence, brutality, perversity and similar elements which were only the surface of what Miller and Moore wanted to do. As Miller says:

> I'm very disturbed by the way that Marvel and DC looked at *Watchmen* and *Dark Knight*. All they got from them is that they were naughtier and a bit more brutal than other comics. They're interpreting stuff that was admittedly violent but they're making it all vicious and very small. (Miller, 1991: 45)

Moore continues in much the same way as Miller:

> [...] obviously, we've [he and Frank Miller] to some extent doomed the mainstream comics medium to a parade of violent, depressing postmodern superheroes, a lot of whom, in addition to those other faults, are incredibly pretentious. I stand accused. (Moore, quoted in Reynolds, 1992: 117)

Clearly both of them are complaining about the wrong readings of their works and people's failure to respond to them in the right way. It seems that both writers had hoped for a better understanding of the criticism they both leveled against the industry, and are disillusioned that they seemingly only made things worse. On the other hand, while the impact of the texts were at first either a lackluster copying of the more obvious elements and a worsening of the public perception of superhero comics, in the long run some things did change for the better. The incredible success of these comics warranted their collected publication in a graphic novel, something which had not occurred before and was only just happening with Art Spiegelman's *Maus*. However, the success of *Maus* is far less unexpected or unpredictable, as it deals with the prosecution of Jews during WWII, a topic which always attracts both critical and popular attention. The fact that *Watchmen* was suddenly included in book clubs' offers was much more unexpected and unusual and helped show that comics, even superhero comics with violence and colorful costumes, can be considered serious literature. The paratextual presentation of comics changed, in large part due to Moore's and Miller's work.

Not only were the series collected in a graphic novel, but there were no adds in it, something even extending to Moore's Batman comic *Killing Joke*, which was released in prestige-format at more than double the typical price, not to mention that the collected *Watchmen* costs 20$. Even the price range shows that this is not just for kids. But even more unusual both Alan Moore and Dave Gibbons are given photographs and biographies on the back of *Watchmen*, which clearly identifies the creators of the text, a deviation of the far more face-less creators at the time they were rarely clearly identified with their work. All of these things point to a greater degree of acceptance into contemporary culture, and importantly not in the way Superman and Batman have done it as popular icons; instead *Watchmen* stand as an artistic achievement, a literary work of art.

However, the greatest influence on both comicbook culture and contemporary culture by a British comicbook writer came not from Alan Moore but instead from Neil Gaiman and *The Sandman*. The reception and influence of *The Sandman* is practically unprecedented in scope, reaching far beyond what it is typical of any type of comicbook. Originally, *The Sandman* was to be the first American assignment given to young Neil Gaiman and he intended it to be based on an old DC character of the same name. He was told to make instead his own character, and while he kept the name, nothing much else survived. Already here, we can see the same interest in re-doing an origin story quite similar to that of Moore's impulse. It is quite likely that DC Comics hoped to achieve a similar type of success with this new writer as they had with Moore, who no longer worked for them. Gaiman had affiliations with Moore, and Moore had written the introduction for Gaiman's first independent comic *Violent Cases* published 1987 in Britain. When published in the US in 1991, it had blurbs recommending it by Alan Moore as well, but also Bill Sienkiewicz and Clive Barker along with reviews from Midweek and Melody Maker, which are significantly not comicbook journals. Here we see how the status of the work is drawn towards the alternative, important comics by the references to Moore and Sienkiewicz and even away from the 'just comics' group by Barker and the non-comics magazines.

While *The Sandman* begins within the DC universe, such as the encounter with John Constantine (of *Hellblazer* fame) and John Jones/Martian Manhunter (of *JLA* fame), it soon becomes evident that *The Sandman* is not a superhero comic and does not really fit into the typical continuity. Gaiman is allowed to ignore the continuity and write outside it, again emphasizing the ambiguous relationship the British writers had with the established continuities.

The Sandman, however, does not orient itself towards the superhero genre other than in these first few issues, and so the more textual side to it will not be detailed, simply because its revision turns toward horror and fantasy comics, and even more towards the literary tradition. One issue is titled "Sound and Fury" reminiscent of William Faulkner's *The Sound and the Fury* and another provides an alternate take on *A Midsummer Night's Dream*, as if Oberon, Titania and the rest of the fairies were real. This story even won the 1991 World Fantasy Award for best short story (www.locusmag.com/

SFAwards/Db/Wfa1991.html), becoming the first comicbook to win a literary award. Probably as much because of this focus on canonized literature, *The Sandman* is collected in graphic novels but in this case with introductions by well-known writers Clive Barker again, Harlan Ellison, Samuel R. Delany, Stephen King, and others. Norman Mailer even contributed a blurb for the fourth collection *Season of Mist*. All authors write fantasy/sf themselves and so provide authentication for Gaiman's creation.

But the influence and extratextual instances of *The Sandman* do not stop at the collections themselves. DC also licensed Titan Books to publish *The Sandman Companion* and recently also a new collection of stories written by Gaiman but illustrated by famous artists such as Sienkewicz again and Milo Manara. Even further, a collection of short stories entitled *The Sandman: Book of Dreams* (1997) was published by HaperPrism rather than DC, which shows the creation following the creator rather than the publisher. Writers who contributed to the collection include John M. Ford, Tad Williams, and Nancy A. Collins, again all writers known for their horror/fantasy works. The collection ends with a reprint of Tori Amos' introduction to Gaiman's spin-off comic *Death: The High Cost of Living*, where Amos writes a brief piece on her relation to the character Death. This connection is furthermore echoed on Tori Amos' album *Little Earthquakes* in the line "me and neil'll be hangin' out with the DREAM KING / neil says hi by the way" from the song "Tear In Your Hand" (Amos, 1992).

It may seem inconsequential that a comics writer and a popular singer know each other, but the fact that Amos contributes to Gaiman's work and he is brought into hers does indicate a certain shift in the status of comicbooks. The same is the case with the other writers providing introductions and blurbs, and their very presence also furthers the status which Gaiman's comics achieve and by association all comics do. Tori Amos is quite interesting in this regard, since her presence represents an unusual contribution to the paratext of *The Sandman*. As she is a singer/songwriter her presence comes from a completely unrelated medium and genre. Whereas most of the people who introduce or recommend Gaiman's works are connected either through the medium (Moore, Sienkewicz, etc) or the genre of the fantastic (Barker, Collins, Delany, Williams, etc), Amos stands out. This is clearly an advantage when trying to establish comics as literary works of art, since her presence broadens the field within which the comic is potentially received. Obviously, from the point of view of the publisher such a connection outside the field is valuable since it might sell more comics. The indirect effect, however, is that the reception of the comics extends beyond the genre field and so reaches into a larger field of production.

As we have seen, the area where the British writers' work has extended into is mainly that of a more literary readership. Along with Spiegelman's *Maus*, who in winning the Pulitzer Prize also broke down certain barriers for comicbooks, Moore and Gaiman have carved out a niche for comicbooks in the literary field. No longer regarded merely as escapist power fantasies, comicbooks found their way into the mainstream in the 1980s. It has been clearly stated by DC that they would not have risked the 1989 *Batman* film, had it not been for Miller's work, and while neither *The Sandman* nor *Watchmen* have been adapted for cinema yet (despite constant rumors), the impact of their work is undeniable. Whether this impact came from their work being particularly British seems dubious, instead there are a number of similar features for the British writers.

First off, both Moore and Gaiman had published successful comics in Britain prior to publishing in the US. This automatically placed them in the category of writers who were allowed some degree of freedom in their work, and allowed their names to be strongly identified with the characters and stories they created. Just as there have been no spin-offs or continued storyline of *Watchmen* without Alan Moore, nor has there been a *Sandman* line without Gaiman (although the line *The Dreaming* comes close, it is a completely different type with no specific continuity between issues). What is so particular about the fact that both Moore and Gaiman were publishing comics in Britain prior to the US, is that this meant they were generally working outside the superhero genre. Despite having to enter that field, at least provisionally, when turning to the US, they both attempt a reworking of the tradition. Gaiman first wrote *Black Orchid*, a rather minor character in the DC universe, and created a different origin for her, just as Moore did with *Swamp Thing*. While certainly not his strongest work, it is significant that even here Gaiman exposes the superhero genre in a metafictive move, when Black Orchid is caught and the villain says the following:

> I know how much you super-people like your secrets. [...] I've read the comics. So you know what I'm *not* gonna do? I'm not going to lock you up in the basement before interrogating you. I'm not going to set up some kind of complicated laser beam deathtrap, then leave you alone to escape. That stuff is so dumb. But you know what I *am* going to do? I'm going to kill you. Now. (Gaiman & McKean, 1989/1991: 6)

And then he does kill Black Orchid. Of course Black Orchid survives (after all, only poor sales can kill a superhero, and even that only lasts until a re-issuing), but the fact that she is simply shot rather than miraculously escaping, somehow kills off the genre conventions alongside it. Gaiman clearly attempts a destructive revision, though the rest of the text generally follows the conventions and so is representative of yet another double-coded text. Both Moore and Gaiman, then, contaminate the superhero genre with their work. Not only do they create a completely new continuity, different from DC's established universe, but they also employ devices from other fields and genres. While this is perhaps most evident in Gaiman's case, most of *Watchmen* is in fact a detective story, with very little action and much more investigation.

The creation of a new continuity can be seen as the second particular feature of the British writers, although this is not as specific since Moore took over *Swamp Thing* first. However, what is clear is the revision of the superhero tradition, specifically in the case of Moore, and the broadening of what types of comicbooks DC would publish in the case of Gaiman. *The Sandman* spawned its own spin-offs with the *Death* graphic novels, but just as importantly it paved the way for the founding of DC's Vertigo line, a new line of more adult-oriented comicbooks, most of them outside the super-hero genre or at least presenting different views of the superhero genre.

This founding of a new line indicates the third particular element about the British writers, which is the change in paratext. Not just making graphic novels or collections more popular, but also the use of introductions, blurbs and other endorsements intended to let the comics enter a new cultural fields, but also the realization that comics can appeal to those older than 12-year old kids. The Vertigo line is the clearest example of this and by issuing comics which do not fall, and are not meant to fall, within DC continuity, it represents a quite radical departure from previous publishing practices. Even alternate visions of superheroes have a new home, which is best represented by the third of the British writers to enter US publishing, Grant Morrison.

His arrival was slightly later than Moore's and to some extent he re-presented the idea of getting British writers to the US, since Moore had done so well. Morrison had also written comics in Britain with *2000AD* and wrote *Doom Patrols* and *The Invisibles*, both of which were his creations with new continuities, along with *Animal Man* and *Arkham Asylum*, a Batman graphic novel, placed within official continuity. Morrison's work is in many ways quite similar to Moore's and Gaiman's in his reworking of tradition, but is perhaps best regarded as a continuation of Moore's deconstruction of the genre. Morrison revels in explicit metafiction even to the extent of having Animal Man encounter Morrison himself as the writer of the comic; apart from taking many of Moore's ideas even further. However, *Arkham Asylum* along with one of Moore's *Superman* stories ("Whatever Happened to the Man of Tomorrow?") were so explicit departures from official continuity, along with Miller's *Dark Knight* that DC also felt it necessary to create the *Elseworlds* imprint, in which stories may take place outside official continuity.

All these changes in paratext show the impact which the British writers had, forcing the US superhero publishers to change the parameters of the genre which they invented. Because of this change, superhero comics have established themselves in popular culture as more worthy of attention, and have even entered literary culture to the extent that a novel may be about superhero comicbook creators and still win the Pulitzer Prize: Michael Chabon's *The Amazing Adventures of Kavalier & Clay*.

The British revision of US superheroes, then, represents both a textual subversion of the genre's conventions, but just as importantly it also affects the cultural field in which comics have usually been placed. The genre was opened up to a whole new readership and its status as solely a popular culture artifact was revised. Clearly this massive change cannot be placed solely at the feet of two or three writers, but in a medium where one genre dominates so much as superhero comics do, any type of revision of that particular genre will have a broader impact than work outside it. Although Spiegelman's *Maus* is the most canonized comic available, the British writers have reached a much larger percentage of comic readers and changed their view of what comics can do.

The transformation which these British writers had on the comicbook culture and medium extends beyond the field itself. Not only have Moore, Gaiman and Morrison crossed over into the American comics field, they have also all expanded into other area and media. Neil Gaiman has written novels, short stories, radio plays, film and TV scripts. Alan Moore has written film scripts, stage plays, made spoken word recordings and short stories. Grant Morrison has written film scripts, TV scripts and newspaper columns. Evidently, they cross not only national borders but also generic and medium borders.

This crossing, however, has not been unproblematic. While Gaiman has generally fared quite well, particularly that portion of Moore's work which has crossed the Atlantic without his control, essentially the adaptations of his comics, has generally been poorly received by both himself and his fans. So while his comics are quite popular, and although the adaptations have also been commercially successful, there is little overlap between the audiences. In this way, there is little exchange between the two versions of the same story, and the mediation must be regarded as unsuccessful in bridging both media. The original film projects which the three writers have been involved with have not achieved the same success as their comics. Instead, these works have remained more obscure and with limited availability, often having more of a cult-following by those who are fans of their comics. Gaiman's and McKean's *Mirrormask* film has been received as a surreal work rather than the fantasy-oriented work which is usual for Gaiman. It seems as if the particular style of Gaiman's writing cannot easily cross into a different medium with the same effect as in the comics.

What we see from this is that the flow across the Atlantic of the writers' other work has been less successful than their work in comics. It seems that there is a greater acceptance of exchange between UK and US in the comics field, where even later British comicbook writers such as Warren Ellis have also been transformed into a major figure. Why this is particularly so seems difficult to define. While the comicbook field is certainly much larger in the US, so is the film industry and here British talents in any medium have had less success in redefining their specific area. Perhaps one must consider the fact that the mid-80s came just after two musical movements from UK to the US: Punk and the New Wave of British Heavy Metal, both of which also redefined the American rock scene. It certainly seems as if practically all the British writers who crossed the Atlantic have been seen as rebellious, often part of a subculture and resisting the American influence by revising the tradition. Also, they have all remained in the UK rather than physically relocating to the US, thus further emphasizing their resistance to the American culture.

References

Amos, Tori (1992) *Little Earthquakes*. Warner Music Manufacturing Europe
Bennett, Tony (1991) "Holy Shifting Signifiers: Foreword". Roberta Pearson
    & William Uricchio (eds.) (1991) *The Many Lives of the Batman: Critical
    Approaches to a Superhero and his Media*. New York: Routledge & London:
    BFI Publishing

Bloom, Harold (1973/1997) *The Anxiety of Influence: A Theory of Poetry, Second Edition*, New York & Oxford: Oxford UP

Boichel, Bill (1991) "Batman: Commodity as Myth". Roberta Pearson & William Uricchio (eds.) (1991) *The Many Lives of the Batman: Critical Approaches to a Superhero and his Media*. New York: Routledge & London: BFI Publishing

Bongco, Mila (2000) *Reading Comics: Language, Culture, and the Concept of the Superhero in Comic Books*. New York & London: Garland Publishing, Inc

Eco, Umberto (1979/1984) *The Role of the Reader: Explorations in the Semiotics of Texts*. Bloomington: Indiana UP

Gaiman, Neil & McKean, Dave (1989/1991) *Black Orchid*. New York: DC Comics

Hutcheon, Linda (1989) *The Politics of Postmodernism, 2nd edition*. London & New York: Routledge 2002

Klock, Geoff (2002) *How to Read Superhero Comics and Why*. New York & London: Continuum

McCloud, Scott (1993) *Understanding Comics*. New York: Kitchen Sink Press/ Harper Perennial

McCloud, Scott (2000) *Reinventing Comics*. New York: Paradox Press/DC Comics

Miller, Frank (1986) *The Dark Knight Returns*. London: Titan Books, 1997.

Miller, Frank (1991) "Batman and the Twilight of the Idols: An Interview with Frank Miller". Roberta Pearson & William Uricchio (eds.) (1991) *The Many Lives of the Batman: Critical Approaches to a Superhero and his Media*. New York: Routledge & London: BFI Publishing

Moore, Alan & Gibbons, Dave (1986) *Watchmen*. New York: DC Comics

O'Neil, Dennis (1991) "Notes from the Batcave: An Interview with Dennis O'Neil". Roberta Pearson & William Uricchio (eds.) (1991) *The Many Lives of the Batman: Critical Approaches to a Superhero and his Media*. New York: Routledge & London: BFI Publishing

Pearson, Roberta E. & Uricchio, William (eds) (1991) *The Many Lives of the Batman: Critical Approaches to a Superhero and his Media*. New York: Routledge & London: BFI Publishing

Reynolds, Richard (1992) *Super Heroes: A Modern Mythology*. Jackson: University Press of Mississippi

Wertham, Fredric (1954) *Seduction of the Innocent*. New York & Toronto: Rinehart and Company, Inc.

Song of the Silenced:
American Performance of Baltic Choral Music

MARIAN E. DOLAN AND J. KAY KEELS

The choral tradition and music of the Baltic countries – Estonia, Latvia, and Lithuania – embodies an exceptionally unique history and cultural context and presents the non-Baltic conductor and singer with a unique set of performance and interpretive challenges. The 'traditional' experience of choral singers and conductors in western Europe and the Americas usually includes singing western choral classics of composers such as Bach, Handel, Mozart, Brahms, Britten, Schubert, Fauré or Orff. We study melodies, tune harmonies, balance and shape fugues, and hone our enunciation of English, Latin, or possibly German. In the emerging field of multicultural choral music, however, both conductor and singers are challenged by melodies and harmonic structures informed by cultures other than theirs, by unusually metered poetic texts, and by lesser-known languages spoken by small numbers of peoples. Choral interpreters, especially those who are from outside the composer's own culture, are also deeply pressed to study how cultural contexts inform not only the writing of but also the representing of this music in a concert.

We, the joint authors here, are an American conductor and a singer who journeyed rehearsing and performing Baltic music in the same choral ensemble and who now write about this experience from our unique perspectives. The conductor, Marian Dolan, is an academic choral conductor and editor by vocation. The singer, Kay Keels, is a choral singer by avocation and business professor by vocation.[1] In journeying Baltic scores, we encoun-

---

[1] Dolan earned masters and doctoral degrees in choral conducting from Yale University and taught at Haverford/Bryn Mawr Colleges and Emory University. Keels is Chair, Graduate Business Administration Department and Director of the MBA program at Brenau University.

tered a whole new paradigm of how an American choir learns and performs this music in a way that reflects and honors the choral music tradition of the Baltics. Three issues of particular importance emerged for us: the context in which the music is composed and sung, the language in which it is written, and the concept of "community" and its importance in conveying the music's intent. Each of these issues has a root origin in the Baltics with a parallel incarnation in the U.S. For example, the score is rooted in and informed by Baltic cultural contexts, yet the reinterpretation of that score is by American singers for American listeners, all of whom are shaped by American cultural contexts. Likewise, the score's original Baltic-based language, with all of its inherent culturally informed Baltic sounds and images, may or may not be readily grasped by either the American singer or listener. And finally, Baltic ideals of "community" as expressed via Baltic choral music is a concept which offers a new challenge to American singers whose culture speaks more of rugged individuality than of community. Thus, multiple levels of cultural "informance" shape every possible element of both the music and its transatlantic journey of interpretation.

The Cultural Context

The Conductor's Perspective: Silencing to Sounding

Music, whether choral or instrumental, grows out of and terminates in silence. Every performer knows this truth, whether s/he is an orchestral, choral, solo, wind, string, brass, percussion, or vocal musician. There is silence before there is musical sound. I learned this first as a flutist; then as a choral conductor: the breathless seconds between a conductor's bow to acknowledge the audience's welcoming applause, a reassuring glance around the assembled musicians, the final inward focus, the upward gesture, and, on the downbeat, *sound* – perhaps Mozart's or Bach's, Puccini's or Stravinsky's sound. The preceding silence, electric anticipation of what comes next, is often the same; the sound following, however, is unique.

But what if the *silence* were unique? What if the stillness in the concert hall before the downbeat was not the only type of silence? How is music affected when the noun 'silence' – that is, the absence of sound – becomes the verb 'to silence', that is, to make something not 'sound', to *not* be heard or understood by another? What if a composer's process was so altered that the musical expression itself was 'silenced'? What if a composer was not able – not allowed – to write the kind and type of music that s/he heard in his/her 'inner ear'?

What if not only the composer but also the reproducers of this music were silenced? A written score does, after all, need another person or group to 'bring it to life' again as musicians say. The performer/s take the graphic notation on the page and literally transform it into sound. What if those people were also silenced – threatened with loss of jobs, families, housing or even imprisonment for 'sounding' a piece of forbidden music, whether that music was from the pen of a known composer or from the anonymous folk tradition of that culture?

And what does it mean when that 'silenced' music finally *is* heard – when the musical style that was 'silenced' finally does get written down, rehearsed, and ultimately, sung? How are the composer, performer and listener affected? To take this idea to yet another level, what if this once-silenced music were represented in another country or culture, especially one whose history had not experienced a similar national, political and artistic silencing? What process must those singers undertake in order to represent the *context* of the music as well as its notes? In short, what is this journey from silencing to sounding?

The Singer's Perspective: A Silenced History

A choral singer stands as the mediator and translator between the silent score and the sounding music. In order to be a clear communicator of the score, a singer's mission is at least three-fold.[2] First, the singer must practice the music by him/herself in order to give an accurate vocal rendering of the composer's notes. Second, each choral singer must work *together* with the other choir members in a rehearsal setting in order to achieve a synergistic presentation of the music; i.e., many voices work to perform as one. Third and most importantly, each singer must internalize the music so thoroughly that s/he can understand the composer's original inspiration, and then convey that vision to the listener. In order to clearly translate the score, the singer must not only understand pitch, rhythm and text, but also the various cultural contexts out of which the music was composed. If the entire en-

---

[2] I am indebted to Dr. Dolan for explaining and teaching the choir this multi-faceted approach to learning music.

semble of singers is able to achieve this level of understanding and interpretation, the composer is honored and the real importance of singing the music is communicated. The importance of this third component is even more crucial when the music is of a culture other than that of the members of the choir.

This three-fold paradigm is particularly apt when applied to an American choir's experience with a Baltic choral score. In addition to the musical details, the cultural-context must be learned also. The vital importance of choral singing in the Baltics can be appreciated only when one understands these countries' silenced history. Until the early 1990s, the three Baltic States – Estonia, Latvia and Lithuania – were under Soviet domination. The Soviets attempted to 'Russify' all of Baltic culture. Baltic peoples were required to speak Russian in public settings, the open practice of religion was banned, all economic activity was organized in service to the Soviet system, and many citizens of the Baltic countries were apprehended on false charges and sent to Siberia – particularly those people who dared advocate the preservation of Baltic culture or religion. So, how did the Balts manage to survive and preserve their rich culture? In large part by singing, not only in their national Song Festivals, but whenever people gathered.

By contrast, singing for most Americans – even for those who love choral singing – is simply a casual and pleasant pastime. So, if an American choral singer is to represent faithfully a Baltic composer's musical intent, s/he needs to learn and understand how crucially important the history of communal singing is to the Balts. The American singer who truly understands this silenced history is, at once, both humbled and challenged at the prospect of attempting to convey its message to listeners on this side of the Atlantic.

The Conductor's Perspective: Representing the Silenced

Unlike in American culture, Baltic communal singing is not singing for entertainment; it is singing *to affirm cultural identity in the face of oppression and extermination of that identity*. Such purpose is a profoundly different approach to choral singing for Americans. Most academic, community or professional choirs and their conductors on both sides of the Atlantic experience a joyful journey in learning and performing a great choral masterwork from the western canon such as Mozart's *Requiem*, Orff's *Carmina Burana*, Handel's *Messiah* or Beethoven's 9th Symphony. Knowing the historic context of the piece – how old the composer was, where s/he was living or working, the circumstances surrounding the writing of the piece, for example – is certainly interesting and informative for both performer and listener. But there are musical compositions that also demand *cultural* contextualizing for their understanding. We, in the U.S., tend to de-emphasize the cultural contexts of our western art music. We speak of the artistic crafting or beauty of the piece, or we critique the interpretive savvy and exactitude of the performers. But the concept of studying the cultural context of a work, especially a composition from 'different' cultural origin, such as the Baltics, is a rather new construct for the American choral musician.

For example, in response to the italicized opening statement above, how do we Americans interpret and understand music that was birthed from a womb of cultural silencing? As a conductor, I could program Mozart's *Coronation Mass* and Estonian composer Urmas Sisask's *Eesti Missa #3* on the same concert. Both pieces have identical musical sections and texts, and both were written for specific parishes to sing in a service of worship, albeit Mozart's in a Catholic liturgy and Sisask's in a Lutheran setting. One of these masses, however, was written after forty years of 'silencing', during which time liturgical music was not allowed to be performed or composed. Is there then a difference in the way a conductor or singer approaches and interprets these two pieces?

I would argue yes. As a conductor, I approach any score with the same 'score study' skills, whether the piece is by Mozart or Sisask. Mozart's mass score and its style bear the influence of late 18c Viennese musical culture: the popularity of opera and its drama, the framework and timing constraints of the cathedral liturgy, the availability and ability of instrumentalists, choristers and soloists. By contrast, the mass setting by Sisask demands a set of interpretive meanings viewed, taught and presented through the lens of its contemporary cultural context: the mass was written for a local Lutheran church in the capital city of Tallinn shortly after the downfall of 40+ years of Soviet occupation and years of liturgical/musical silencing. The traditional pedagogical skills of a choral conductor – the study of music history, the understanding of music theory, and the knowledge of various musical structures (such as sonata, chorale, rondo, minuet, through-composed) – are thereby stretched and amplified to include study of the *cultural* contexts of 'silenced' Baltic music. This concept will become clearer by looking briefly at two of the most basic elements in a choral score: language/text and melody.

Language of the Silenced

The Conductor's Perspective

For the nations of the world with smaller populations, one of their greatest unifiers is language. The ability to speak it – to communicate stories, songs, narratives, laments, news or history – marks one as being of that group. To have one's native tongue silenced and replaced by a completely different language is culturally shattering. During the decades of Sovietization, in places of business, education, government, and outward society, one of the most important cultural markers for each of the Baltic countries – their languages and all of the inherent dialects – was stripped away and subverted with one language, Russian.

The language of Sisask's *Eesti Missa / Estonian Mass*, however, is not Russian. Composed in 1992–93 on the cusp of independence from the Soviets, the mass uses the vernacular language once silenced, Estonian, rather than Russian or even traditional liturgical Latin. The classically trained conductor is therefore challenged to learn the mass text in Estonian with all of its verbal colors, characteristics, and nuances as thoroughly as s/he knows the "traditional liturgical Latin" mass text used by Mozart. A mass setting begins with the prayer "Lord, have mercy" which, in the traditional text, is "Kyrie eleison". This text begins with a hard, crisp phonation of 'k' followed by a rolled 'r' sung on the given pitch; the vowels are mostly bright in tone; and the 's' is sung as a voiced 'z' to the pitch of that note. Contrast this with the Estonian text "Issand, halasta": the vowels are mostly open 'ah' (the vowel that singers love!), and the consonants are mostly <u>un</u>voiced 's' or 'h' sounds. One might say the Estonian text conveys a gentler and almost inward-focused spirit as compared to the edgier, bolder traditional liturgical text's statement. The sounds of these two languages could not be more different, and this is without adding the elements of pitch and rhythm. One can see from this simple example that the Baltic composer's choice of language – ie., the native tongue that was once silenced – now becomes a literal cultural 'study' for the American conductor and choral singers.

The Singer's Perspective: the Challenge of Sounding a Silenced Language

Singing in any non-English language presents an added challenge for most American singers. Many (perhaps even most) Americans are uni-lingual; there is no particular pressure or urgency to learn a second language in this country. Even when guests in another country, most American tourists expect the local citizens to speak English to them. By contrast, many Baltic citizens are bi-, if not tri- or quad-lingual. Only 1 or 2 million people might speak their native tongue, so Balts learn and speak other western languages in order to communicate more broadly. The roots and use of their own indigenous language, however, is never lost.

The American singer must work especially hard to understand and present accurately the native language when singing Baltic music. Baltic languages are somewhat challenging for an American to speak. Some of this challenge may be attributed to certain sounds in a given Baltic language that do not have equivalents in English. Another factor may be that most Baltic languages are not closely related to a more widely spoken language. Lithuanian, for example, traces its ancient roots to Sanskrit. The American singer must come to realize that the strange words and syllables that s/he struggles to form and sing have deep meaning for the Baltic peoples. For example, for me to sing the text "Holy, Holy, Holy" (the Sanctus text in a mass) evokes a deep connection to my faith and to my understanding of Trinitarian doctrine and the triune God. It was a startling revelation for me to realize that an Estonian who sings, "Püha, Püha, Püha" makes the same sort of deep connection. Singing Urmas Sisask's "Püha" in Estonian meant that first I needed to understand what the unfamiliar text meant, and then I had to internalize those sounds until they were comfortable to me until finally I could sing them with meaning and full understanding for myself and for the listener. The process was one of moving from merely the mechanical representation of unfamiliar sounds to words with context and meaning for both the native speaker and me.

Further, knowing what Baltic composers and singers endured in their recent history in order to be able to sing these words gives this Estonian text an even deeper meaning than the familiar English words I might casually mouth on a Sunday morning. It is, then, with a deep sense of mission and commitment that I struggle to learn and sing the languages of the Baltics. The sometimes arduous process of learning to sing the language of another is a sign of respect as well as solidarity. Imagine the joy experienced by an Estonian listener upon hearing a choir from the U.S. sing the Estonian national anthem or a runic-tune arrangement by Veljo Tormis! The ensemble is no longer singing *at* an audience, but *for* them and *with* them. Language, then, is one of the most significant elements in shaping and forming community, as explained further in the ensuing discussion.

The Silenced Melody

The Conductor's Perspective

A conductor who chooses to program a Baltic work often finds him/herself needing to study the use and context of Baltic runic or folk tunes. These tunes, unique to each country, commonly have small ranges and repetitive patterns. Their use in a contemporary composition harkens back to the ancient use of such tunes within a community to tell a story or share some news. When applied to contemporary choral music, such tunes give an added layer of cultural meaning. For example, in Sisask's mass, the traditional Estonian *regilaul* or runic tune pervades both the Kyrie and Credo movements. Exploring the overlap of the *regilaul's* cultural context with these liturgical movements prompts the question of whether there is a deeper connection between the use of these folk idioms and their application to the mass texts. Does the music teach and sing differently because of this contextual overlap? Yes, it does. For example, if the runic tune and its cultural context is explained to the singers and then applied to their understanding of the Credo text (the creed, or confession of faith said by the worshipping community), a very profound insight occurs. The "Credo/we believe" text is itself an expression of communal faith: within the context of a worship service, the Credo text is spoken together by everyone present. In Sisask's mass, this communally spoken text is now overlaid with a melody of the ancestors – literally a folk melody of the peoples, which, in *its* ancient cultural and historic context, was sung communally. Furthermore, for decades the Soviet oppressors silenced not only runic tunes such as this one but also stifled the gathering of worshipping communities. Native Balts were not only forbidden to sing the prayer "Lord, have mercy" or "we believe", they were also not allowed to sing it *together* as a worshipping community. Not only was the song of the individual singer silenced, so also was the corporate song of the community. So here in Sisask's "Kyrie" and "Credo" we have the re-emergence of a communally sung folk melody, set to a text about a community's faith, both of which, once silenced, now emerge in a powerful combination. And the entire choir sings all of this *in unison* – together, as *one* melody with no harmony. What emerges here, not once but twice, is an extraordinary statement about the strength and endurance of community: they sing, together, in community, the words of faith to the song of the generations – neither text nor tune silenced, but sung by all in fully-voiced faith and freedom.

The Singer's Perspective

A singer approaches any new piece of music, including a Baltic score, with a number of goals. First, the singer must master a "literal" translation of the notational language on the page into the melodic sounds the composer intended. Consciously or subconsciously, singers will bring their own culturally informed ideas about melody to a new piece of music regardless of whether that score is written by a U.S. composer or by someone outside of the American culture. The melodies we grow up hearing here in the U.S. are quite different in style and structure from the Lithuanian *sutartines* tunes.

The Conductor's Perspective

In order to help the choir better understand some of our Lithuanian scores, I asked them to learn and perform a *sutartines* melody. These ancient folk tunes are not sung in the same way nor do they sound like American folk songs or the latter's western European prototypes. American folk music tends to have melodies of a moderate range, with a balanced arch shape, sung over a series of simple harmonies often played by a keyboard instrument or guitar. By contrast, *sutartines* do not have instrumental accompaniment; they are a purely vocal, melodic idiom. *Sutartines* are actually a pair of melodies, sung one against the other as one would sing a round or a canon. Each melody is well shaped and of modest range. When sung together, however, the two tunes produce harmonic clashes of 2nds and 7ths – very dissonant sounds to an American singer's ear conditioned by the style of popular American song idioms that avoid such pungent clashes.

The Singer's Perspective

The *sutartines* we learned sounded strange in my ear. It felt like this melody was not resolved in the way that I am accustomed to hearing in an American tune. Because the sound of the *sutartines* literally clashed with what my culture had taught me to understand as 'melody', internalizing the *sutartines* tune and its inherent dissonances was quite a challenge for me. I realized that the issue was not a matter of a 'good' vs. 'bad' melody; it was instead a matter of my being able to step beyond my own culturally informed ideas of what constitutes 'melody' and literally re-tune my ears in order to internalize and interpret the Lithuanian sound of these melodies.

Vocally reproducing notes accurately and confidently, however, is only the beginning of a singer's melodic interpretation. In order to represent the composer's intent correctly, sometimes the singer must adjust his/her vocal color to a darker, brighter, edgier, rounder or more nasal sound. For example, singing with a more nasal quality in the U.S. is likely to draw forth jokes about country music; however, in other nations' languages or dialects, a nasal tone quality may be normative and therefore quite acceptable. The choral singer must understand the cultural context of the melody and how its unique colorings may be the driving inspiration for the composer. The choral singer has a responsibility to sing accurately not only the language but also the vocal tone colorings that will reproduce most accurately a Baltic score, even if the language and color stretches the singer beyond his/her own cultural comfort-zone.

The Silenced Community

The Conductor's Perspective

Communal singing is found in most countries: informal gatherings such as a birthday or family celebration, political rallies, the singing of a national anthem at a sporting event, songs of people gathered for worship, or formal high-art choral concerts. To silence forcibly such singing is also to silence the community and its identity. Take, for example, this simple story of a Lithuanian woman, recalling her earliest musical memory from a childhood defined by Soviet occupation: "One day at school, as [I] had started to sing a Lithuanian song, [my] mother, a teacher in the Kindergarten, placed her hand very tightly over [my] mouth. Singing in Lithuanian was of course forbidden under the Soviet regime and [my] mother had had to teach [these songs] secretly to [me]. If the song had been overheard, [my] mother would have lost the right to ever work again" (Hill, 2003: 23–4). This type of self-silencing unfortunately had become normative. One would imagine that this harsh process, carried out over and over again in a small country, would literally, within a few decades, eradicate a large portion of the culture. One extraordinarily unique event prevented this permanent silencing.

The national song and dance festivals of Estonia, Latvia and Lithuania, first held at the end of the 19th century, are unique and vibrant phenomena. Each country has a specially designed outdoor amphitheater that holds some 20,000+ performers plus an audience of 200,000-300,000! The history of each country's song festivals is slightly different, but the overall gathering of that country's population to sing together is rooted in the same ideal: to reaffirm cultural roots, to pass along the songs from generation to generation, and, as a gathered people, to sustain the culture's value and unique identity. During the years of independence in the early 20th century, the Baltic countries' national song festivals undoubtedly drew on such songs as that mentioned in the mother-daughter story above. These national festivals, begun during the early years of independence, continued during occupation – albeit with compositions 'approved' by Moscow. During the national fervor of the late 1980s and early 1990s, the tradition of communal singing carried over into the large gatherings of people protesting Soviet occupation. The fall of the Soviet system in the Baltics is known literally as the "Singing Revolution" because, as the Balts say, they sang their way to freedom and independence. Communal singing literally formed and re-formed three entire countries by affirming and reaffirming national identity and unity. In 2003, UNESCO (the United Nations Educational, Scientific and Cultural Organization) designated the Baltic Song Festivals as "Masterpieces of the Oral and Intangible Heritage of Humanity" so that their cultural heritage might be safeguarded for future generations.

Can this ideal of Baltic communal singing be conveyed to an American choir – in its understanding as well as its performance? Doing so would be a challenge. The Baltic Song and Dance Festivals, exceptional musical and cultural phenomena, have no North American cultural or historic equivalent. Our closest historic paradigm is perhaps the civil rights movement of the 1960s and 70s where large protest gatherings also included communal singing. Our closest contemporary cultural equivalents of massed gatherings of people are not musical but rather political rallies and sporting events. Yet to conceptualize a public gathering of over 200,000 is difficult for an American because even the largest sports stadium in the U.S. holds only just over 100,000. Sharing video footage of Baltic Song Festivals with American singers is a helpful pedagogical tool for framing the sheer magnitude of these events. Another helpful analogy for understanding the size of a Baltic Song Festival is to compare event attendance vs. national population. If approximately one-third of the Estonian population attended the 1988 *Laulupidu*, the equivalent 33% of the 1988 U.S. population is 83 *million* people! Having this percentage of the U.S. population participate in a joint activity is measurable not in communal singing but only in terms of entertainment, specifically television viewing: 83 million Americans watched the Olympics, the Super Bowl, and the finale of "Cheers".

The Singer's Perspective

Choral singing is, by its very nature, communal. However, typically Americans are individualistic by nature. So, it is not too surprising that many American singers often try to impose their individualistic voices on a choral ensemble; literally, one singer tries to out-sing those around him/her. Rather than a unified whole, the choir can become a cacophony of competing single voices – a situation that a composer of choral music rarely if ever intends. American choirs often must put forth extra effort to build a sense of community and oneness-of-voice that seems to come more naturally to Baltic choirs and singers. One need only witness the singing at one of the Baltic music festivals to understand true community. As noted earlier, gathering together to sing the traditional music, in their own country's language, was not a casual exercise for the Baltic peoples; it was a matter of cultural survival. As a singer, I have been a part of a choir of 25–30 singers who were able to achieve that single communal 'voice' when we worked at being more committed to the whole than to each individual singer. At the Baltic Song Festivals, the choir may number 15,000 – 20,000 ... and yes, *they do sing as one*. Not only does the choir achieve this sense of community, but those in the audience of thousands often join in the singing as well!

The Journey from Silence to Sound

The Conductor's Perspective

What, then, does the experience of singing the music of the Baltics, in all of their rich cultural contexts, 'sound' like for an American singer or conductor? Is it possible for one culture to 'sing with understanding' this unique and very culturally contextualized music? In 1994 with a chamber choir of undergraduate liberal arts students and their very patient Estonian classmate, I journeyed the teaching of Veljo Tormis' *Inkerin Illat/Ingrian Evenings*, a 15+ minute unaccompanied work of Estonian folk song settings. In 1997 with a chamber choir of graduate theology students, we lived with the Sisask *Eesti Missa #3* cited earlier, also sung in Estonian with the assistance of an Estonian-speaking classmate. And in 2003, different singers from this same theology school premiered Lithuanian composer Kristina Vasiliauskaite's *Mišios šv. Cecilijos garbei / Mass in Honor of St. Cecilia*, for choir and organ in a newly translated English version. For each concert cited above, we rehearsed the usual musical elements, but also made the added investment of cultural contextualization in our rehearsals. For these mostly middle-class white American singers, most of whom spoke no language other than English, the challenge of a new language, no less an unusual and unique one, left them with a newfound respect for being a 'minority' whose voice is often not heard or understood. Other singers commented on wanting to sing well for the native-speaking classmate in order to honor and support her/his tradition, history, and the years of silencing. Yet others found it fascinating to sing a familiar text in an unfamiliar language, to 'hear' theology in another 'tongue' – not just the sound in the ear, but literally the shape of the mouth while singing the text. Some singers commented on their shift in perspective from singing 'at' an audience to singing 'in' community. Others were moved by learning that the composer of the Lithuanian mass could neither write nor publish the sacred choral music harbored in her heart and ear until the Soviet occupation ended and freedom of expression, including the composition of sacred music, was restored. What then does it mean for American singers to honor Baltic music once silenced? One articulate bass described his experience as follows:

> Music is a perfect way to evoke generative themes and issues in a non-violent way. We tapped into a 'historical lament' that not only caused us to

remember but caused us to vision our ministry as sociologically, politically and morally accountable to the world (Sandow, n.d.).

The American musical culture, so often defined by the individual soloist and by music-as-entertainment, has much to learn from the ancient and contemporary Baltic song traditions. The American conductor who boldly programs this music – whether Estonian, Latvian or Lithuanian – allows his/her choir an opportunity to explore the edges of their own comfort zones, to identify the influences and values of their own culture, and to explore how communally performed music forms and shapes a society. Baltic song, rooted in the oldest tunes of the culture, sounds a word of truth to power, and images identity in the face of oppression. The nearly five-decade history of silenced Baltic choral music and the unflagging tradition of the Baltic national song festivals speak to the vision, tenacity and strength of the Balts *and* of the model they offer to all who will listen. If we listen, we hear not only the silence but also the songs.

References:

Daitz, Mimi. (2004) *Ancient Song Recovered: The Life and Music of Veljo Tormis.* Hillsdale, NY: Pendragon Press

Hill, Joy (2003) "The Freedom to Sing". *International Choral Bulletin.* Vol.10, 23–4 Sandow, Keith (1997). Unpublished and untitled written academic assignment; Candler School of Theology. Atlanta, Georgia: Emory University

Kuutma, Kristin. (n.d.) "Cultural Identity, Nationalism and Changes in Singing Traditions". (*Folklore*) [http://www.folklore.ee/folklore/] (Accessed: 2005, April 5)

Kuutma, Kristin. (n.d.) "Festival as communicative performance and celebration of ethnicity". (*Folklore*)[http://www.folklore.ee/folklore/] (Accessed: 2005, April 5)

Misiunas, Romauld J. & Taagepera, Rein (1993) *The Baltic States: Years of Dependence 1940–1990.* Berkeley and Los Angeles: University of California Press

Entrepreneurship in Lithuania: Embracing a Western Tradition[1]

J. Kay Keels

Entrepreneurship is not uniquely a product of the US, nonetheless, it is often associated with the "rugged individualist" image of many US businesspersons. For the process of entrepreneurship to occur, three sets of interactive factors must be present: individual-level factors, interpersonal-level factors and societal-level factors (Baron & Shane, 2005). These interactions are nearly taken for granted in a free-market capitalist society. Individuals are encouraged to be creative, free-thinking risk-takers. At the interpersonal level, families and other support networks are available to promote the entrepreneur's efforts. In Western society, there is a level of trust in the free market system and those who participate in it. In addition, the larger environment has been shaped economically and politically to drive entrepreneurial activity.

In a situation where none of these factors exist – at least, not in a supportive sense – how does a country go about developing an entrepreneurial culture? Until 1990, Lithuania had been a part of the former USSR and was operated as a planned socialist economy – every business decision was made centrally in Moscow, and all decisions were made for the good of the Soviet state.

An entire generation of Lithuanians had been discouraged from the kind of individualistic thinking that engenders entrepreneurial activity. Further, there were no support networks for individual business activity, and the

---

[1] I want to express my deep appreciation to Ms. Alge Budryte, PhD candidate, Vilnius University, for providing a wealth of sources and information. I am also very appreciative of the constant support and encouragement offered by Dean Andrea Birch, Brenau University. Without the assistance of these two individuals, the completion of this paper would not have been possible.

oppressive rule of the Soviets had taught Lithuanians to trust no one and to be fearful of strangers. Clearly, Lithuania did not seem to have a context that was conducive to the development and nurture of entrepreneurs. How, then, in the short span of its newly-gained independence, did Lithuania move from being just another cog in the Soviet industrial machine to assuming an impressive position among the top twenty economies of the world for ease of doing business (Easen, 2004)?

The Importance of Entrepreneurship

What Is Entrepreneurship? The first question nearly always draws a response that begins with "there is no universally agreed-upon definition of entrepreneurship" (Baron & Shane, 2005; Peng, 2000). Nonetheless, the study of entrepreneurship, a relatively new academic field, has generated some interesting findings regarding who an entrepreneur is and what it is that is unique and descriptive of what an entrepreneur does. Peng (2000) adopts the simple definition of *entrepreneurship* as "the creation of new enterprise". Somewhat similarly but more descriptively, Baron and Shane offer the following: "entrepreneurship, as a field of business, seeks to understand how opportunities to create something new arise and are discovered or created by specific persons, who then use various means to exploit or develop them, thus producing a wide range of effects" (2005: 4). One of those desired effects, particularly as understood in market economies, is the creation of value and as a consequence the accumulation of wealth. Entrepreneurs, then, are those specific persons who recognize the aforementioned opportunities and engage in processes necessary to produce the desired effects. Essential personal characteristics include the ability to recognize opportunities and the skill and knowledge to execute the necessary processes.

Why Is Entrepreneurship Important? More specifically, for this paper the important question is: "why is entrepreneurship important in a transition economy?" 'Transition economy' is a label often applied to the Baltics as well as other former Soviet-controlled countries that are undergoing significant changes in their economic systems after gaining independence from Russia (see Peng's [2000] explanation). Grennes (1994) provides a very clear answer to why entrepreneurship is important: "Entrepreneurship is an essential function in a market economy, and the emergence of entrepreneurs is important for the development of a prosperous market economy in Lithuania". Following the difficult years under the centralized communist economic system imposed by the soviets on all of these former SSRs, including Lithuania, one would assume that these newly independent states would rush to embrace some form of market economy. However, some states were more enthusiastic and progressed more quickly than others. In Lithuania, there was some ambivalence toward capitalism initially (Grennes, 1994) and economic reform came more slowly than in the Lithuania's Baltic neighbors, Lativa and Estonia. However, in the early days of independence, experts warned, "If economic policy does not reward entrepreneurship, entrepreneurs will not be forthcoming in Lithuania" (Grennes, 1994).

Emerging from the Soviet System

In the late 1990s, Vichas and colleagues (Vichas, Klimaviciene, Crawford & Klein, 1997) identified some of the barriers hindering Lithuania's transition to capitalism. Many of these barriers also represented impediments to the development of a successful entrepreneurial climate, for example, the socialist mindset had been ingrained into the Lithuanian's approach to economics for an entire generation. Consequently, there was a basic lack of understanding of the concept of capitalism. The little-known languages of the Baltics also posed barriers to entrepreneurial and economic development. The greatest barriers were presented by a lack of legal and social conditions conducive to developing a market economy, and the Soviets had left the Lithuanian infrastructure in poor condition.

Vichas et al (1997) pointed to a prevailing socialist mindset combined with a lack of familiarity with capitalist ideas and thinking. "The process of Sovietization in the Baltics involved russification, industrialization and the imposition of a secular ideology on agricultural societies which were ethnically homogeneous and, in the case of Lithuania, fervently Catholic" (Viesulas, 1995). In short, the Soviet system sought to erase all of the sociocultural vestiges of what it meant to be Lithuanian.

In addition, individuals in Lithuania lacked the kind of foreign language skills that were appropriate for conducting business outside the country's borders. The Soviets required that everyone speak Russian, an element of "russification". Children were educated in Russian, and Russian was the language of the Soviet economic system. To Lithuanians, as well as to natives of the other two Baltic states, Russian was a <u>very</u> foreign language that had little in common with their own (Idzelis, 1984). Idzelis (1984) highlighted some of the more obvious differences: Baltic languages are written in Latin script; Russian, in Cyrillic. Lithuanian, one of the oldest languages in Europe (Vinchas et al, 1997), traces its roots to Sanskrit and other Indo-European influences; Russian is Slavic. Furthermore, given the Soviet's rather insular economic system, Russian was certainly not a widely accepted language for conducting international business.

The aforementioned lack of trust of strangers as well as an absence of networks to encourage entrepreneurial development represented significant impediments to entrepreneurial development. Moreover, there was a prevailing mood of uncertainty about the newly emerging political and economic systems. The kind of self-confidence required to undertake an entrepreneurial venture is often fostered by an individual's experience in a family business or a relationship with a mentor who was an entrepreneur. Obviously, there had been no such supportive relational systems in Lithuania for fifty years – an entire generation had no opportunity to experience family or entrepreneurial business relationships. The current generation of adults in Lithuania had no frame of reference for economic endeavor. Vinchas and colleagues (1997) specifically noted that all business decisions under the socialist system were made in service to the needs of the state, including all production and distribution decisions. Consequently, a whole generation that grew up under these planned economies either lost or never developed the kinds of free enterprise capabilities and processes that had existed before the imposition of the socialist system.

The comparative scarcity of entrepreneurs in Lithuania as well as the relative lack of market activity as compared to its other Baltic counterparts has been noted by many authors, and Lithuanian attitudes toward economic activity have been characterized as ambivalent or even negative (Grennes, 1994).

As Soviet domination ended, Lithuania seemed to lack nearly all the ingredients that make an economy attractive to entrepreneurs and to those who would seek to invest in entrepreneurial activity. Its banking system was inadequate; its infrastructure was in poor repair; its legal system was not well-developed nor was it conducive to the needs of business; and, its industrial sector was not market-oriented (Cizauskas, 1992). All of these shortcomings represented serious impediments to Lithuania's entrepreneurial development; yet its infrastructure, especially its highway system, was in better shape than many of the other SSRs (Budryte, 2005).

The Effects of Cultural Context

Beyond the absence of social structures to support entrepreneurship, prevailing cultural values stood somewhat in opposition to the core objectives of entrepreneurs. Grennes (1994) pointed out specifically that Lithuanians tended to harbor a strong resentment and bitterness toward anyone who accumulated excessive wealth, either under the old Soviet system or too rapidly under the newly emerging economic system. In a competitive environment, however, the most basic goal is to create value that generates wealth, and often the key to creating value and accumulating wealth is to identify and satisfy an unmet need. Culturally, however, there appears to persist among Lithuanians a strong tendency toward communal sharing in times of need rather than exploitation of that need.

> I personally witnessed some evidence of this mindset when I visited Lithuania in the summer of 2003 to attend the country's national music festival. At some of the evening outdoor performances, the night air tended to be rather cool. On such occasions, young people would appear with large coffee urns strapped to their backs like backpacks, and they would circulate through the crowd dispensing free coffee complete with the accompanying packets of sugar and creamer which they dug from their pockets! To an American who had become at least somewhat desensitized to the notion of paying $4.00 for a gourmet cup of coffee, the possibility that someone would give away coffee for free, especially on a chilly evening, was astonishing. Although not an entrepreneur myself, entrepreneurial detection signals were flashing in my brain: hot coffee on a chilly evening was most definitely an entrepreneurial opportunity that could be exploited. On another evening during the festival when the weather was not only chilly but rainy as well, people stood near the entrance to the performance venue distributing free umbrellas!! (Author)[2]

Two cultural phenomena for which the Balts are well-known may have contributed to this non-competitive, communal mindset: the *Singing Revolution* and the *Baltic Way*. The Singing Revolution grew out of the national

---

[2] The preceding account was based solely upon my observation. More recently, I have learned that the real reason for the lack of entrepreneurial activity was that it was prohibited by the organizers of the festival. Some of the largest impediments to entrepreneurial development are actually the legal and regulatory environment in Lithuania (Budryte, 2005).

song festivals that had occurred in each of the Baltic countries for many years. The strong desire for independence in Estonia, Latvia and Lithuania gave these festivals a heightened importance in the years just prior to independence. Westcott (2004) noted that the music at the earlier Estonian festivals was "sung in subjugation" to Soviet domination whereas at the festival in 1989, the Estonian people "sang in defiance". The Lithuanian counterpart is described below:

> In the late 1980s Lithuanians organized an independence movement called *Sajudis* (Movement). In 1988, people gathered in large, peaceful rallies to sing their national songs and give voice to their frustrations. These rallies were the only way Lithuanians could express their nationalism and cultural pride during the Soviet occupation. The rallies came to be known as the Singing Revolution. (Voras Internet Services, Ltd, 1998)

The second phenomenon, the Baltic Way, stands as a most amazing demonstration of solidarity and a visual embodiment of the intensity of the desire for independence. Professor Vaira Vike-Freiberga, describes the Baltic Way and attests to its significance:

> The Baltic Way of 1989 was a singular event in itself. It was a unique, non-violent form of protest against the Soviet occupying regime, uniting hundreds of thousands of Latvians, Estonians and Lithuanians in a human chain that stretched for 600 kilometres through the three Baltic capitals. The Baltic Way has since led to the reappearance of the three Baltic countries on the map of Europe and to their evolution into full member states of the European Union and the NATO Alliance. (2005)

The strong sense of community and cooperation exemplified in these two cultural phenomena, while truly remarkable, represented almost the antithesis of the kind of competitive spirit that is the hallmark of capitalism and entrepreneurship. On the other hand, one could also argue that such fierce pride and determination in the face of seemingly insurmountable odds could be one of an entrepreneur's most valuable assets.

Development of an Entrepreneurial Culture

Lithuania declared its independence in 1990, and that declaration was generally recognized by 1991, especially since the USSR's attempt to re-establish its domination failed, and in 1993, the last of the Russian soldiers left Lithuania. In the early years of its independence, many scholars speculated as to whether Lithuania would model its economy after the free market systems of the west or whether it would revert to a model more closely reminiscent of the centralized economy from which it had just emerged. There was some genuine concern that Lithuanians would gravitate toward the eastern model despite its flaws, because it was what they knew. In 1993, the Lithuanian economy hung in a sort of limbo between communism and capitalism (Grenne, 1994).

No matter what kind of economic system eventually emerged or what kind of transition the country went through to achieve it, every one of the former soviet states was bound to continue to bear the marks of the socialist system for some time (Peng, 2000; Grenne, 1994). Comparatively, the Baltics actually fared better than the other countries under Soviet domination, but there was nonetheless an ever-widening disparity between income levels in the Baltics as compared to most western market economies.

Given their country's long history of being dominated, not only by the Russians, but earlier by the Poles and Germans, the Lithuanian people had developed a very strong sense of mistrust of any country or system that might seek to exert too much influence on the country's economic development. In fact, there was some concern that the country would turn inward and become highly protectionist, thus discouraging the healthy growth and development of its economy (Grenne, 1994).

Lithuania had been less subject to a large influx of "russified" Balts as its two Baltic neighbors had been. While this circumstance may have helped to preserve Lithuanian culture under the Soviets, it also tended to lessen the intensity of the negative feeling against the Russians and "russified" imports. Some observers were concerned that the Lithuanians had been lulled into a sort of political complacency that allowed the communists to retain control, thus slowing progress toward economic reform and a market economy (Viesulas, 1995).

Looking to the Future

Despite all of the previously mentioned impediments, Lithuania did make progress toward the development of a free market economy and the development of an entrepreneurial culture. Progress, however, was slow and in a comparative study of small business characteristics in Lithuania, Minkus-McKenna (2000) found very little change between 1993 and 1998.

She mentioned three areas of particular concern: (1) lack of business education, (2) little to no progress in the development of new sources of funding for small businesses and (3) a continuing paucity of new entrepreneurs.

Nonetheless, Lithuania continued its forward progress, and by the early 2000s, it had instituted economic and social changes significant enough to earn itself a place among the top twenty countries noted for ease of starting a new business (World Bank, 2004). There were several forces that mostly likely contributed to the forward progress of Lithuania's transitional economy: (1) the deep recession of 1998 triggered by the Russian financial crisis, (2) Lithuania's application and acceptance for membership in the European Union, (3) programs such as The United States Agency for International Development (USAID) and (4) World Bank support.

Russian Financial Crisis. Although Russia's financial crisis brought on economic hardship and recession for all of the Baltic countries (Fairlamb, 2003), this short-term difficulty may have been one of the best things that could have happened to these three former Soviet states. They finally realized that they could no longer tie their own future economic health and success to Russia. Consequently, the press for EU membership became even more urgent. Fairlamb (2003) noted, "[…] since they threw off the Soviet yoke, the three tiny countries have embraced change with a relish that puts Old Europe to shame. Almost all of their industry has been privatized. Most markets have been deregulated. Capital controls have been abolished. Their economies have been opened up to foreign competition" (unpaged).

European Union Membership. Application to the European Union brought with it exactly the kind of economic, political and legal discipline that Lithuania and its Baltic neighbors needed (Lainela, 2000; Easen, 2004). Working toward EU membership was no small feat for the Baltics; they began with almost no knowledge of or experience in developing a free market economy. Leinela (2000) noted: "Accession to the EU has proven important for applicants in their transition to a market economy. It offers countries a clear economic and political target for transition and motivates them to continue with their reforms. EU legislation also provides a tested framework for the creation of coherent legal systems in transition economies, where Western-type economic legislation has been largely absent".

"If there's one thing that has helped the Baltic states [sic] transform their economies, it is their commitment to sound government finances and strong currencies. The three countries have their budget deficits well under control[…]" (Fairlamb, 2003). He goes on to explain, "The Lithuanian and Estonian currencies are tied to the euro, and all three countries will meet the criteria to adopt the euro by mid-2006 if they keep up their current pace.[3] Most tariffs between the EU and the Baltic countries have already been swept away, and more than 70% of their exports already head west. When they become members, trade is expected to increase further" (unpaged).

The prospect of EU membership also seemed to provide strong incentive for stimulating entrepreneurial activity. Writing for *Business Week Online* in 2003 in an article titled "The Blooming of the Baltics", Fairlamb was very optimistic about the prospects for the future of entrepreneurship and economic development in these three small countries. He wrote: "The three countries' combined population may be tiny, at just 7.3 million, and much of their economic growth is driven by investment from Swedish and Finnish companies attracted by their low wages and taxes … [b]ut the Baltic states [sic] also have more than their fair share of home-grown entrepreneurs". Fairlamb (2003) continued, "Thanks to such entrepreneurial vigor, the Baltics are already the fastest-growing and most economically dynamic of the EU's 10 future members. Together, they clocked an average growth rate of 6.1% in 2002. When they join the EU next year, the Baltics, which not long ago were oppressed members of the Soviet Empire, will add a heavy dose of free-market ideology to the union" (unpaged website).[4]

USAID. By turning its economic and political aspirations toward western models, Lithuania attracted the assistance of agencies such as The United States Agency for International Development (USAID). USAID's website explains its role in Lithuania's development in the following statement:

---

[3] Ahead of Fairlamb's suggested schedule, Latvia pegged its currency to the euro at the beginning of 2005. In the next few years (Lithuania and Estonia in 2007; Latvia in 2008), all 3 Baltic countries are expected to replace their national currencies with the euro (Budryte, 2005).

[4] Lumping all three of the Baltics together for observation and commentary, as Fairlamb does here, is somewhat misleading. Post independence, cooperation among the three countries has diminished considerably. Increasingly, each Baltic country wants to be evaluated as a separate entity for its own accomplishments (Budryte, 2005). While such desire for individual recognition is admirable, it could also be detrimental for these small, emerging economies to lose completely the spirit of cooperation that helped usher in their cherished independence.

> [USAID] has played a major role in the economic, political and social development of Lithuania since 1992. The primary goals have been to stimulate the growth of a free market economy, promote strong democratic institutions and a dynamic civil society, improve environmental protection, and strengthen the social safety net. USAID assistance has enhanced Lithuania's capacity to integrate into Western political and security structures, develop a healthy economy, and achieve democratic reforms which rival many Central and Eastern European countries (unpaged website).

One important facet of the USAID mission was a broad-based training program. "Since 1993, over 1,500 Lithuanian professionals have had the opportunity to develop their knowledge, skills and attitudes in their particular areas of expertise, and to increase the capacity of their organizations by paving the way for indigenous, sustainable development" (USAID website).

Of particular interest in the training mission was a program known as Entrepreneurial Management and Executive Development (EMED). The USAID website explains,

> When USAID began the EMED program in Lithuania in 1994, World Learning staff canvassed the country to find entrepreneurs with small and medium businesses who would benefit from meeting with counterparts in the United States. Through an open and carefully targeted selection process, entrepreneurs were identified for an EMED program that would enable the trainees to improve their business operations, discover new ideas that could lead to expansion, and develop lasting and valuable contacts with American leaders in their fields (unpaged website).

EMED produced many positive results that helped to spur a surge in entrepreneurial development in Lithuania including increased profitability for many small companies, increased job creation and employment, and a rise in the number of women starting and operating businesses. In general, program participants gained experience, knowledge and confidence. Many of them also cultivated productive partnerships and relationships with U.S. counterparts.

World Bank. One program of particular importance to the development of entrepreneurship in Lithuania was the collaboration of a team from the World Bank with a Lithuanian Knowledge Economy Team. Its commitment to the development of a knowledge-based economy is further testament to Lithuania's determination to become a world-class economy driven by an entrepreneurial culture. The report issued by the World Bank in 2003 emphasized the importance of the development of a knowledge-based economy:

> The ability to acquire and use knowledge is increasingly important for countries' economic competitiveness. Moreover, the importance of knowledge for development will likely continue to grow—possibly making the difference between prosperity and poverty, both between and within countries. Acquiring and using knowledge require access to and the ability to use information and communications technology. But they also require efficient education systems that provide opportunities for life-long learning, new approaches to innovation that bring together researchers and entrepreneurs, and an economic and institutional framework that supports the use of knowledge to provide new and competitive products and services (2003: i).

Conclusion

Clearly, entrepreneurs will be in the forefront of Lithuania's future economic growth and development. If the country's recent progress is any indication, that future will certainly be bright. Lithuania had a choice when it gained its independence; it could have chosen to model its economy after its old Soviet suppressor or it could have chosen to look to the west for a new model. Lithuania cast its economic lot with the west and is well on its way to taking its place among the growing and dynamic economies of the European Union.

References

Baron, Robert A. & Scott A. Shane (2005) *Entrepreneurship: A Process Perspective*. Thomson – Southwestern.

Budryte, Alge (2005) PhD candidate. Vilnius University. Personal Communication.

Cizauskas, Albert (1992) "The Political Economy of Lithuania". *Lituanus: Lithuanian Quarterly Journal of Arts and Sciences*. 39 (1) [http://www.lituanus.org/.]

Easen, Nick (2004) "Where best to base your business". For CNN. Friday, September 10, 2004 Posted: 1602 GMT (0002 HKT). [http://edition.cnn.com/2004/BUSINESS/09/08/go.world.bank.report/]

Fairlamb, David (2003) "The Blooming of the Baltics". *International – European Business* (July 14, 2003) *BusinessWeek Online*. [http://businessweek.com/magazine/content/03_28/b3841150_mz034.htm]

Grennes, Thomas (1994) "The Lithuanian Economy in Transition". *Lituanus: Lithuanian Quarterly Journal of Arts and Sciences.* 40 (2) [http://www.lituanus.org/]

Idzelis, Augustine (1984) "Industrialization and Population Change in the Baltic Republics". *Lituanus: Lithuanian Quarterly Journal of Arts and Sciences.* 30 (2) [http://www.lituanus.org/]

Kutma, Kristin "Festival as Communicative Performance and Celebration of Ethnicity" [http://haldjas.folklore.ee/folklore/vol7/festiva.htm]

Lainela, Seija (2000) "Baltic Accession to the European Union". *Lituanus: Lithuanian Quarterly Journal of Arts and Sciences.* 46 (3) [http://www.lituanus.org/]

Minkus-McKenna (2000) "Characteristics of Small Businesses in Lithuania: 1993–1998". *Lituanus: Lithuanian Quarterly Journal of Arts and Sciences.* 46 (3) [http://www.lituanus.org/]

Peng, Michael W. (2000) *Business Strategies in Transition Economies.* Thousand Oaks, CA: Sage Publications, Inc.

USAID. Mission to Lithuania. [http://www.usaid.gov/locations/europe_eurasia/countries/lt/index.html]

Vichas, Robert, Klimaviciene, Ausra, Crawford, Gerald & Klein, Hans E. (1997) "Practical Barriers in the Transition to Capitalism: The Case of Lithuania". Conference paper presented at The World Association for Case Method Research and Application (WACRA) [unpaged].

Viesulas, Romas Tauras (1995) "The Politics of Macroeconomic Stabilization in the Baltic States". *Lituanus: Lithuanian Quarterly Journal of Arts and Sciences.* 41(1) [http://www.lituanus.org/]

Vike-Freiberga, Vaira (2005) "The Baltic way in Europe. Revolution and Evolution". Baltic Studies Conference. Vidzeme University College Valmiera. June 17-19. [http://www.va.lv/cbse/]

Voras Internet Services, Ltd. (August 24, 1998) [http://lithuanian-american.org/folklife/lithuania.htm]

Westcott, Kathryn (2004) "Revolutions: What's in a Name?" BBC News (Friday, 26 November, 2004) [http://news.bbc.co.uk/1/hi/world/europe/4041157.stm]

Why to Invest in Lithuania. [http://www.vilnius.lt/dipolis/dok/02_why_to_invest_in_lithuania.pdf]

World Bank (2003) "Lithuania Aiming for a Knowledge Economy". Severin Kodderitzsch (Team Leader)

The Transatlantic Flow of Morality: A Case Study of Abortion Politics

Heather Gollmar Casey

Much has been written lately, both in popular media and more scholarly works, about the growing schism between the United States and its land of origin, Europe. A divergence of views is evident in a variety of contexts. US foreign policy has become increasingly unilateral while Europe's has assumed a multilateral approach. Europe is eliminating trade barriers while the US enacts new restrictions. The European Union encourages tight debt margins while the US deficit has skyrocketed. European leaders who are perceived as blindly following the US's lead face growing domestic opposition. Do these differences indicate a halt in the transatlantic flow of political ideology and practices? A close examination of abortion rhetoric and legislation in the United States, United Kingdom (excluding Northern Ireland), France, and Germany suggests that rather than the US gradually adopting European practices or vice versa, the countries are arriving concurrently at similar formal outcomes (abortion legislation) but significantly different political and social contexts (discourse).

Why would the countries studied here have arrived at such common abortion legislation? The United States often follows Europe's lead in matters of social policy; unemployment benefits, health care, government secured pensions, even extension of suffrage beyond upper class males, all began first in Europe and slowly flowed, becoming diluted along the way, over to America. But then why such dramatic differences in the discourse which surrounds abortion legislation? There are three factors which could explain this phenomenon: history of women's rights, women's political representation, and state-church relations.

Each country's abortion policy can be expected to reflect that country's history of women's advocacy and a presence or absence of an audible women's discourse.[1] The availability of abortion and other reproductive technologies promotes women's equality and promotes, in Myra Marx Ferree's terms, women's "full personhood" (2003). On the other hand, the possible termination of a potential life has far reaching ethical concerns which can push religious organizations to pressure the state to restrict abortion. Thus when there is no clear separation between church and state, one would expect more restrictive abortion policies. In the countries being studied here, each of these characteristics can help explain why despite similarities in abortion legislation, the discourse in which abortion is discussed is dissimilar.

One, the rhetoric surrounding women's purpose/position in society has a shared history for many countries. Regardless of region, periods of revolution or increased nationalism have been identified as moments of visibility and potential for women's rights advocates. The similarities of the French and American Revolutions are more obvious but women in other European countries have had like experiences.[2] It is precisely when conceptions of citizenship are changing, either in terms or an individual's position vis-à-vis state institutions or the position of a particular group of individuals vis-à-vis perceived "others", that women's potential and the surrounding discourse are recognized. The political and social elite are willing to accept an increase in women's public visibility when it is framed within a non-threatening discourse, educated mother as the educator of citizens.

In the case of the French and American revolutions, political discourse originated in Europe (Thomas Paine's *Common Sense*, *Declaration of the Rights of Man*) and migrated across the Atlantic to be mimicked by the rebellious colonists. Ironically, though each revolution relied upon nationalist appeals, political discourse focused on universal human liberties. French revolutionaries, echoed by the colonists, spoke of the new ideals and values of republicanism. Part of the revolutions' joint promise was to change notions of citizenship, allowing common individuals to participate in the highest political functions. Women, as mothers of the nation, were also included in this discourse. When political regimes are fighting for their national identity,

---

[1] Of course, this relationship is a complicated one. Countries with the highest rates of abortion (China, India) are also the ones in which women are clearly subjugated to men. The high rate of abortion however is not a result of permissive state policies but the overwhelming preference to have sons.

[2] Karen Offen (1998) discusses the effect of political change of women in Italy, Poland, Finland, and Sweden. Barbara Einhorn (1993) makes the case for women in democratizing Eastern Europe; Wendy Bracewell (1996) for women in Serbia.

both the physical bodies and symbolic roles of both men and women are called into service for the state. Men will be asked to serve their country on the battlefield, and women from the home. As Nira Yuval-Davis (1996) states, "within the logic of nationalism, women, as the subjects who physically give birth and symbolically reproduce the citizenry, are marked as vessels of the nation's moral integrity, survival, and coherence".

As is the case today, political discourse then was watered down as it crossed the Atlantic, though in both US and France the notion of republican motherhood was held in high regard. While America limited republican motherhood to a gentle encouragement for mothers to educate their (male) children to be virtuous citizens, in France the discourse centered more directly on the female body. Not only were goddess figures used to represent the new Republic, revolutionary publications included images of fountains in which the milk from virtuous mothers' bare breasts streamed directly into the mouths of eager new(born) statesmen (Jacobus, 1992). Sara Melzer explains the importance of women: "women as an allegorical figure came more and more persuasively to stand for Liberty, Equality, republican virtues, and the Republic itself in the men's representations of their new political order" (1992: 5). A similar distinction can be seen in abortion rhetoric today. In Europe, particularly France and Germany, while the moral questions surrounding the termination of a pregnancy are recognized, the debate is focused on more tangible things – physical bodies, monetary supports, meeting certain definitions of "need". In the US, the debate has become more and more metaphysical, centering on questions of equality and individual freedom.

The second potential explanation for the divergence in European and American abortion discourse is women's political representation. Here the trend seems to parallel that of abortion policy; the outcome (level of representation) is similar on both sides of the Atlantic, but the discourse is not. Though women's political representation is generally higher in the rest of Europe, the countries studied here, with the exception of Germany, share the US's shamefully low levels. In the US, women hold 14.8% of the seats in the House of Representatives, and 14% in the Senate (Center for American Women and Politics). In the United Kingdom, women held 17.9% of seats in the House of Commons and 17.8% in House of Lords. In France, the respective percentages are 12.2% (National Assembly) and 16.9% (Senate). Germany, the exception, has 32.2% in Bundestag and 24.6% in Bundesrat (IPU). The formal political status of women, measured only by percentage of legislature, is fairly similar with Germany ranking at the top, and the United States towards the bottom. Defying the logic of a direct correlation to abortion policy however, the US on paper ranks as the most liberal abortion policy while Germany's is the most restrictive.

The discourse which surrounds ensuring women's representation is very different between the European countries and the US. In Germany, many of the political parties guarantee women a percentage of slots in party electoral lists (http://www.quotaproject.org/displayCountry.cfm?CountryCode=DE). In France, parity reform in 1999 ensured "equal access of women and men to electoral mandates and elective functions" and holds political parties financially responsible for facilitating equal access (Quota Project). The United Kingdom for a short time also required electoral quotas but the policy was found to violate employment equality laws (Gelb, 2002). Since that time, the Liberal and Labour parties have adopted voluntary quotas for their electoral lists (Quota Project). In these countries, discussions of women's inclusion are centered on state protection of women's rights. In the US, no such policies formally protect women's inclusion. While direct quotas would be impossible given that the US does not use proportional representation, political parties themselves are often reluctant to recruit and encourage women candidates. American political discourse there is focused on individual rights, any guaranteed protection for one group is considered an infringement on the rights of others. As indicated below, a parallel distinction separates abortion discourse in the US from that in the European countries.

The third characteristic to be considered is the church-state relationship. Michael Minkenberg (2003) examines how church-state relations impact abortion policy in the United Kingdom (excluding Northern Ireland), France, Germany, and other European countries. He found that with the exception of France, a conservative family policy exists in all countries with a strict separation of church and state (2003: 207). Though his study does not include the US, using his descriptions and terminology it would fit this conclusion.[3] In Germany, which is described as having some overlap between the church and state, and the United Kingdom, with a state-sponsored church, family policy is more moderate. As with women's political representation, this finding also directly contradicts what would

---

[3] Here I consider US abortion policy to be conservative not as it exists on the national level, but as it is carried out on the state level.

seem to be a more logical correlation, a higher degree of separation leading to more moderate policies.

A second discovery in the Minkenberg study is that in none of the three European countries studied here did the churches play a leading role in the pro-life/abortion restricting movement. Looking at anti-abortion discourse in each country, he found a reliance on scientific rather than "religious-moral" terms was more successful (2003: 210–211). US anti-abortion discourse is deeply embedded in religious-moral terms however. In fact, women activists lament the religious right's dominance in abortion discourse (Wolf 1995, Duden 1993, Feldt 2004, Roth 2000, Schroedel 2000).

Current Status of Abortion Legislation

Looking at the United Nations's country profiles on abortion, the four countries being studied look very similar. In each, abortions are available prior to an indicated gestational age. In Germany and France some type of pre-procedure counseling is required. In France and the United Kingdom, two medical practitioners must attest that certain requirements indicate an abortion is needed. Abortion legislation is a bit more complicated in the United States because of its federal structure. While the Supreme Court has guaranteed a basic right to abortion services, states possess a great deal of discretion in setting the availability of abortions.

United States: Abortion is theoretically available in all states on request prior to fetal viability. States may and have imposed any number of the following conditions/restrictions as long as they do not impose an "undue burden": mandatory waiting periods (19 states), limits on public funding of abortions (35 states), conscience-based exemptions to medical personnel or health facilities to refuse to perform an abortion (46 states), counseling ban to prohibit health care providers from informing adult women about abortion services (6 states), spousal consent/notification (9 states), requiring payment of extra insurance premiums (5 states), limits on public employees' insurance coverage (8 states), mandatory counseling (30 states) (Schroedel, 2000).

United Kingdom: According the 1990 Human Fertilization and Embryology Act (stem cell 2004), abortion is permissible prior to the viability of the fetus, designated at twenty-four weeks, if two (one in an emergency situation) registered medical practitioners testify the social, environmental, or living conditions of either the mother or her existing children would worsen if the pregnancy were to continue. In cases where the mother's health or life is in grave danger, or the fetus would be seriously handicapped, there is no time limit. According to the National Health Services Act of 1977, many abortions will be covered by the National Health Service.

France: Until ten weeks gestational age, abortion access is unlimited as long as the woman is willing to state the pregnancy has placed her in a state of "distress". After that time, abortion may be permitted only if two physicians attest to the risk to the health of the woman or fetus. A "social interview", in which a physician must describe the physical risks associated with abortion and financial assistance available if the pregnancy were to continue, is also mandatory.

Germany: Abortion is unlawful with a possible jail term of three years (Stem Cell 2004). However, abortion is legal in the case of rape or incest. Even unlawful abortion will not be prosecuted if the birth would gravely impair the physical or emotional health of the mother. Other conditions which must be met in order to avoid prosecution include gestational age (before twelve weeks), and mandatory counseling which includes a discussion of fetal development at least three days prior to the procedure. In some instances of financial need, the cost of the abortion will be covered by the state.

Abortion Discourse

United States: Abortion discourse shies away from ethical or moral considerations and relies upon principles of equality and individual freedom. Abortion discourse includes phrases such as "constitutional right to choose", "women's basic liberties", "reproductive justice", and "fundamental American values" (National Organization of Women, NARAL). Many abortion rights advocates criticize the dominant Republican agenda for replacing science with ideology (Feldt 2004). After the 2004 elections, it has been suggested that the discourse used to promote women's equality, including but not limited to abortion access, has been defeated by the moral discourse of the religious right. Even candidates for the leadership of the national Democratic Party, most notably Vermont Governor Howard Dean and Indiana Representative Timothy Roemer, criticized abortion discourse for dominating the political agenda.

United Kingdom: Abortion discourse in the UK is most similar to that in the US. Pro-choice organizations do address individual rights, they state emphatically rights can not exist until after birth; a fetus is not an actual human *being*, but is only human *tissue* inside the body of an *actual* human being. For many groups, the question about whether a fetus is in fact a living being has already been decided. Attempts to argue otherwise are not very productive. In fact, a recent political debate about the nature of abortion was decried as "US style election" debate and the public was reminded that 76% of all British support a woman's right to choose (www.abortionrights.org.uk). In the UK, the call is for all women to have equal access to safe, legal, and free abortion.

France: Abortion discourse in France undoubtedly follows a secular tone. There is a dual emphasis on individual privacy and state protection. According to Dominique Memmi (2003), state funding of abortion is akin to financial supervision of a recognized practice and legal protection of abortion justifies self-determination in procreation (653). Some theorists even portray abortion as a scientific response to a "biological complication". The framework of ethics and morality which dominates abortion discourse in the United States is absent.

Germany: Abortion discourse addresses both women's autonomy and state protection. German abortion supporters concede the moral implications of abortion. Myra Marx Ferree cites a speech by a female Bundestag representative that "every termination of a pregnancy is a kind of partial suicide for the mother, a destruction of a piece of her own self and is also perceived to be exactly this by the pregnant woman" (Ferree, 2003: 333). Rather than pushing for abortion rights in a moral vacuum, German women stress government responsibility in supporting women, pregnant or not. German abortion legislation then emphasizes public health and humanitarian justifications. The need for an abortion is not the result of an individual woman's character flaw but of the state's inability to create an environment in which she can have children.

Concluding Remarks

Historically the transatlantic flow of both political discourse and outcomes has been from Europe to the US, with the US waiting to see how innovative (liberal) policies played out in Europe before adopting a milder version. In most policies today, at least in the eyes of Europeans, the opposite seems to be true. The US espouses more radical (conservative) beliefs and practices and Europe is begrudgingly towed along behind. Liberal winds blew from the continent to the New World, while conservative gales originate in the US. In the context of abortion legislation however, all the countries studied here are simultaneously moving in the same direction towards more restrictive abortion policies. In each case, gestational periods within which abortions may be permitted have been shortened and criteria to indicate "need" have increased. Though there are specific restrictions unique to each country's political context, the overall tone remains constant.

Perhaps this is not a transatlantic phenomenon but part of a larger global movement in which access to abortion services is universally restricted. The increase in abortion rates in parts of Asia and Africa contradict this possibility. Perhaps both sides of the Atlantic have come to an agreement about which individual freedoms should be extended and which retracted. The variation in abortion discourse in each country studied contradicts this possibility.

This variation can not be explained by history of women's rights though it can explain restrictive abortion policies. Women were included in revolutions in both Europe and US but as agents of and for the state. In all countries, political rights, most notably suffrage, were granted to men of all races and economic class before they were given to women. A similar lack of women's political representation in each country further supports similarities in abortion legislation. In none of the countries studied does the percentage of women in the legislature approximate women's percentage of the population. Three of the countries studied have never had a female head of government. The United Kingdom did but of course Margaret "The Milk Snatcher" Thatcher was not exactly an advocate for women's complete (political, social, and economic) equality. The lack of a commitment to women's full incorporation into political life therefore is paralleled by lack of a commitment to women's maximum rights and freedoms. Though each country studied has a slightly different church-state relationship, there is no correlation between degree of separation and abortion discourse.

An examination of the discourse in each of these areas can help us understand the variations found in abortion discourse. In the United States, discussion of women's rights (whether that be in a revolution, political representation, or access to abortion) is focused on abstract individual rights. It is argued that prioritizing women's concerns inherently limits the rights of others (future statesmen, general population, or a fetus). In the European countries, discussion of women's rights is focused on state responsibility (to protect mothers). The question there is to what lengths the state is obligated to protect women's particular freedoms.

Thus transatlantic flow of morality discourse has shifted and does not flow directly east to west nor west to east. Instead countries on both sides are using slightly different justifications to arrive at fairly similar outcomes. What can not yet be discerned is whether European nations are following the US's lead but adapting the rhetoric to fit their context or whether the reverse is true. Looking at international politics and recent changes in European domestic policies (slight reductions in benefits provided by the state to offset budget deficits), it appears the US is the point of origin. Clearly, the current US administration believes this to be the case.

References

Bracewell, Wendy (1996) "Women, motherhood, and contemporary Serbian nationalism". *Women's Studies International Forum.* Vol.19. No. 1/2

Duden, Barbara (1993) *Disembodying Women: Perspectives on Pregnancy and the Unborn.* Cambridge: Harvard University Press

Einhorn, Barbara (1993) *Cinderella Goes to Market: Citizenship, Gender and Women's Movement's in East Central Europe.* London: Verso

Feldt, Gloria (2004) *The War on Choice: The Right-wing attack on Women's Rights and How to Fight Back.* New York: Bantam Books

Ferree, Myra Marx (2003) "Resonance and Radicalism: Feminist Framing in the Abortion Debates of the United States and Germany". *American Journal of Sociology* Vol.109. No.2

Gelb, Joyce (2002) "Representing Women in Britain and the United States: The Quest for Numbers and Power". CS Rosenthal (ed.) *Women Transforming Congress.* Norman: University of Oklahoma Press

Jacobus, Mary L (1992) "Incorruptible Milk: Breast-feeding and the French Revolution". Sara E Melzer (ed.) *Rebel Daughters: Women and the French Revolution.* Cambridge: Oxford University Press

Landes, Joan (1988) *Women and the Public Sphere in the Age of the French Revolution.* Ithaca: Cornell University Press

Melzer, Sara E (1992) "Introduction". *Rebel Daughters: Women and the French Revolution.* Cambridge: Oxford University Press

Minkenberg, Michael (2003) "The Policy Impact of Church-State Relations: Family Policy and Abortion in Britain, France, and Germany". *Western European Politics.* Vol. 26. No.1

Offen, Karen (1998) "Contextualizing the Theory and Practice of Feminism in Nineteenth-Century Europe (1789–1914)". R. Bridenthal, SM Stuard, M. Wiesner (eds.) *Becoming Visible: Women in European History.* Boston: Houghton Mifflin Company

Offen, Karen (1990) "The New Sexual Politics of French Revolutionary Historiography". *French Historical Studies.* Vol. 16. No. 4, 909–922

Roth, Rachel (2000) *Making Women Pay: The Hidden Costs of Fetal Rights.* Ithaca: Cornell University Press

Schroedel, Jean Reith (2000) *Is the fetus a person? A Comparison of Policies across the Fifty States.* Ithaca: Cornell University Press

"Stem Cell Division: Abortion Law and Its Influence on the Adoption of Radically Different Embryonic Stem Cell Legislation in the United States, the United Kingdom, and Germany" (2004) *Texas International Law Journal.* Vol. 39. No. 3, 479–520

Wolf, Naomi (1995) "Our Bodies, Our Souls". *The New Republic.* October 16: 26–35

Yuval-Davis, Nira (1996) "Women and the Biological Reproduction of 'the Nation'". *Women's Studies International Forum.* Vol. 19. No. 1/2

Dove sono le donne artisti?...and Other Questions Regarding Revisionist Art History and Italian Women

Mary Beth Looney

Not unlike Linda Nochlin's pivotal essay "Why Have There Been No Great Women Artists?" of 1970, this contribution is also an analysis that poses more questions and possible theories than definitive answers (Nochlin, 1988: 147–158). The following discussion of differences between the art historical and museum climates of the United States and Italy, with specific attention paid to the study and exhibition of works by women artists of the Italian Renaissance and Baroque periods as well as feminist-inspired research, acknowledges the limitations from which the original idea stemmed. Taking undergraduate-level students to three Italian cities in one week is by no means an exhaustive treatment of our studied subject. However, this essay is written with those students' experiences in mind, to perhaps more accurately assess the novice traveler's perceptions of seeking out the works of a particular class of artists amidst the vast amount of art shown in Italian exhibition spaces.

Students, faculty and friends of Brenau University of Gainesville, Georgia, embarked on a trip to Italy during their so-called Spring Break in the first week of March, 2004. A significant number of these travelers had never been to the country, much less Europe, so they were naturally excited to visit the famous sights of Rome, Florence and Bologna. A smaller fraction of the group of thirty-five was more uniquely prepared than the rest: these students had been studying the art of Italian women in a Special Topics in Art History class for eight weeks prior to the trip. Course content included women as art makers and as art subjects in the Renaissance and Baroque eras, with substantial focus given to the works of artists Sofonisba Anguissola, Lavinia Fontana, Giovanna Garzoni, Artemisia Gentileschi, Barbara Longhi, Properzia de Rossi and Elisabetta Sirani.[1] We closely examined the biographies and careers of these groundbreaking, professional women artists of the Western world. We made careful notes on respective Italian museum collection holdings, and we left for our trip with grand expectations to view works of art that were so celebrated in English language textbooks, journals and articles. The results of our forays in search of 'the women' were both exhilarating and disappointing for the same reason: it is very difficult to locate them, and if and when they are located, the seekers must bring their own fanfare.

A number of explanations for this challenge were supplied well before embarking upon the physical search. Named women artists of the preceding historical periods are very few in number, and even though their ranks swelled in the Renaissance and Baroque eras thanks in large part to the uniquely progressive attitudes towards the education of upper-class women, there is but a handful who lived long enough and were productive enough to leave behind a substantial body of work. The historical rarity of these women artists is compounded by history's treatment and recognition of them: they have been forgotten, overlooked, downplayed – and because of societal restrictions on their education, subject matter and financial freedoms – they have been undervalued. In the last thirty years, research, restoration and conservation efforts to correct this problem have been significant, if not arduous.

Present-day art historical scholarship continually strives to correct serious misattributions of women artists' works to their more visible male contemporaries. Yet scholars continue to disagree over attributions, particularly in the case of artists whose work is understood to be uneven in quality, such as that of Elisabetta Sirani (1638–1665), a woman who was known to create pictures with record speed, which may have aided in her money-making capacities, but may not have resulted in stylistic consistency. With the establishment of ever-mounting information on (and the ever-growing renown of) these artists, researchers are now faced with an additional, reversed problem of connoisseurship: newly emerging works of art transferring from private ownership to more public collections may arrive

---

[1] Please see the addendum of working bibliography sources for the course.

as wrongly attributed to women artists.[2] Numerous pieces which have been finally, properly attributed to their female authors may have sustained physical damage while they lingered in improper storage facilities or hung neglected in less-than-ideal conditions. Current attempts to restore such works remain expensive and time-consuming, therefore requiring removal from public view while they either await or undergo restoration. Some paintings and drawings remain too fragile and beyond the scope of proper repair; they too rest in the dark recesses of collection storage units and may only receive attention from the inquirer who must make special arrangements with an institution to view an object for a brief period of time. Finally, there remain the women artists' works in less-frequented Italian churches. Sometimes properly identified, labeled and on display in the settings for which they were perhaps originally designed, these darkening and sometimes damaged paintings have yet to receive the attentions of a restorer for any number of reasons, the greatest of which is probably the need for funding. On our trip, we did happen to notice a large painting by Teresa Muratori in the chapel complex of San Stefano in Bologna. A very large, altar-sized painting situated on a left-side wall close to a vestibule, the darkening painting is additionally very difficult to see in the murky depths of the building. It is even more difficult to uncover much information on the artist.

All of the aforementioned problems with the scholarship on women artists of the Italian Renaissance and Baroque eras were discussed in the Special Topics class prior to the trip. Since it is virtually impossible to discern what a given Italian institution will or will not have on display

---

[2] A case in point: the Brenau University Permanent Art Collection received a 17th century oil painting of the Madonna, Child and an Angel from Dr. and Mrs. Roy A. Varner in 2001. A plaque on the lower frame reads: Elisabetta Sirani (1638–1665), Madonna, Child and Saint. My research of this painting – which included consultations with scholars Babette Bohn of the United States, Sir Denis Mahon of England and Adelina Modesti (who published a monograph on Sirani in November 2005: Elisabetta Sirani: *A Virtuous Woman of the Bolognese 17th Century*, Bologna: Editrice Compositori) of Australia has yielded a different identification of the artist in question. Based on favorable comparisons, I agree with Modesti's assertion that the image is, pending restoration, most likely by Girolamo Donnini (Correggio 1681–Bologna 1743).

during a visit,[3] students were made aware of the potential for disappointment. The chance to view certain major works was all we could realistically anticipate. However, there is no complete way to prepare 21st-century American students for the experience of cultural difference in museum practices. They have been uniquely conditioned to consider the 'other' in most aspects of life, and they expect that consideration to bear out in institutionalized displays of art and culturally significant objects.

Guided by revisionist historical practices, United States art exhibitions featuring the works of women, African Americans, Latino Americans and other minorities have been staged since the 1970s. Numerous books, articles and journals inspired by or in support of these exhibitions continue to be published. Our nation's capital hosts whole museums dedicated to the historical and contemporary works of exclusive factions of our population.[4] Such reflections of this country's multiculturalism make for a unique tourist experience, with many opportunities for concentrated exposure and focused study. The endeavor to serve audiences of various interest levels (from the introductory to the more specialized) also appears in the form of guided tours (either with a live guide or an audiocassette player) and sometimes copious amounts of wall text. Both forms of directed observation and engagement with particular works of art ensure that the novice museum-goer finds that which is deemed important; the can't-miss works of art therefore receive due attention. While this practice has become more common in museums around the world, Italy's unique slice of Western art and its museum policies still make for a more challenging experience.

---

[3] Consulting museum websites is sometimes helpful. The Uffizi Gallery of Florence maintains a very good website that does update information on what is on display room by room as well as temporarily closed rooms. Bologna's Pinacoteca Nazionale also has a website, but it does not exhaustively list or feature illustrations of works by room. While this is frustrating, it is understandable as the digital photography of every work of art in a large collection is time-consuming and expensive to accommodate in terms of band-width. Smaller Italian galleries and museums may have an introductory website only, which includes entry fees, hours of operation and the announcements of special exhibitions. Yet, while sites such as that of Casa Buonarroti in Florence include a color-coded map and some descriptions of works in various rooms, this does not aid in the location of the Artemisia Gentileschi painting of *The Inclination* (1615–1616), as it is pictured as being part of the collection but not placed in any specific room.

[4] These include (but are not limited to) the National Museum of Women in the Arts (opened in 1987), The Smithsonian's Anacostia Museum and Center for African American Art (opened in 1967) as well as The National Museum of African Art, the Black Fashion Museum (founded in 1979), and the very recently inaugurated National Museum of the American Indian.

Despite the fact that Italy boasts this rare group of women artists from centuries that saw so few of them in the rest of the Western world, it has no museums exclusively dedicated to them or later generations of women artists. As for the former collective, there are, quite possibly, too few of their works in Italy to comprise a museum collection. With the aforementioned reasons for that limitation in mind, yet another factor bears mentioning: the Renaissance or Baroque Italian woman artist may have traveled to seek work, as in the case of Artemisia Gentileschi (who spent time working in England with her painter father Orazio)[5]; or she may have sold commissioned works to collectors in other countries. Before Sofonisba Anguissola went to Spain to work in the court of Philip II,[6] she fulfilled self-portrait requests from various foreign collectors who specifically aimed to acquire a painting made by such an unusual creature as a woman artist. For these reasons – as well as the more obvious fact that art frequently changes hands in the global market – scholars looking to uncover the heretofore unpublished Anguissola or Fontana must search the entire world. Locating and viewing works of art by women already published in Italian collections presents further challenges.

As evidenced in the Brenau University 2004 trip to Italy, the few works of art by women on view in major museums of Rome, Florence and Bologna receive little special attention. Museum literature, such as maps, exhibition materials and collection guides, do not spell out where these unique works are located within the exhibition spaces. Typically found in the midst of other chronologically ordered works of similar styles, they silently await discovery. Wall text – in any language – on a singular work is extremely rare. While museum-goers in a few of these major institutions could be seen wearing rented headphones plugged into audiocassette players, no telltale headphone icons – intended to bring attention to specific discussion on the recording – rested above the label information of works by women artists. As might be imagined, our American "blue-light special" predispo-

---

[5] For instance, without knowing the provenance of Artemisia's *Self-Portrait as the Allegory of Painting* (1638/9), one could speculate that the Royal Collection of England acquired it while the painter lived and worked in that country. Charles I has been documented as one of her patrons at this time.

[6] Unfortunately, many of Sofonisba's paintings from her Spanish period were destroyed by a fire in the 17th century.

sition met with serious frustration.[7] The most dedicated seekers of our group resorted to methodical search tactics, examining each work of art for any familiarity with previous study. They painstakingly read all labels.

Perhaps the Italian mode of museum exhibition design (or a lack thereof) discourages the impatient American viewer. Still, the value of this experience rests with a number of points up for consideration. We learned a lot about ourselves and the ways in which a museum can be a surprisingly exciting place to visit.

Such painstaking search yielded a great deal of exposure to everything in the exhibitions. We all saw much more than we might have otherwise seen. If someone in our group made faster progress through the exhibition, they returned to the remainder of the group with advance reports on what was ahead. Had one of our savvy students not exhaustively looked into all of the Pitti Palace collection's nooks and crannies, we might have missed a glass-shelved room with a dozen or more Giovanna Garzoni (1600–1670) still life paintings first commissioned by the Medici family for their historically famous library. A greater sense of joy in discovery came about from this repeated experience of stumbling upon something rewarding. Such an exercise in museum exploration instilled a measure of excitement that just might be lacking in American institutions, where so much of a display is mapped and accompanied by written and spoken text that the viewer has no choice but to acknowledge what he or she is *told* to recognize as "important".

As has been mentioned, acute curiosity led us into spaces we might not have otherwise ventured. In one case this practice proved to be even more rewarding than the Garzoni images in the Pitti. After an early visit to the Vatican Museums and Saint Peter's Cathedral in Rome, members of our group walked from our hotel to the medieval neighborhood of Trastavere in search of Stefano Maderno's marble effigy of Saint Cecilia (1600). Navigation of the narrow cobblestone streets led to the church of Saint Cecilia, fronted by an open courtyard with a tinkling fountain. The city-noise of Rome faded. We respectfully entered the darkening church to find what we sought, the marble 'record' of the incorruptible patron saint of music as she

---

[7] I refer here to the old sale strategy of Kmart stores, in which a flashing blue light – similar to the red lights atop police cars – was placed in a particular aisle in order to advertise the extremely short-term sale of specific merchandise. Shoppers would be told over the store loudspeaker that a blue light special was underway for the next several minutes in a specific location.

was reportedly found when her body was exhumed in 1599. We also admired the polychrome marble installed beneath the altar, the wonderful mosaics behind it and the paintings in the side aisles. As one might expect of student tourists, they frequented the church gift shop. There, they noticed a sign and a door: for two Euros, the visitor could descend into the crypt below the church. At least ten adventurous souls went downstairs to discover a room with a map in Italian. Our group's guide began to translate the text, explaining that this site was ancient, the undermost layer of the church. A middle-aged, bespectacled man appeared, carrying a large ring of keys. He smiled and asked us in broken English if we wanted to know more about what we were seeing. Our *real* tour then began.

For the next hour and a half, we were treated to a thorough exploration and explanation of the legendary house of Saint Cecilia's family, probably built in the second century AD. We were shown a room with rounded holes in the floor – intended for cold storage of food and wine. We saw the space of the family's former, very modern lift (elevator). We viewed what was Cecilia's bedroom and a beautiful, mosaic-encrusted wedding chapel (decorated in the 19th century). The complexity of the space seemed endless. Our impromptu guide would gesture to yet another locked room with his ring of keys, and we would nod yes, we wanted to see that, too. When we emerged from the so-called crypt, believing our tour had ended, we prepared to exit the church. The guide called to us that we had not yet seen the site of Cecilia's martyrdom and the two Guido Reni paintings that decorated the space. Again, he gestured with keys to a gated door that led off of the main church interior. Again, we followed. We examined the calidarium of her bath, where her persecutors attempted to suffocate her with hot steam (or scald her, depending on the source). We touched the stone slab upon which the saint's throat was slit three times after the hot steam failed to kill her. We squinted in the darkness at the two Reni paintings. We finally had to leave. As we bid our goodbyes, our accompanying tour guide remarked that the man with the keys had asked him a question in Italian as we moved from room to room in the crypt: why do Americans laugh so much?

Our accompanying guide tried to explain that we were simply happy. My answer was a bit more considered: we were laughing with joy at the mere experience of discovery. Thanks to a stranger armed with information and keys to more discoveries, we were further delighted to understand what we were seeing, whether or not the stories were more legend than fact. History – however it is interpreted – had come alive, and it was enchanting.

It occurred to us that we had been incredibly fortunate to receive our impromptu tour. We might have otherwise spent all of fifteen minutes in the crypt, not comprehending what we were seeing. Our willingness to thoroughly explore a given space yielded the 'blue-light special' experience we were more accustomed to receiving in American museums and galleries. After this and our additionally frustrating museum visits, looking high and low for the women artists, we began to flex our intellectual muscles of critical thinking: we wondered why these women artists received so little fanfare in twenty-first century Italy. One possible answer may rest with the state and character of feminism in that country. If American scholarly regard for minority factions of our population prompts the building and support of institutions that bring greater focus to that scholarly regard, then what of our Italian neighbors' socio-cultural-political concerns and their resulting impact on museums and exhibitions?

The concept of Italian feminism may strike some as ironic, given the country's deeply Catholic (and therefore highly paternalistic) roots, which touch upon so many of its social constructs. Italian feminism has nonetheless developed in its own way and with its own unique character. The movement first achieved momentum in the 1940s as a political response to Fascist restrictions placed upon women in the workplace (Hellman, 1987: 31–33), and along with many other countries' feminist platform developments, gained further ground in the 1960s, 1970s and 1980s (Chiavola, 1986). The essential nature of Italian feminism parallels its American counterpart as it serves to promote women, their work and their disadvantaged position in society. However, contrasts arise in the recognition of gender diversity. In very simplistic terms, American feminism seeks societal regard for equality. Italian feminism acknowledges (and embraces?) the dissimilarity of genders, recognizing that regardless of the ambition for a more elevated position in society, women remain different from men.

As characterized by Lucia Chiavola, Italian feminism is unusual in its non-institutional basis, with interested parties coming from a variety of class backgrounds and pursuits who do not necessarily seek a formal unity under one group name or sanction by any authority. Chiavola's more general statements about the nature and practices of Italian feminists in academia further illuminate this case as well as strike some parallels with the historical presence of Italian women artists:

> There are, of course, women in academia, many of whom have an interest in studying or teaching other women's work, or in bringing their lives as women

> to bear upon their subject disciplines and their modes of research. Instead of trying to institutionalize these issues, however, they manage to carve out a space in the curriculum *as it is*. In this respect, they infiltrate and exploit the grey areas of academic organization[....] They have been intellectual commuters: traveling in and out of those domains of culture and politics where they mixed with men and became part of 'the system.' (Chiavola, 1986: 3–4)

Contemporary Italian women in academia mimic their historical, artistic counterparts in their more subversive methods of approaching the canon of their chosen field. They work and serve their own cause while abiding by standardized practices and traditions. They are quiet, unobtrusive renegades.

How this unique feminist outlook impacts Italian museum practices could possibly extend to that same quiet presence of the work of one 17th century woman artist among the many Caravaggios at the Ufizzi.[8] Yes, Artemisia Gentileschi was a remarkable artist – but she produced her works in the highly male-oriented, competitive realm of Italian Baroque painting, adopting the established treatments of popular subject matter published by her masculine contemporaries *as well as* surpassing those traditions with new innovations. In her own letters we read about her bitter struggles to compete with men, yet her strategies for such competition involved 'playing the game' the way it had been played by men and for men. And so perhaps Italian feminists would advise that we can't *not* appreciate her efforts and accomplishments against this particular backdrop. To give her the 'blue light special' treatment would be to remove her from the appropriate context.

Ultimately, my tour group's combined states of exhilaration and disappointment in seeking and only occasionally finding a work of art by a woman artist of the Italian Renaissance and Baroque periods illustrates and reinforces the 'other's position in history, a case made all the more exceptional in the face of 21st century women's college students from America. Our magical experience in Saint Cecilia in Rome advances the notion that the demonstration of sincere interest can yield the reward of a private, privileged adventure. Unlike the typical art museum experience in America – where information is overtly conveyed and the visitor's encounter can be wholly controlled – the Italian version facilitates a more active and individualized

---

[8] Gentileschi's *Judith Slaying Holofernes* (1612–21) is exhibited (along with one or two of her other, lesser pictures) in a part of the museum that is undergoing construction. If one proceeds too quickly to what appears to be the end of the collection rooms, these paintings may be missed.

pursuit of the subject. Indeed, the 'blue-light special' tour can be had for the asking. The essentially cultural differences between these two countries' museum practices rest with their respective approaches to modes of curiosity and kinesthetic learning. In a way, the American museum visitor desires a sort of "armchair" equivalency to their experience: they expect comfort and convenience. They dislike too much work for what they want to know. Yet this can make for too-rapidly gained – and ultimately lost – information. Should they adjust to the very different Italian museum experience and become absorbed in the business of true engagement with their subject, they may return home with renewed vigor for eschewing the rented headphones and audiotape in favor of seeking profound enrichment.

References

Apostolos-Cappadona, Diane (1998) *Dictionary of Women in Religious Art.* Oxford: University Press Oxford

Bolland, Andrea (2000) "*Desiderio* and *diletto*: vision, touch, and the poetics of Bernini's *Apollo and Daphne*". *Art Bulletin* 82. No. 2. June, 309–330

Bond, Paula and Kemp, Sandra (eds) (1991) *Italian Feminist Thought: A Reader*. Oxford, United Kingdom: Basil Blackwell, Inc.

Broude, Norma and Garrard, Mary G. (eds) (1992) *The Expanding Discourse: Feminism and Art History.* New York: HarperCollins Publishers

Chadwick, Whitney (2002) *Women, Art and Society.* 3rd edn. New York: Thames and Hudson

Chiavola, Lucia (1986) *Liberazione della donna: Feminism in Italy*. Middletown, CT: Wesleyan University Press

Cole, Michael (1999) "Cellini's Blood". *Art Bulletin* 81. No. 2. June, 215–235

Dixon, Annette (2002) *Women Who Ruled: Queens, Goddesses, Amazons in Renaissance and Baroque Art.* London: Merrell Publishers, Ltd.

Dunn, Marilyn (1994) "Piety and Patronage in Seicento Rome: Two Noblewomen and Their Convents". *Art Bulletin*. 76. No. 4. December, 644–663

Frederickson, Kristen, and Webb, Sarah E. (eds) (2003) *Singular Women: Writing the Artist.* Berkeley: University of California Press

Garrard, Mary D. (1992) "Artemisia and Susanna". *The Expanding Discourse: Feminism and Art History.* Broude, Norma and Mary G. Garrard (eds). NY: HarperCollins Publishers. 147+

Garrard, Mary D. (1994) "Here's Looking at Me: Sofonisba Anguissola and the Problem of the Woman Artist". *Renaissance Quarterly* 47. No. 3. Fall, 556–622.

Greer, Germaine (1979) *The Obstacle Race: The Fortunes of Women Painters and Their Work.* New York: Farrar Straus Giroux

Heller, Nancy (1995) *Women Artists: An Illustrated History.* 3rd ed. New York: Abbeville Press

Hellman, Judith Adler (1987) *Journeys Among Women: Feminism in Five Italian Cities.* New York: Oxford University Press

Holman, Beth L. (1999) "*Exemplum* and *Imitatio*: Countess Matilda and Lucrezia Pico dell Mirandola at Polirone" *Art Bulletin* 81. No. 4. December, 637–664

Jacobs, Frederika H. (1997) *Defining the Renaissance Virtuosa: Women Artists and the Language of Art History and Criticism.* Cambridge: Cambridge University Press

Johnson, Geraldine A., and Grieco, Sara F. Matthews (eds) (1997) *Picturing Women in Renaissance and Baroque Italy.* Cambridge: Cambridge University Press

King, Catherine (1994) "Looking a Sight: Sixteenth-Century Portraits of Women Artists". *Zeitschrift Fur Kunstgestschichte* 58. No. 3, 381–406

May, Stephen (1998) "Against All Odds". *Art and Antiques.* February, 44–51

McHam, Sarah B. (2001) "Donatello's Bronze *David* and *Judith* as Metaphors of Medici Rule in Florence". *Art Bulletin* 83. No. 1. March, 32–47

Murphy, Caroline P. (1997) "Lavinia Fontana and the Female Life Cycle Experience In Late Sixteenth Century Bologna". *Picturing Women in Renaissance and Baroque Italy.* Johnson, Geraldine A. and Grieco, Sara F. Matthews (eds). Cambridge: Cambridge University Press

Nochlin, Linda (1988) *Women, Art, Power and Other Essays.* NY: Westview Press

O'Neill, Mary (2001) "Virtue and Beauty: The Renaissance Image of the Ideal Woman". *Smithsonian.* 32. No. 6. September, 62+

Opfell, Olga (1991) *Special Visions: Profiles of Fifteen Women Artists from the Renaissance to the Present Day.* London: MacFarland and Co., Inc.

Petersen, Lauren H., (2003) "The Baker, His Tomb, His Wife and Her Breadbasket: The Monument of Eurysaces in Rome". *Art Bulletin* 85. No.2. June 230–257

Stapen, Nancy (1994) "Who Are the Women Old Masters?" *ArtNews* 93. No. 3. March, 87–94

Suleiman, Susan Robin (ed) (1986) *The Female Body in Western Culture: Contemporary Perspectives*. Harvard, CT: Harvard University Press

Syson, Luke and Thornton, Dora (2001) *Objects of Virtue: Art in Renaissance Italy*. Los Angeles, California: J.Paul Getty Museum

Tinagli, Paola (1997) *Women in Italian Renaissance Art: Gender, Representation and Identity*. Manchester: Manchester University Press

Valone, Carolyn (1994) "Women on the Quirinal Hill: Patronage in Rome, 1560–1630". *Art Bulletin* 76. No. 1. March, 129–146

Walker, Barbara G., (1988) *The Woman's Dictionary of Symbols and Sacred Objects*. New York: HarperCollins Publishers

Weil, Rex, (1995) "Sofonisba Anguissola: A Renaissance Woman". *ArtNews* 94. No.7. September, 91

Witcombe, Christopher L. C. E. (2002) "The Chapel of the Courtesan and the Quarrel of the Magdelens". *Art Bulletin* 84. No. 2. June, 273–292

Travels with Merrill (and the Athena Project)

Jean Westmacott

In mid-June of 1995, Merrill Hayes and I were standing at a counter in the aptly named Malpensa Airport in Milan haggling over the conditions of our car rental. Fading from jet lag and lack of sleep, all Merrill and I wanted to do was to find a place to rest in the city. Once ensconced in our pristine, spacious (much larger than ordered) rental car, we decided instead to begin our drive across northern Italy to Venice and escape from the smog laden air sunk in the valley bowl surrounding Milan. Reinvigorated by our goal, we headed east and onto the mêlée of the A4 'autostrada'. Before continuing with the story of our journey, I must explain how a project concerning the Greek goddess Athena provided the reason two American women from Georgia were traveling in Italy that summer.

In 1994, a group of dedicated Athens, Georgia, citizens led by lawyer Clay Bryant decided that their fair city needed a piece of public sculpture to celebrate the classical origins of its name. During the spring of 1994, I was asked to send slides and a resume to the Athena Project Committee to be considered for – and was fortunate to receive – the sculpture commission for an image of the mythical Greek goddess Athena for the city of Athens, Georgia. The sculpture, to be eight feet tall and carved from Italian Carrara marble, was to be installed on a pedestal of Georgia granite in the forecourt of the new Classic Center, a complex containing a theatre, restored firehouse and conference center.

What did I know about Athena? I knew she was associated with wisdom and war. I knew she was the patron deity of the city of Athens, Greece and that the famous frieze from the Parthenon recorded and celebrated that fact. The legend about her springing fully grown and fully armed from the head of Zeus was also familiar to me. What I did not realize were several of Athe-na's other attributes which made her ideally suited as a symbol for the Georgia Piedmont town. As the goddess of wisdom, she was also believed to have an inventive and creative mind. She was credited with the invention of the plow and the oxen's yoke among others. More than the goddess of war, she was seen more accurately as the goddess of victory for athletes and poets as well as soldiers. The contestants of the first Olympics looked to her for success in their various events. The virgin goddess, ironically, was also seen as the chaste protector of the domestic hearth and the family.

For Athens, Georgia – a seat of learning housing the University of Georgia, surrounded by productive farmland, a site for some events for the 1996 Olympics and with a citizenry that cherishes strong family values

– what could be a more appropriate symbol than her namesake, Athena? Despite any active belief in the Greek pantheon of gods and goddesses, polytheism generally being a practice of the distant past, we still draw upon many symbols and ideas of classical times, both Greek and Roman. In the United States, Greek porticoes mark entryways of many homes, businesses, government buildings and churches, not to mention the influence of democratic ideals. To note more mundane references, the FTD Florist Company uses the symbol of Hermes/Mercury in their advertising and what seaside resort would be complete without a restaurant named for Neptune brandishing his trident?

Athena has been depicted many ways by many different artists. The image I selected was inspired by the final panel of the frieze from the Parthenon, in which the citizens of Athens present Athena with a gift of a new 'peplos' or Archaic Period dress. My version of Athena shows her striding forward with the new peplos over her shoulder, wearing the splendid Greek horsehair-trimmed helmet and steadying a shield that serves as a protective symbol. On the shield is a wreath of laurel leaves. The citizens of Athens chose Athena over Poseidon as their patron, because she brought them the gift of the olive tree to be cultivated. I stretched the botanical link from olive tree leaves to laurel leaves, to connect with the Olympics and the traditional prize of laurel wreaths awarded to the event winners.

Lara Magzan, a student at Brenau University, was the inspiring model for Athena. Lara's qualities of character, intelligence and courage in addition to strong yet feminine beauty, paralleled those I saw Athena possessing. Lara struggled successfully against serious financial and emotional difficulties. Born in Sarajevo in former Yugoslavia, her life was torn apart by the then emerging conflict in the Balkans. While a full time student, Lara supported herself with multiple jobs as a dormitory counselor, as an assistant with Brenau University Galleries and the Wages House (a clothing and textile museum on campus), working in the cafeteria and babysitting. Remarkably, she always managed to maintain a high grade point average and graduated with honors.

Following approval of the small twelve inch maquette by the Project Athena committee, I completed the bulk of the four foot version while staying at my mother's home on Long Beach Island in New Jersey. After the figure's steel armature was covered in plasticine (an oil based clay), Lara Magzan came to stay for two weeks to model. With Lara's help, I concentrated on the head and the anatomy of the figure. Our conversations while working revealed much about how Lara's character was formed – her early life in Sarajevo, the influence of her grandmother, her father's death during her early childhood and the example of her mother's resolve to provide for her family as best she could. Her mother worked as a nurse for an oil company. They lived in Egypt and Greece. When her mother was sent to work at the company's offices in Tripoli, Libya, Lara attended school in Malta, where she first heard about Brenau University. Despite Lara's fascination with and ambition to acquire material success, maintaining friendships have remained a core value. At the end of the summer of 1994, I loaded the clay figure into my station wagon and headed south, feeling sure I would arouse the curiosity of state police. The covered prostrate form of the sculpture certainly looked as if I were transporting a body!

Back in Georgia, I hired another Brenau University student, Merrill Hayes, as studio assistant for the project. Merrill was a sculpture major in the Art & Design Department and my advisee. She was very bright but had been having difficulty with her life's direction until she focused on sculpture. Merrill and I set to work on adding Athena's dress and accoutrements – the bristling horse hair decorated helmet, shield and the gift of her new peplos draped over her shoulder. Merrill's attention to detail was invaluable particularly in creating the many leaves needed for the laurel wreath decorating the shield. By October we were done and ready for final approval from the Athena Project Committee, which to our relief was readily given. The next step was to make the rubber mold and plaster supporting 'mother' mold with the help of Jack Ward, a sculptor and owner of a foundry in Holly Springs, Georgia. Jack cast two plaster copies of Athena from the mold. One remained in Georgia for the committee to use for fund raising purposes. The other cast was shipped to the Nicoli Studios in Carrara, Italy to be the model for the final marble copy.

Throughout the winter of 1994–95, Merrill and I were on tenterhooks about the progress of the final marble Athena – speaking to Signor Carlo Nicoli about every other week. He wanted me to come to Carrara to collaborate on the finishing details of the Athena as soon as they completed the roughing out stage of the enlargement. He certainly enlarged my ego by telling me that when they opened the crate with the plaster cast, his first words on seeing the Athena model were "Aah, Maestra!" – high praise coming from someone whose business makes officially approved copies of Renaissance and Baroque masterworks for museums around the world.

Merrill and I began planning our trip for late spring or early summer. Her two requests, beside the business portion in Carrara, were to visit Venice and to see Michelangelo's David at the Galleria dell'Accademia in Florence (Firenze). Finally we received word that Signor Nicoli would be ready for us to come to Carrara in mid-June. Merrill and I made arrangements to rent a car in Milan and use it while in Italy and, after our stay in Carrara, drive through France to Calais where we would return the car. Our plan was to cross the Channel to England, where I would meet my husband, who is English, and visit relatives. Merrill wanted to visit a family friend in London.

And so we found ourselves leaving the Malpensa airport in Milan and threading our way onto the A4 in our rental car. Merrill and I were finally headed east to Venice! Our route took us by Brescia and along the southern edge of Lake Garda. We indulged in a spontaneous detour off the autostrada to a smaller road closer to the lake. We drove up a narrow peninsula to the picturesque town of Sirmione at the tip, dominated by the castle of Rocca Scaligera. After getting through some congestion near Peschiera we rejoined the A4 and continued to Verona. We paid a quick visit to the city of Romeo and Juliet and, for a time, Dante's home. We succeeded in getting totally lost – crossing and re-crossing the Adige River many more times than we intended! Having decided to reach Bassano del Grappa by nightfall, we reluctantly left the lovely pale rose-colored city behind as we drove up into more mountainous terrain. It was getting dark by the time we drove into the small town nestled in the foothills of the Dolomites and settled into a small pensione. The sole reason for visiting Bassano del Grappa was to eat at a small restaurant recommended by some friends. Their specialty was mushrooms and our dinner was well worth the extra drive. It was a small quiet restaurant with elderly and initially austere looking waiters in black pants and vests with very white shirts. During our meal Merrill confessed that she did not like cheese – any sort of cheese. I couldn't imagine enjoying Italian food without eating cheese! Fortunately, with the rich assortment of foods available in Italy, any concern about limited choices proved groundless. Whether it was our frank appreciation of the delicious food or Merrill's youthful charm, by the end of our meal the waiters' initial coolness had completely evaporated and we were offered complimentary desserts and drinks of Grappa, the potent liqueur named for the town of its origin. We tottered off to sleep, dazed by our long and incredibly varied day.

After an early morning walk across a 16th century covered wooden bridge over the Brenta River designed by Palladio, we indulged in some freshly baked apricot brioche and cappuccino. Feeling that life was indeed good, we headed for Venice. The travel agent had booked us into a hotel on the Venice Lido. Although it was a pleasant place, we felt too far from the 'real' Venice. The next day we boarded a vaporetto to take up residence in a small hotel in the Dorsoduro area of the city. Although our room was much smaller, the true Venetian atmosphere was intoxicating – no sounds of cars, the lap of water with echoes of voices and music reverberating in the narrow passages and off the water, and that uniquely luminous moist light. We spent several days there, visiting St. Mark's Square and the Basilica, the Baroque Church of Santa Maria della Salute, the Accademia and the Venice Biennale. Seeing the Biennale in Venice was a collision of time and culture that fascinated Merrill. We saw a global pooling of contemporary work from minimal and conceptual to photorealistic styles, object-making to object-rejecting, beautifully crafted to roughly fashioned, from elegant solidity (GiulianoVangi's stone carvings) to Bill Viola's impalpable yet enveloping video art, and from themes of society's vapidity to the haunting solemnity of Magdalena Abakanowicz's bronze figural husks – truly something for every turn of mind and all in the most achingly beautiful and historic setting. On our last day in Venice, we went to the nearby island of Murano as Merrill wanted to buy glass with her graduation money. Her choice was an enigma to the salespeople at the glass studio where she finally made her selection. In demonstrating the process of making their glass, the salesperson showed Merrill the uncut crystal glasses first blown by the artisans before finishing. Merrill insisted amidst strong protests that she wanted to purchase four glasses in that raw unfinished state. Merrill won and those glasses still occupy a place of pride in her dining room.

Leaving Venice, our next destination was Florence or rather, Firenze. Why is it that city names can't retain the same spelling and pronunciation in all languages as in their country of origin? Dr. William Eiland, Director of the Georgia Museum of Art, was spending a month working on a research project in Firenze and invited us to visit en route to Carrara for a tour of the city and an early dinner. We arrived at Dr. Eiland's lodgings in the mid-afternoon. He immediately led us on the most fast-paced, one hour walking tour I have ever experienced. Beginning with the Duomo and Baptistery, he led us around Orsanmichele, through the Piazza della Signoria by the

Palazzo Vecchio, by the Uffizi, onto the Ponte Vecchio for a glimpse of San Miniato al Monte on a distant hill across the Arno River, back by the Palazzos Davanzati and Strozzi, a quick pause for us to kiss the snout of a bronze boar in the midst of a market area, and over to San Lorenzo for quick views of Michangelo's library with the Mannerist staircase and the nearby Medici Chapel – all this while keeping up the most erudite, interesting, non-stop commentary. Returning to the Duomo area, Dr. Eiland left us with directions on how to get to the Galleria dell'Accademia (assuring us it would certainly be open) while he went to prepare dinner. Merrill and I dashed to the Accademia. Upon arriving at the entrance, a guard halted us and said the museum was closing. I begged him to let Merrill see the David, telling him that it was her whole reason for coming to Firenze! She looked so stricken that the guard took pity on her and re-opened the doors. He led us into a long room, but said we could not go any farther. We could see the magnificent figure clearly at the end of the space just as some long curtains dividing the area were released. I will never forget the rapt look on Merrill's face as she gazed at Michelangelo's masterpiece while the curtains slowly joined, finally obscuring our view. With a great sense of fulfillment, we thanked the guard and made our way to Dr. Eiland's place for a delightful dinner.

Being June, the evening was still light when we left for Carrara. Once on the autostrada we quickly passed by Prato and Lucca and found ourselves driving along the coast paralleling a long mountain range – the Alpi Apuane, according to the map. They seemed very high, actually about 5–6,000 feet. We had the impression they were capped by snow. As we drew closer, we realized the 'snow' was marble. The quarries (first opened in 27 B.C.E. in the reign of the Emperor Augustus) were at the tops of the mountains, glistening with the rays of the setting sun.

We drove into Carrara assured by Signor Nicoli that we could "ask anyone for directions" to his place (it was not a small town, but he was right). The piazza where he lived was bordered on three sides by his home, office and studios. The strains of a Cole Porter song being played on a piano drifted across the piazza as we approached in the twilight what we assumed to be the door to his home. When we knocked, the music abruptly stopped and Signor Nicoli appeared. He welcomed us in the friendliest manner and invited us up to the family's beautiful apartment filled with antique furniture, Turkish carpets and a stunningly eclectic array of art. We expressed our eagerness to see the marble Athena. As there were no electric lights in the studios (the carvers worked only by natural light), we moved carefully into the darkening workspace. Slowly our eyes focused and we could see the shadowy forms of the two Athenas, one large and one smaller, side by side in the ghostly crepuscular light. Satisfied, we were then quickly settled into our own separate apartment (with a trapdoor entrance through one of the studios below) before whisking us off to a late dinner in a nearby taverna. The next day, we saw the studios and Athenas by bright daylight. Plaster models of former projects were stored on massive shelves along two walls – many were recognizable works like the *Pieta*. The Nicoli Studios' expertise in reproducing copies of masterworks as well as contemporary artists' commissions in marble and other stone was overwhelmingly evident. Merrill and I were in awe. We were introduced to the master carver, Nino Paolino, and his apprentices. A young man named Gino was working on the roughing out of the Athena. As I reviewed the progress of the carving, he and I managed to communicate remarkably well despite our lack of knowledge about each other's languages. He handed me a pencil and showed me how to mark where I wanted more stone removed and where to be careful not to take more away. The carvers there still use the same method of enlarging work as the ancient Greeks based on the theory of triangulation – measuring the angles and distances of 3 points on the original then increasing them proportionately on the final piece. They make notations of the measurements along two long angled lines with chalk on a large piece of slate. Both the model to be copied and the marble copy have three points, literally small columnar bumps, established on the same corresponding locations. The process is still mystifying to me.

One among many high points of our stay in Carrara was an exciting visit to the quarries where the marble for the Athena was extracted. Carrara marble has the advantage of being a very clear color with no strong patterns and therefore excellent for figurative work. It is also very weather resistant as it doesn't absorb a lot of water as it is fairly non-porous. We were driven in a small car up very steep and narrow graveled roads towards the quarries near the top of the mountains above the city. Instead of leveling the mountains, I was surprised to see the stone quarried out of cavernous openings in the sides. The enormous trucks and equipment being used inside were dwarfed by the size of the "cave di marmo"– appearing more like Tonka toy vehicles. By contrast, in Georgia, marble and granite are quarried from dizzyingly deep pits. Merrill recalled how impressed she was by a demonstration of how to test stone for its soundness for carving. One of the quarry workers picked up a large hammer and banged it on a large block of marble. We were told to listen for the ringing sound, which indeed we heard. If there are fractures in the stone, the sound would be a dull 'thunk'. Quarry work is dangerous business. As testament, one of the projects at the Nicoli Studios was a commission for a memorial to quarry workers who have lost their lives. On a lighter note, Signor Nicoli told us about one quarry owner's son who was learning the trade. To get to the work site, the workers took a short cut by means of a sort of basket hooked to some wire that transported them like a ski lift across a deep ravine to the quarry. One day, the son was the last to leave the site and used the basket to cross. Halfway across the engine stopped and he spent the night suspended over the gorge. In the morning, the workers rescued him. After stepping out of the basket, he thanked them and walked away never to return to the quarry business or the area again!

During our stay, I received word that my mother-in-law had died. This was devastating news as we were very close. I arranged to fly to England to join my husband and family for the funeral then return to Italy to finish my part of the Athena work. Merrill decided to come with me to England and stay with friends in London until my return from Italy and our scheduled departure later from England for the United States. Signor Nicoli graciously offered to treat Merrill and me to dinner in Lerici before leaving for England the next day. Lerici was a resort town not too far north of Carrara on the coast favored by 19th and 20th century writers and poets Shelley, Yeats, D.H. Lawrence as well as Sartre and Simone de Beauvoir. Shelley lived there for four years before his tragic death by drowning in the bay when his boat capsized while sailing to a meeting with Leigh Hunt. The ride proved to be even shorter than we anticipated since Signor Nicoli drove according to a theory that if he maintained a speed of 200 kilometers per hour on the autostrada, the polizia would not be able to track him on radar. It took a certain period of recovery time walking around the harbor area of Lerici before Merrill and I thought we could handle digesting food. The return trip after a delicious dinner of risotto and seafood was blessedly slower. The Nicoli family could not have been kinder or more hospitable. Merrill said she still has a vivid memory of seeing the gleaming cathedral of Pisa beside its improbably tilted campanile as our plane lifted off the runway.

The completed Athena sculpture arrived in Athens, Georgia later that year in October, having been delivered first by boat to Savannah. Over the winter, the Keystone Company of Elberton, Georgia created an elegant granite pedestal. The pedestal was inscribed with the Athenian code of citizenship sworn as an oath by the youth of ancient Athens at the age of seventeen. Sentiments we would do well to emulate today.

> We will never bring disgrace on this our City of an act of dishonesty or cowardice.
> We will fight for the ideals and sacred things of the City both alone and with many.
> We will revere and obey the city's laws, and will do our best to incite a like reverence and respect in those above us who are prone to annul them or set them at naught.
> We will strive increasingly to quicken the public's sense of civic duty.
> Thus in all these ways, we will transmit this City, not only not less, but greater and more beautiful than it was transmitted to us.

The official dedication and unveiling took place on May 3, 1996. In addition to Athena Project Committee members and chair, Clay Bryant, Lara Magzan, Merrill Hayes and myself, there were in attendance many Athens area residents, the mayor and other public dignitaries, the Classic Center director and staff, some University of Georgia students and faculty, and most heartening to me – family, friends and a large contingent of faculty, students and staff from Brenau University including the President and two Vice Presidents. Merrill said her father was the most impressed by the presence of Vince Dooley, the legendary University of Georgia football coach. Following the speeches, receptions, and a flurry of press coverage, the dust settled.

There had been some voices of protest during the course of the project that the erection of a statue of a Greek goddess might be seen to encourage "pagan worship and ideas" in our largely Christian community but those few outcries fell silent as Athena became an accepted part of the landscape in Athens, Georgia. Perhaps those protesters had a point as people have taken to leaving gifts on the pedestal at Athena's feet – usually flowers, although someone did once leave a tribute of a bound length of hair! It still gives me a great deal of pleasure to drive by the Classic Center and see tourists taking pictures of one another in front of the Athena statue. She has been featured on magazine covers, in advertisements and was the subject of a hilarious April Fools' Day story in a local paper called the *Flagpole* (in which she was accused of kidnapping another local sculpture called "The Spirit of Athens"). Athena even appeared on the CD cover for a recent release by the band, *Widespread Panic*. After a stint working with a foundry program at Johnson Atelier in New Jersey, Merrill Hayes returned to England for a Master of Fine Arts degree in sculpture from the University of Kent. She recently opened a gallery in Charlotte, North Carolina. Lara Magzan moved to New York City where she works for CNN. The Athena Project experience and the friendships formed with Merrill, Lara, and Signor Nicoli created a lasting impression for the author of the importance and benefits of global interrelationships. Athena herself stands serenely resolute in front of the Classic Center of Athens, Georgia, an embodiment of Euro-American confluence.

'Crossing a Bare Common': Emerson's Ironic Negotiation of the Sublime

SØREN HATTESEN BALLE

> Hegel remarks somewhere that all great world-historic facts and personages appear, so to speak, twice. He forgot to add: the first time as tragedy, the second time as farce.
>
> Karl Marx, *The Eighteenth Brumaire of Louis Napoleon* (1852)

This paper deals among other things with the notion of the American sublime and thus carries on an already ongoing debate which in recent years has reached its highpoint in Harold Bloom's strongly affirmative remarks on the subject. In this paper, I shall focus on perhaps the most well-known attempt to discuss the possibility of sublimity in an American context, namely the one found in the writings of Ralph Waldo Emerson. The main claim of this paper is that Emerson's version of the American sublime represents a transatlantic negotiating of the European and not least English romantic development within the tradition of writing and thinking about the sublime. To put it very simply, this means to present a version of the sublime in which transcendence is transposed "into a naturalistic key" – to use Thomas Weiskel's apt phrase. Admittedly, this is hardly a new, nor a very original way of situating Emerson's sublime. Here I follow a number of predecessors – among them most notably Harold Bloom, but also more recently Eric Wilson's book *Emerson's Sublime Science* (1999).

A prominent feature of Emerson's discourse of the sublime – also noted by Bloom and Wilson – is his "protrusive" rhetoric (Bloom). A widespread tendency exists among Emerson critics to construe his exorbitant rhetorical style as somehow perfectly conducive to achieving the sense of transcendence that his effort to convey an American's experience of the sublime would have to involve. Characteristically, Emerson's highly charged eloquence on the sublime is more often than not described as a "sublime rhetoric". From the stock of rhetorical tropes, the most favored by Emerson and picked out as the trademark of his rhetorical sublimity, critics mention in particular his use of hyperbole and chiasmus. Common to both tropes is said to be their ability on the rhetorical level to accomplish the kind of *crossing into transcendence* that describes the sublime experience on the thematic level of Emerson's texts.

The second main claim of my paper, however, is to propose that Emerson does not use these tropes in an unreserved apotheosis of the sublime. Although acknowledging Bloom's point that Emerson's American sublime is achieved in an *agon* with English Romantic poetry, I shall demonstrate that his sublime rhetoric is much more circumspect than is usually recognized by his critics, including Bloom. Not least shall I analyze the manner in which his blustering rhetoric of crossing – notably through the figures of hyperbole and chiasmus – represents a kind of double talk, where its assertions of sublimity are made ironically so as to suggest their potentially self-canceling nature. In this context I shall investigate some of the paratextual and intertextual framing devices used by Emerson in order to question the authority of his own discourse. Among those of most importance will be included ones such as warped allusions to classic sublime texts, the choice of the essay genre in preference to the poetic genre, etc. Thus I hope to tell another less authoritative story of American Transcendentalism than the one a certain tradition of Emerson criticism has told. In order to contextualize my reading I shall consider echoes of Emerson's ironic and self-critical sublime in one of his heirs, Wallace Stevens.

In a wider perspective, which also includes Stevens's belaboring of it, Emerson's double talk on the sublime can be read as an early example of postcolonial 'writing back' across the Atlantic to the colonial metropolis in Europe. This latter suggestion will be my third main claim of this paper. There is, however, a snag about such a claim. America was not a British colony anymore when Emerson and American Transcendentalism had their heyday in the early and mid 19th century. Furthermore, America was a settlement colony, so the need for complete cultural and literary severance from a European, especially British heritage would not appear as imminent as with native populations subjugated by a colonial power. As Robert Weisbuch has pointed out apropos of Emerson:

> Race and language do not have the same kind of terrible play in settlement colonies, and the settlers themselves, however much they experience themselves as dominated by the metropolis of the empire, are an extension of that empire in the eyes of the native inhabitants – American Indians, for example, or imported slaves; reciprocally, early settlers in New England took pains to insure that they were not viewed in London as "going savage." (Weisbuch in Porte and Morris, 1999: 195)

It would be very difficult not to find Weisbuch's comments applicable to Emerson – even without the native American or the imported slave's testimony to quote in evidence of his cultural ties with the British empire. Imbued with the rhetoric of the sublime, his writings cannot help inscribing themselves firmly in a long unmistakably Eurocentric tradition going back at least to Longinus's *On the Sublime*. In fact, the integration of that tradition with his own writing goes so far that he palimpsests its texts almost verbatim sometimes. Yet, as Weisbuch is also quick to add:

> Some, not all, post-colonial generalities nonetheless apply, most notoriously the monopolizing of prestige by imported models of high culture; the encouraging of third-rate imitations of these models; and thus a long lag between political independence and its cultural counterpart. Whatever we see as complications to the claim, Euro-Americans vehemently expressed their sense of being post-colonial in just these ways. (195)

Emerson's time was, indeed, an era with an anxious sense of and attempts to move American writing out from under the hegemony of British models, now that the country was no longer just a province of the British empire. Emerson would himself contribute to them in his essay "The Poet" by writing that "[w]e have yet had no genius in America, [...]" (Emerson in Ziff, 1982: 281). And in "Self-Reliance" he voiced a sense that America remained intellectually colonized because its schools still taught an Anglo-European curriculum. Writes Emerson: "The intellect is a vagabond, and our system of education fosters restlessness. Our minds travel when our bodies are forced to stay at home. We imitate; and what is imitation but the traveling of the mind" (198).

The paradox of Emerson's American version of the sublime is precisely that it very much identifies with a European tradition, while at same time displacing its own authority as an expression of sublimity. This feature does not bode particularly well for considering it in a postcolonial context of writing back. I shall, however, argue that it is when Emerson is truest to the European tradition of the sublime *and* most calls his own rhetoric of sublimity into question that it makes sense to speak of his discourse as postcolonial. Adopting Homi K. Bhabha's notion of *mimicry*, I would like to suggest that we can begin to understand Emerson's double talk on the sublime in a more comprehensive manner. In fact, the ambivalence that Bhabha claims emerges between the civility of colonial discourse and its mockery by the colonial subject seems to replay itself with respect to what happens in Emerson's writing when he hyperbolically insists on an American sublime, but also surreptitiously exposes his own hyperbole. The usefulness of Bhabha's term to a reading of the sublime in Emerson perhaps becomes even clearer when one realizes that in his essays he always poses in the dual role of both colonizer and colonized, as we saw Weisbuch mentioned as a peculiar characteristic of Euro-Americans. On the one hand, he figures as a representative of European culture and, on the other, as its not quite Europeanized colonial subject. As I shall demonstrate, this aspect manifests itself with added prominence to the extent that Emerson very strongly marries his notion of an American sublime to its traditional one of what Jan Rosiek has called a "successfully dramatize[d] [...] sense of bond with the un-limited or in-finite" (Rosiek, 2000: 16–17), even as the latter grotesquely hypertrophies. Thus, I would argue, Emerson shows the implication of his own writing with the dominant discourse of European culture, just as he deauthorizes its historical priority and exposes its facticity.

If Bhabha's notion of 'mimicry' is preferable as a tool to analyze the status of American sublime in Emerson, compared to Harold Bloom's use of the notion of 'misreading', this is to do with the importance Bhabha attaches to its cultural historical scope and its splitting and de-naturalizing function. When Bloom reads Emerson's American sublime as a misreading reversal of British Romantic articulations of it, he confines its cultural meaning to a frame of reference that is strictly psycho-poetical. Not least does he point to it as an example of how the sublime achieves a new and essential aesthetico-historical reality because it represents a poetic "refusal of history, particularly literary history" (Bloom, 1976: 254) and thus becomes a "hyperbolical trope of self-rebegetting" (244). Bloom therefore never seriously ponders the possibility that the very legitimacy of the 'reality' of an American sublime may be at stake in Emerson's rearticulation of it, if read within an American postcolonial context. Instead, Bloom holds onto the conventional religio-literary rhetoric of power and infinity which surrounds most European accounts and representations of the sublime. In his essay "Emerson: The American Religion" there is strong evidence of that in his characterization of a passage from *Nature* (1836), which is the most well-known instance of the Emersonian sublime:

> Not upon an elevation, but taking his stance upon the bare American ground, Emerson demands Victory, to his senses as to his soul. The perfect exhilaration of a perpetual youth which comes to him is akin to what Hart Crane was to term an improved infancy. Against Wordsworth, Coleridge, Carlyle, the seer Emerson celebrates the American difference of *discontinuity*. (Bloom, 1982: 159)

Bloom's capitalization of the word 'victory' very much contributes to stressing the continued association of the sublime with real force and omnipotence, however much it has been reconfigured and re-contextualized in Emerson's American imitation of it. My contention would be that the American difference that Bloom argues characterizes Emerson's notion of the sublime stays securely within a concept of artistic expression as a sign of naturalizable national aesthetic distinctness.

Bhabha, on the other hand, offers an analytic term through his concept of 'mimicry' which when applied to Emerson's work opens onto a reading of it where its rhetoric of the sublime represents a misreading of a central notion in European aesthetic discourse that can be viewed as partaking of what Bhabha has called "the ambivalence of colonial discourse" (Bhabha, 1994: 126). According to Bhabha, colonial discourse always attempts to civilize the colonial subject by having him imitate its norms, but not quite. The desire of the colonial master is to impose his norms on the colonial subject, but at same time to indicate a discriminatory difference that relegates the native's imitation of them to the position of being inferior, primitive, savage, distorted, unnatural, exiled, etc. But it is precisely also this mockery of colonial discourse in the colonial subject's adoption of it which marks not only its continued assertion, but also its splitting from itself. For, in Leela Gandhi's apt formulation:

> Mimicry is also the sly weapon of anti-colonial civility, an ambivalent mixture of deference and disobedience. The native subject appears to observe the political and semantic imperatives of colonial discourse. But at the same time, she systematically misrepresents the foundational assumptions of this discourse by articulating it, as Bhabha puts it, 'syntagmatically with a range of differential knowledges and positionalities that both estrange its "iden-

tity" and produce new forms of knowledge, new modes of differentiation, new sites of power.' (Gandhi, 1998: 149–150)

Chief among the effects which result from the colonial subject's disrupting the "identity" of colonial discourse is a loss of all its reality, authenticity, authority and normativity. Instead of powerfully affirming the claim of colonial discourse to representing 'the real thing', the colonial subject "rearticulates, repeats 'reality' as mimicry" (Bhabha, 1994: 130).

In the following I shall demonstrate that Emerson's rhetoric of an American sublime is an example of such sly civility. This I propose to do, however, by stressing the internal contradictions of his postcoloniality, insofar as the "ambivalent mixture of deference and disobedience" alluded to by Ghandi necessarily manifests itself the more strongly with respect to a writer from a settlement colony. For – as already pointed out – the need among early 19th century Euro-American artists to turn away from European models at the same time collides with a desire to be reckoned on equal terms with them because their cultural codes never stopped being suspiciously European and never even had begun to be indigenously American. Therefore, I will argue that the sublime in Emerson's American version becomes slyly civil in the sense that it politely mirrors its European counterpart by double-crossing it. It does not, in other words, represent a completely novel, uniquely American instance of it, but by being a less respectable respectful extension of its European precursor more likely exposes a subversive underside already belonging to the latter. I would thus venture the proposition that the sublime in Emerson becomes indistinguishable from its own mimicry or parodying double.

In order to explain what Emerson's *mimicry* of the sublime means within a postcolonial context of this kind, I shall begin by considering some passages from his writings where he discusses the theme of transatlantic relations between Europe and America in more general terms. Here I hope to provide a framework that will help to situate Emerson as an American postcolonial writer, whose point of view reflects a transatlantically hybrid or double-crossing perspective rather than an unequivocally American one, as has been most wont in discussions of the American sublime.

Robert Weisbuch has proposed the term "Atlantic double-cross" to characterize such a perspective, but he prefers to interpret it in a much more benignly figurative sense than I believe is possible. Weisbuch tends to view the literary crossing between Europe and America in 19th century writing as one centered on "a battle for cultural existence" between two independent Romantic traditions with Emerson initiating "an American attempt to throw off British literary influence" (Weisbuch, 1986: 295).[1] If, as Paul Giles has done in his *Transatlantic Insurrections* (2001), we understand the cross-Atlantic connection between European and American literature in this period as primarily of a postcolonial nature, then the two traditions turn out to intersect more intimately "through various forms of entanglement", but also more deceptively (Giles, 2001: 9). "Atlantic double-cross" will for that reason have to be interpreted in its literal sense as a dead metaphor, stressing that both traditions parasitically contaminate and are contaminated by each other across the Atlantic. They have no essence on their own. Bhabha's notion of *mimicry* is, as I have already intimated, a very useful equivalent term to employ, if we wish to characterize the postcoloniality of the transatlantic Euro-American literary relations in this manner. In Emerson's case it is especially in his book *English Traits* (1856) that we find the most illustrative examples of how we may begin to analyze his writings from a transatlantic and postcolonial point of view, which may eventually be extended with a view to revising the mainly Bloomian interpretation of the Emersonian sublime as a purely American Romantic literary phenomenon.

Emerson's Double(-)Crossings

Emerson's *English Traits* is a travel book based on his observations from two visits to England in 1833 and 1847. Its first chapter opens with a sentence stating: "I have been twice in England" (Emerson, 1983: 767). So, in a quite literal fashion is it a book about a double crossing – namely, that which its opening sentence would necessarily allude to in 1856, the year of his work's publication when Emerson had become so much of an icon to the culturally literate public in America and Europe to be known to have to cross the Atlantic for a European visit.

This is, however, not the only way in which the theme of double crossing is introduced in the early sections of the book. The two opening chapters

---

[1] In his eponymous book *Atlantic Double-Cross: American Literature and British Influence in the Age of Emerson* (1986) Weisbuch spells out his view of Euro-American literary relations in the following manner: "I believe that the American writer begins from a defensive position and that the achievements of British literature and British national life are the chief intimidations against which he, as American representative, defends himself" (Weisbuch, 1986: xii).

"Ch. 1: First Visit to England" and "Ch. 2: Voyage to England" function peritextually as a kind of prologue to the book, even though they have not been textually marked off as such, but are integrated with the remaining sixteen chapters. Both chapters in turn deal with the American writer and traveler's experience of crossing over from America to England on the two separate occasions of 1833 and 1847. Whereas the first chapter only spends two introductory paragraphs on depicting the actual journey and the author's reflections on reasons for going to England as a "young [American] scholar" (Emerson, 1983: 767), the whole second chapter is a very detailed report of his second crossing onboard "the packet-ship Washington Irving [...] from Boston" (779). What is interesting about this prologue is not only its division into two separate chapters, formally indicating the temporal gap between the first and the second crossing. More important is the slightly lopsided manner in which the two crossings are presented, which includes more than just the difference in number of detail with which they are treated. There is also a difference in how Emerson crosses over to England the first and the second time.

Emerson's narrative of his first visit to England creates a sense that its transatlantic nature is less straightforward than might appear to be the case. Instead of arriving in the country from the Atlantic side, he enters it as if from the backdoor via the English Channel since, as he puts it, "[...] I crossed from Boulogne, and landed in London at the Tower stairs" (Emerson, 1983: 767). In fact, the effect that Emerson's narrative seems intended to have is initially to conjure up an image of himself in the role of the American tourist who has been visiting Europe and on his way back to America decides to make a stopover in England before continuing his journey back across the Atlantic ("In 1833, on my return from a short tour in Sicily, Italy, and France, I crossed from Boulogne, and landed in London at the Tower stairs" (767)). In this way England is troped upon as a topography of modern tourism, as the visit to England is metonymically linked to Emerson's tour of Sicily, Italy and France through the narrative device of the Channel crossing. But what in particular goes to characterize England as a touristic space for Emerson is the perceptual mode which the description of his journey to the country hints at. According to theorists of travel writing, the experience of the tourist in the 19th century introduces a "panoramization of the world" and an ensuing "panoramic view" of it (Schiffer in Korte, 2000: 94). This experience is generally seen as resulting from the "accelerated mode of perception offered by railway travel" (94) which industrial society increasingly facilitated. The "sense of fleetingness, change and a foreground distorted by speed" which Reinhold Schiffer claims for the panoramic view of the tourist is perfectly true of Emerson's account as well. Not only is his tour of Sicily, Italy and France "short", the three countries he travels in are described in no great detail, but merely very superficially referred to by way of their proper names. Similarly, it is the cartographic specifics of the ports of departure and arrival that are highlighted, so that it is the typical 19th century tourist's routine of crossing from the Continent to England rather than the mythic dimension of the American's first encounter with his ancestral homeland.

This framing of England within a touristic perceptual context is further stressed by the remaining sentences of the first paragraph. The impression is that Emerson and his "companion, an American artist" have come to England on no other business than as tourists. First of all, what Emerson remembers from the visit is what the typical 19th century tourist would remember. As Barbara Korte points out in *English Travel Writing from Pilgrimages to Postcolonial Explorations*, the tourist's panoramic view of the landscape he traverses involves nothing more than "the pure pleasure of seeing" (Korte, 2000: 94). The latter aspect of the touristic experience is unmistakably present in Emerson's account of the walk he and his American artist companion take from the landing place at the Tower stairs to their sleeping quarters in Russell Square:

> It was a dark Sunday morning; there were few people in the streets; and I remember the pleasure of that first walk on English ground, with my companion, an American artist, from the Tower up through Cheapside and the Strand, to a house in Russell Square, whither we had been recommended to good chambers. (Emerson, 1983: 767)

The pleasure of walking noted by Emerson is definitely linked to the visual aesthetics of the scene encountering the two strollers, produced by its morning darkness and depopulated appearance.

Furthermore, Emerson's account produces what Korte claims "resemble[s] typical tourist behavior: the text moves, with the traveler, from one view to the next, from sight to sight" (Korte, 2000: 96). It points out what using Jonathan Culler's term she calls "'markers' for sights" (96) and acquires a guiding function for whichever tourist might visit London in the future. The implied reader of tourist guides and regular visitor to London would also know that this function is foregrounded by Emerson, since a cursory look at a contemporary map of the city would reveal the route taken by him and his companion not to be shortest, but a rather lengthy detour. Just as Emerson and his traveling companion have had their stay in London programmed through prior recommendation of where to put up for the night, so his own book inscribes itself in the conventions of 19th century travelogues and tourist guides by implicitly narrating how best to experience the city as a pedestrian. Thus, at first Emerson's business in London comes across as touristic in the sense that it is the protracted delight of pedestrian sightseeing and the comforts of accommodation for the night that appear to be central.

What is interesting about Emerson's touristic description of first arriving in England is, however, the double-edged function it seems to have in a context of transatlantic relations between America and England. On the one hand, it leaves no doubt that the experience of modern tourist writing constitutes the generic frame for his manner of telling how he and his travel companion crossed from Europe to England and spent their first hours in London.[2] The effect of such a narrative frame is to transform England from a 'real' country into a picturesque landscape, "draw[ing] on traditional patterns of picturesque landscape depiction" (Korte, 2000: 92). Indeed, looking for sights is for the 19th century tourist writer "the importance of the visual, of seeing *pictures*, as an essential experience of tourist travel" (my emphasis) (94). As Barbara Korte remarks in her book, this "allows the writers to avoid the portrayal of culture *contact* [...]. [The] writing strategy [...] is the strict separation of descriptions of a country's population from geographical and topographical descriptions, so that the country, [...] comes across as 'unpopulated'" (Korte's emphasis) (92).

Sightseeing predominates in the opening sentences of *English Traits*, which is underscored by its reference to the almost complete absence of people in the streets, and tends to replace a desire to strike up any other kind relationship with the place and its population. In this way London

---

[2] Here it is worth recalling the marked increase in numbers of American tourists to Britain around the time when Emerson traveled there and wrote his book; steam ship passage had not only become faster, but cheaper, thus enabling thousands of Americans to cross the Atlantic. Cf. Benjamin Goluboff's remarks in "'Latent Preparedness': Allusions in American Literature on Britain", *American Studies* Vol. 31, No. 1 (1990): "After 1840 (the year in which Samuel Cunard's shipping line was established) American tourism in Britain increased dramatically. Encouraged by the relatively cheap and rapid steam ship passages, and attracted by the London Exhibition of 1851, Americans annually went to the Old Home in thousands. For the most part, this second wave of Americans came purely to see sights, many to write about them. It was these tourists who were responsible for the great proliferation of British travel accounts at mid-century [...]" (66).

becomes a culturally invested space where a strong focus on its picturesque features suppresses mention of its contemporary and historical realities. Similarly, Emerson himself is portrayed as upholding a safe position as the observing outsider with a tourist's discriminating eye for the sights of London. The conflicted transatlantic cultural connection between Britain and America is thus backgrounded by his narrative, which instead prefers to highlight the much more pleasurable viewpoint of a Channel-crossing tourist. But Emerson's picturesque rendition of London still has a certain American tinge to it, threatening to conjure up the complexities of British-American relations and the postcolonial American writer's mimicry of British cultural domination.

For it is also clear that Emerson's reasons for depicting England as a site for picturesque sightseeing appear – at least at first sight – to be especially like those of other contemporary American tourist travel writers. According to Benjamin Goluboff, there is a common characteristic of 19th century American travel literature on Britain:

> The American experience of travel in Britain was attended by an enchantment of the familiar. American travellers arrived there prepared to see sights and hear voices already well known to them. It is a familiar irony that people travel to confirm their expectations of the foreign. But in no other avenue of travel were those expectations so vivid as for the nineteenth-century American en route to Britain. "The Old Home" might thrill Americans but it could rarely surprise, rarely defy their expectations. (Goluboff, 1990: 65–66)

Goluboff further notes that if Americans traveled to Britain in order to see the Britain they were already latently prepared to expect finding, this was mainly due to their reading about it. Most of them raised on the canon of British literature, their image of the land tended to be informed by its literary representation in the works of classic British writers. Thus, American travel accounts came to institute a convention of literary allusion as a means of rendering their experience of Britain, and their experience in turn to be wholly Anglophile and textualized. English literature was in a sense the American traveler's prime tourist guide to Britain *faut de mieux*.

Now, Goluboff points to three different functions of literary reference in 19th century American travel writing about Britain. First of all, it worked as a mimicking device for the culturally insecure mid-century American travel writer who, as Goluboff emphasizes, "appear[s] to have felt that to travel in Britain constituted a sort of examination in cultural literacy" (Goluboff,

1990: 66–67). Due to the cultural hegemony of British literature in post-Revolutionary America, many American travel writers bore witness to a strong sense of belatedness and a desire to update themselves culturally. In order to make up for their sense of being latecomers on the cultural scene, their travel narratives were mainly means by which they could record their experience of England as a display of "conversancy with the canon of British literature" (67). Secondly, literary reference helped them situate themselves familiarly on British land. Thirdly, but most importantly, it was through allusion to the English literary canon that American travel writers neither expected to see nor saw contemporary 19th century England, but rather "the image of a placid rural England" they had already encountered in the literature of "Shakespeare, Milton, Addison, Pope and Scott" (67, 68). Thus, according to Goluboff, they would be able to dissemble their own cultural belatedness and escape to "a fictive Old England" already familiar to them through their readings of English literature.

As appears from Goluboff's account of American travel writing from the time when Emerson published *English Traits*, the American tourist's relation to Britain is not very different from any other 19th century tourist's relation to the places he or she visits, insofar as "it is a familiar irony that people travel to confirm their expectations of the foreign" (Goluboff, 1990: 65–66). Employing Jonathan Culler's cultural semiotics of tourism in general to Goluboff's notion of a 'latent preparedness' in American tourists for England, literally mediated through their reading of the English literary canon, 'the real England' they narrate having encountered is a "sign relation" as are all so-called authentic sights and places tourists quest for on their visits. According to Culler,

> [...] 'the real thing' must be marked as real, as sight-worthy; if it is not marked or differentiated, it is not a notable sight, even though it may be [e.g.] Japanese by virtue of its location in Japan. The authentic is not something unmarked or undifferentiated; authenticity is a sign relation. (Culler, 1988: 161)

In other words, if the mid-century American tourist was latently prepared for seeing 'the real England' when going there, it is primarily because English literature had always already signified or marked out for him where to find it and what it looked like. Any other visitor who went there would be likewise prepared, but more likely through the reading of tourist guides.

Taking into account Culler's reflections on the essentially mediated nature of the touristic experience, its semiotic structure, it is not possible to speak about a more or less immediate access to the authenticity of a certain place. For the very idea of the authentic and the real is a construction produced by modern tourism, and in that sense it constitutes an intrinsic part of its sign system or cultural code. The tourist's hunt for the authentic sight is therefore caught in a double bind, since, claims Culler, "[t]he authentic sight requires markers, but our notion of the authentic is the unmarked [sic!]" (Culler, 1988: 164). Thus, the "modern quest for [authentic] experience" is really "a quest for the experience of signs" – of the real (165). The latter semiotic aspect of the touristic experience is also what is implied in Barbara Korte's notion of the tourist's picturesque vision, insofar as it goes to characterize the way in which tourism constructs the experience of the 'real' as an aesthetically pleasing sight. But in relation to Culler's insight one must, however, add that the cultural semiosis of the authentic is also differentially culturally coded. In line with how Goluboff characterizes American travel writing at mid-century, it is worth noting that the American tourist's experience of 'the real England' tends to be mediated by his chronic allusions to representations of the land in classic English literature. In this way, what counts as 'the real England' for the American travel writer is never just a question of the typical 19th century tourist's quest for the sights of England, but largely depends upon the postcolonial American's particular cultural coding of England.

What characterizes the American travel writer's cultural semiosis of authentic England in more specific terms is its postcoloniality according to Goluboff. His argument is in some respects, I would argue, very close to Homi Bhabha's definition of postcolonial culture as hybrid and mimic. For as already pointed out, there is nothing indigenously American about the American travel writer's experience of England. 'The England' he (re)visits is the one he has already encountered in the canon of older English literature and is in that sense more British than American. On the other hand, the literalness with which he recognizes the correspondence between 'the fictive England' he has read about and 'the real England' he actually sees adds a distinctively other touch to his English experience. Goluboff does not mention the basically catachrestic nature of this experience, but he is very much aware of its hybridity, what he calls its "latent preparedness", and that it is only by mimicking the British literary classics as if they signified an original England that the 19th century American travel writer is able to contravene his postcolonial cultural inferiority. Nevertheless, Goluboff does not consider the possibility that the catachrestic element in American travel writing's allusive practice may also be read as mimicry of the privilege of British literary culture in the strong Bhabhian sense. He rather prefers to view this privilege as intact.

Returning to Emerson, it is not immediately obvious that his account in *English Traits* of his first encounter with the country relies upon allusion to English literature in order to confirm that he has found the authentic England. According to Goluboff, "Emerson's *English Traits* (1856) confronted contemporary Britain quite squarely; it was also a work, significantly, that contained very few allusions" (Goluboff, 1990: 80). Both Goluboff's points appear on the face of it very true, but one may nonetheless qualify them somewhat. In any case, though there is no explicit allusion to the canon of English literature, Emerson's narrative does not quite attain to being just another modern tourist's sight-seeing of London. Traces of an allusive practice still remain, so that "a latent preparedness" by English literature for visiting England residually informs his narrative. It is not to classic English literature that he alludes, but to the more recent one of William Wordsworth, more specifically to his poem "Composed upon Westminster Bridge, September 3, 1802". The pristine beauty which this poem ascribes to the modern industrial city of London before the onset of its busy and grimy daily activities in the morning, is obliquely doubled by Emerson in his description of his first early morning walk through an almost unpopulated London.[3] It seems as if Emerson thus invokes the picturesque image of the American visitor coming upon an aboriginal and authentic England. His references to the "dark Sunday morning" and the few people in the streets carry an almost prelapsarian meaning and turn London into a paradisiacal landscape.

Emerson's more or less submerged allusion to Wordsworth seems to have a double function. If it does not play the role of displaying the culturally insecure American's conversancy with English literature, it nevertheless points to a reflection in Emerson on the hybridity of postcolonial Anglo-American culture. Furthermore, his imitation of Wordsworth's picturesque rhetoric also seems to have another more denaturalizing function. In the sentences immediately following his description of first setting foot on English ground he goes on to comment on the historical contingency of

---

[3] Cf. William Wordsworth, "Composed upon Westminster Bridge, September 3, 1802": "This City now doth, like a garment, wear/The beauty of the morning; silent, bare,/ Ships, towers, domes, theatres, and temples lie/Open unto the fields, and to the sky;/All bright and glittering in the smokeless air" (ll. 4-8) (in M.H. Abrams and Greenblatt, 2000)

English and Americans sharing the same language, noting in turn the disadvantages of no longer being able to behave like a common tourist:

> For the first time for many months we were forced to check the saucy habit of travelers' criticism, as we could no longer speak aloud in the streets without being understood. The shop-signs spoke our language; our country names were on the door-plates; and the public and private buildings wore a more native and wonted front. (Emerson, 1983: 767)

By interposing these remarks, Emerson clearly double-crosses the contemporary American travel writer's convention of alluding to classic English literature, thus problematizing the latter's mistaking its picturesque representations of a placid and rural Old England for the real England. Instead, there announces itself the uncanny realization that English language and culture is more perversely the home of the American than Emerson's initial characterization of his encounter with the country hints at. Emerson exposes the fiction of authentic English (or American) culture as fiction and prefers to think of the transatlantic relation between Britain and America not in binary oppositional terms, but as one of mutual crossing. In this way, the historical realities of an Anglo-American postcolonial legacy are indirectly invoked.

In the chapter on Emerson's second visit to England in 1847 the same demythologizing intent manifests itself. The chapter, which mostly focuses on the transatlantic crossing by boat, ends by telling about the ship's approach to the British Isles. Writes Emerson:

> As we neared the land, its genius was felt. This was inevitably the British side. In every man's thought arises now a new system, English sentiments, English loves and fears, English history and social modes. Yesterday, every passenger had measured the speed of the ship by watching the bubbles over the ship's bulwarks. To-day, instead of bubbles, we measure by Kinsale, Cork, Waterford, and Ardmore. There lay the green shore of Ireland, like some coast of plenty. We see towns, towers, churches, harvests; but the curse of eight hundred years we could not discern. (Emerson, 1983: 783)

It is worth noting that the passage refers to the "latent preparedness" of the American traveler for navigating his visit to Britain. His mind is portrayed as adjusted in advance to recognizing a certain Britain. In particular, we should pay attention to the fact that the Ireland Emerson writes he saw on approaching its coast is primarily a mythic and rural one, which is evidenced by the reference to its green shore, the comparison of its coast to a coast of plenty, and the reference to harvests. Emerson slyly implies that this vision of Ireland represents an aesthetic distortion of a much more violent historical reality – namely, the eight hundred years of Anglo-Norman colonization of Ireland. On the other hand, his narrative at the same time makes it seem relatively unlikely that after removal of English colonial dominance in Ireland a true native Irish culture will emerge. The catch is, of course, as a postcolonial American Emerson glimpses little hope of transcending the insinuations of British cultural influence across the Atlantic; for he can see only the Ireland which British cultural representations of it offer. But mockingly miming the discourse of such aestheticizing representations, nonetheless, tends to weaken their authority in his narrative.

Sublime Negotiations

If we turn to Emerson's 1836 essay "Nature", a similar double crossing of British cultural discourse is evident. A central moment in the essay is Emerson's description of the experience of the sublime and, as I have proposed above, Emerson's rhetoric of the sublime lends itself to a reading where it can be viewed as a transatlantic *mimicry* of its English Romantic version. It is especially the way in which William Wordsworth has proposed a poetic program of the sublime that I would claim Emerson double-crosses in his essay.

In Wordsworth's "Prospectus to *The Recluse*" (1798-1814/1814) one finds the most sustained argument for the sublime. Its prime element is that transposition of the transcendental "into a naturalistic key" which Thomas Weiskel has argued constitutes the romantic sublime (Weiskel, 1986: 4). Crossing into transcendence is for Wordsworth and the Romantics significantly a secular matter and no longer primarily a religious concern. In "Prospectus..." he puts it in the following manner:

> – Beauty – a living Presence of the earth,
> Surpassing the most fair ideal Forms
> Which craft of delicate Spirits hath composed
> From earth's materials – waits upon my steps;
> Pitches her tents before me as I move,
> An hourly neighbour. Paradise, and groves
> Elysian, Fortunate Fields – like those of old

> Sought in the Atlantic Main – why should they be
> A history only of departed things,
> Or a mere fiction of what never was?
> For the discerning intellect of Man,
> When wedded to this goodly universe
> In love and holy passion, shall find these
> A simple produce of the common day.
> (Abrams & Greenblatt, 2000: 302, ll. 42–55)

As is evident from the extract from Wordsworth's poem, the vehicle for attaining the transcendental is the human intellect as it finds the latter not beyond this world, but realized in the everyday world. Wordsworth's poetic argument for the sublime proposes, I would argue, a chiasmatic reversal of the traditionally diametrically opposed poles of the beyond and the mundane. But at the same time such an exchange of properties between them does not present itself as having yet come true. Rather, Wordsworth dons the *persona* of the poet-prophet who authoritatively predicts its coming. In that sense, he institutes a rhetoric of the sublime which does not lose any of its prestige despite its secularization.

Emerson's "Nature" intertextually tropes upon Wordsworth's vision of a naturalistic sublime, on the one hand, by transferring it from the latter's poetic context into his own prosaic context of essay writing and, on the other, by hyperbolically literalizing it in the American landscape. As it stands, Emerson's act of transference appears to affirm the realization of the sublime prophesied by Wordsworth in "Prospectus…" Yet, the hyperbolic manner in which he tells about its happening tends to undercut its grand asseverations. Let us quote the relevant passage:

> Crossing a bare common, in snow puddles, at twilight, under a clouded sky, without having in my thoughts any occurrence of special good fortune, I have enjoyed a perfect exhilaration. I am glad to the brink of fear. In the wood, too, a man casts off his years, as the snake his slough, and at what period soever of life is always a child. In the woods is perpetual youth. Within these plantations of God, a decorum and sanctity reign, a perennial festival is dressed, and the guest sees not how he should tire of them in a thousand years. In the woods, we return to reason and faith. There I feel that nothing can befall me in life, – no disgrace, no calamity (leaving me my eyes), which nature cannot repair. Standing on the bare ground, – my head bathed by the blithe air and uplifted into infinite space, – all mean egotism vanishes. I become a transparent eyeball; I am nothing; I see all; the currents of the Universal Being circulate though me; I am part or parcel of God. The name of the nearest friend sounds then foreign and accidental: to be brothers, to be ac-

quaintances, master or servant, is then a trifle and a disturbance. I am the lover of uncontained and immortal beauty. In the wilderness, I find something more dear and connate than in streets or villages. In the tranquil landscape, and especially in the distant line of the horizon, man beholds somewhat as beautiful as his own nature. (Ziff, 1982: 38–39)

What is worth noticing for a start is that Emerson repeats Wordsworth's use of the trope of chiasmus so as to naturalize the sublime moment. Characteristically, he is very careful to anchor the narrative situation in the context of the quotidian world. The references to walking across a bare common, snow puddles, twilight, cloudy weather and to the writer's ordinary state of mind contribute to this anchoring. But the quite pedestrian activity of crossing a common is simultaneously troped as a crossing into the extraordinary, divinity and immortality. In chiasmatic fashion the sublime thus changes places with the mundane, so that they become hardly distinguishable from each other. "Standing on the bare ground" is only slightly different from having "the currents of the Universal Being circulate through [one]".

The effect created by such a reversal of terms is to introduce a grandiloquent rhetoric of the sublime which uses hyperbole as its preferred figure of speech. The crossing of the ordinary with extraordinary in Emerson's text precisely stands out as "a bold overstatement, or the extravagant exaggeration of fact or of possibility", which is M. H. Abrams's dictionary definition of the term (Abrams, 1999: 120). In line with Wordsworth's denial of the transcendental as "a mere fiction of what never was", Emerson crosses transcendence into the literal fact of lived experience. But instead casting doubt on the credibility of his hyperbolic literalization of the sublime, it seems on the face of it that Emerson's use of the declarative sentence serves to underscore the factuality of the sublime experience. The very amassing of declarative statements in the passage produces an excess of the factual, which in turn collapses the ontological separation between the human and the divine. Essentially, to cross a bare common appears no less factual than becoming a transparent eyeball. And, finally, Emerson's choice of the essay genre is a further contributing factor in this respect. According to Robert L. Root, Jr. and Michael Steinberg, one of the distinguishing features of the essay is that like other creative nonfictional genres it "is reliably factual, firmly anchored in real experience, whether the author has lived it or observed and recorded it" (Root and Steinberg, 1999: xxxvi).

Yet, there is still a question to which extent the discourse of the sublime in Emerson has the authoritative status that its blustering rhetoric sets the stage for. Insofar as chiasmus and hyperbole are the dominating tropes in the passage quoted from "Nature", Emerson's narrative tends to present a grotesque testing of the limits of the factual, while they are also strongly insisted upon. When the experience of the sublime eventually results in virtually transforming the writer into "a transparent eyeball", "nothing", all-seeing and "part or parcel of God", he stands out as a strange hybrid creature, combining the elements of monstrous human physicality, spiritual nothingness and omnipotent divinity. Seen in this light, Emerson's sublime comes to veer towards the unbelievable as he alludes to and realizes Wordsworth's prophetic statement that transcendence will be "a common produce of the simple day".

It is this double-edged character of Emerson's discourse of the sublime that poises it uncertainly between factual statement and inflated rhetoric. In this respect, it divides itself against itself, raising questions about how seriously it should be taken. Does it merely present the transatlantic mimicry of sublimity, thus problematizing the poetic-prophetic authority of Wordsworth's "Prospectus..."? Or does it continue to affirm it, thus extending the dominance of a European literary tradition within an American context?

In concluding this essay, I suggest that part of the answer to these questions can be sought in a poem by one of Emerson's American heirs. Aptly entitled "The American Sublime" (1935), Wallace Stevens's poem opens by asking the question of how to counter the mockery of the sublime:

> How does one stand
> To behold the sublime,
> To confront the mockers,
> The mickey mockers
> And plated pairs?
> (Stevens, 1987: 130, ll. 1–4)

What the rest of Stevens's poem keeps suspended, however, is any definite answer to this question. After all, it turns out that the reader is left to wonder if Stevens himself is not one of those sublime mockers of the sublime that his poem appears to desire to defend itself against. Especially when his poet-speaker in the final two lines of the poem dares ask such everyday questions as to what wine to drink and what bread to eat, while beholding the sublime. Unless, of course, the wine and the bread allude to the Eucharist.

References

Abrams, M. H. (1999) *A Glossary of Literary Terms. Seventh Edition.* Fort Worth: Harcourt Brace College Publishers

Abrams, M.H. and Greenblatt, Stephen (eds.) (2000) *The Norton Anthology of English Literature* Seventh Edition. Vol. 2. New York and London: W.W. Norton & Company

Bhabha, Homi (1994, new ed., 2004) *The Location of Culture.* London and New York: Routledge

Bloom, Harold (1982) *Agon. Towards a Theory of Revisionism.* Oxford: Oxford University Press

Culler, Jonathan (1988) *Framing the Sign. Criticism and its Institututions.* Oxford: Basil Blackwell

Emerson, Ralph Waldo (1983) *Essays and Lectures.* New York: The Library of America

Paul Giles (2001) *Transatlantic Insurrections. British Culture and the Formation of American Literature, 1730-1860.* Philadelphia, Pennsylvania: University of Pennsylvania Press

Goluboff, Benjamin (1990) "'Latent Preparedness': Allusions in American Travel Literature on Britain." *American Studies* Vol. 31. No. 1

Korte, Barbara (2000) *English Travel Writing from Pilgrimages to Postcolonial Explorations.* Trans. Catherine Matthias. London and New York: Macmillan Press Ltd. and St. Martin's Press, Inc.

Root, Jr., Robert L. and Steinberg, Michael (1999) *The Fourth Genre. Contemporary Writers of/on Creative Nonfiction.* Boston: Allyn and Bacon

Rosiek, Jan (2000) *Maintaining the Sublime. Heidegger and Adorno.* Bern: Peter Lang

Weisbuch, Robert (1986) *Atlantic Double-Cross. American Literature and British Influence in the Age of Emerson.* Chicago and London: University of Chicago Press

Stevens, Wallace (1987) *Collected Poems.* London and Boston: Faber and Faber

Weisbuch, Robert (1999) "Post-Colonial Emerson and the Erasure of Europe". Porte, Joel and Morris, Saundra (eds.) *The Cambridge Companion to Ralph Waldo Emerson.* Cambridge: Cambridge University Press

Weiskel, Thomas (1986) *The Romantic Sublime. Studies in the Structure and Psychology of Transcendence.* Baltimore and London: Johns Hopkins University Press

Anxiety Between Europe and America: Reinhold Niebuhr and His Use of Søren Kierkegaard's Concept of Anxiety

Brian C. Barlow

Reinhold Niebuhr lived a life of anxiety between Europe and America. His discovery of Søren Kierkegaard and his existential reflections on anxiety made it possible for him to live and think in a time that (although it is still very much with us) has been called the "age of anxiety". This essay focuses on both his life context and his theological writings to mine the riches of his most famous work *The Nature and Destiny of Man* (1964). This two volume work is surely one of the finest series of reflections to have ever been produced for the prestigious Gifford Lectures. Niebuhr delivered his Gifford Lectures just before and during World War II. Born into the dynamic and tension-filled German pietism of the American Midwest, educated in the still monastic closeness of Yale Divinity School, and schooled in the conflict-ridden and anxious times of the Detroit labor movement as a young pastor, Niebuhr was well-prepared for his first encounter with Kierkegaard's writings (then only available in German translation). But, our focus is on the Gifford Lectures and the contexts of his preparation for them in America, his delivery of them in Europe, and his writing on anxiety "between Europe and America" in his magnum opus with its specific encounter and use of Kierkegaard's concept of anxiety.

Anxiety in America

Niebuhr was only the fifth American to be asked to deliver the Gifford Lectures. The most famous of his predecessors was William James who produced the classic work in psychology of religion, *The Varieties of Religious Experience* (1958). Niebuhr's biographer relates of this moment of his life:

> During the winter [of 1937][…]he accepted an invitation – engineered by his old friend John Baillie, now a powerful figure in the Scottish church – to deliver the prestigious Gifford Lectures at the University of Edinburgh in 1939. Only four other Americans – William James, Josiah Royce, John Dewey, and William Ernest Hocking – had been selected since Lord Gifford endowed the lectures with a grant of 80,000 pounds sterling in 1888. Niebuhr had reason to be anxious in that august company; he had never engaged in a long-term scholarly project in his life. The offer of 1,000 pounds for two sets of ten lectures each made the coming intellectual struggle somewhat more attractive – likewise the prospect of following hard on the heels of his nemesis Karl Barth, scheduled to finish his series of lectures in 1938. Yet, Niebuhr was genuinely humbled and his self-doubt surfaced repeatedly. (Fox, 1985: 178)

Niebuhr's metaphorical thinking led him to see the Giffords as a form of "slavery", a kind of bondage that would keep him from undertaking his more favored practice of extemporaneous speaking, whether in a sermon or political speech. His previous writing had been executed in the form of diary entries (meant for publication) and the essay. His style as well as his lack of rigor in the analysis of concepts had bruised his ego and perhaps reawakened old wounds that reminded him of his less than ideal formal education and essentially only partially completed one. He was given to bouts of insecurity, stewing in states of anger and anxiety (Fox, 1985). Reflections and reading about the state of Europe just prior to World War II, Niebuhr despaired over what he considered the terror of "inevitable catastrophe" (184).

Although he was temperamentally given to action and pressed about by a variety of forces, always clamoring for his immediate attention, he was reminded of the Giffords and brought face to face with their prospect.

> Thinking about them at all was "intellectually and spiritually painful […] I have to force myself to keep at it because every time I try to work out the pattern I become afraid of the magnitude of the job and fear that I can never complete it. (185)

Niebuhr seems to have suffered from a form of writer's block at this time, perhaps due to feelings of inadequacy which were themselves more deeply embedded in anxieties of both primitive and derivative natures.

> By the first week of 1938 his anxiety was beginning to look like panic – even though the lectures were still more than a year away […] The more he read the more he felt he ought to read. He was looking for points of contact between

Greek tragedy and the Hebrew prophets and found it a devil of a job. (186)

But it may have been his discovery of the writings of the Dane, Søren Kierkegaard, in 1937 in German translation (which was Niebuhr's native language) that began the process of creative and paradoxical transformation and finally loosened Niebuhr's shackles and enabled him to burst forth into what most consider today a rhetorical *tour de force* (Brown, 2002). Nevertheless, he was continually beset with health problems due to "overwork" and began a descent into despair at the approaching war. It was the challenge of becoming a father for the second time that, Jamesian like, gave him the necessary struggle and the will to believe in himself so that he could envision the first half of the Gifford Lectures (Fox, 1985).

Anxiety in Europe

Niebuhr's anxiety was not miraculously healed nor did it disappear in any spontaneous moment of transcendence. His reading of Kierkegaard and his life context both continued to cast doubt on this possibility anyway. His actual deliveries of the lectures were themselves moments of anxiety. He appears to have felt them less than satisfactory, reintroducing the shame that goes along with any attempt to autonomously master a task whether it be walking for the first time or walking back and forth while delivering the Giffords in an extemporaneous manner. Many have remarked on Niebuhr's method of lecturing or preaching. He never stood still but was constantly on the move, perhaps dreading the moment when he might get stuck or blocked or fixated on a particular point. The style was part of his great attraction to audience and students alike.

> By the end he was "completely exhausted" and faced the depressing prospect of finishing the second series while meeting a score of other obligations he had incurred both in Britain and on the Continent. One side of him wanted to be rid of the intellectual pressure of the Giffords, to get back into the flow of day-to-day events [...] The other side of him sensed that the scholarly challenge came first: he must establish himself as a thinker as well as a prophet. (188–189)

Although Kierkegaard had helped to enable Niebuhr to confront his demon of anxiety, he was at least as much dominated by these demons as master of them (Fox, 1985). Niebuhr seems to have been "driven by a demon" in order to write the first lecture series (including the important lecture on Kierkegaard and sin). But, one is not sure whether this "demon" was in dread of evil or the good (Kierkegaard, 1980). The "sympathetic antipathy" and "antipathetic sympathy" of Niebuhr's personal anxiety continued to plague him while revising the first lectures for publication even as bombs were dropping on nearby Edinburgh as the war had gotten under way (Fox, 1985).

Niebuhr continued to be plagued with dread, rage, and sorrow as the war became increasingly present during the remaining lectures. But the war also seems to have fueled in Niebuhr what James has called the "moral equivalent of war". His lectures continued on in spite of the war as did his audience who were committed to hear them.

> [T]hese were not standard Gifford lectures; they were inspirational [...] sermons on the Christian view of human destiny. If bombs were going to fall it made sense to make time three afternoons a week for some stirring reflections that went beyond tragedy. (191)

Although Niebuhr's anxiety would continue to plague him throughout life, at times leaving him prostrate with depression, he also continued to struggle toward that vision of moral victory that James had earlier inspired him with.

Anxiety Between Europe and America

As Richard Fox has remarked, *The Nature and Destiny of Man* is a book filled with "tension" both in form and content (Fox, 1985: 202). It is the expression of a man who has experienced personally and deeply the anxieties and tragedies of his own life as well as the world, whether in overt or covert struggle. But, it is also a book steeped in the language and tradition of the Bible and Niebuhr's use of Kierkegaard's concept of anxiety to help him elucidate the dialectical anxiety of original sin is steeped in that tradition as well. If the form and expression of Niebuhr's lectures are existential and dialectical the content is nevertheless thoroughly theological. The theology is still informed and influenced by nineteenth-century liberal theology, but Niebuhr has also begun to depart from that liberalism toward a post-liberal theological orthodoxy. (It remained for Karl Barth to carry out that project more consistently) (Stanley Hauerwas, 2001).

The finished lecture on original sin and anxiety by Niebuhr is the result of anxiety between Europe and America. It is American theology based in part on European sources. The tension between Europe and America is seen in Niebuhr's partial departure from European (and American) liberalism. Yet, his use of Kierkegaard's concept of anxiety reintroduces the tension in Niebuhr's reading, lecturing, and finally writing of *The Nature and Destiny of Man*. Our focus must be selective and thus we will only look at Niebuhr's discussion of Kierkegaard and anxiety in the chapter "Original Sin and Man's Responsibility".

> The Christian doctrine of sin in its classical form offends both the rationalists and moralists by maintaining the seemingly absurd position that man sins inevitably and by a fateful necessity but that he is nevertheless held responsible for actions which are prompted by an ineluctable fate. (Niebuhr, 1964: 241)

Thus begins the chapter on original sin. While Niebuhr is indebted to Kierkegaard on many points it is important to note that Kierkegaard (nor Vigilius Haufniensis, the pseudonymous author of The *Concept of Anxiety*) did not see original sin as either inevitable or necessary. It was the possibility of sin that originally resided with each individual who in anxiety could leap into sin or not (Kierkegaard, 1980).

Niebuhr waffles at times between viewing original sin as an absurd act by a free human being or a *seemingly* absurd act. It is a flaw in logical rigor that permits this inconsistency. His lack of scholarly experience may account for this. His prophetic passion is what fuels his discussion more than dogmatic logic. Nevertheless, if he sometimes misses the clarity and radical originality of Kierkegaard, he does get the passion correct and it is this which makes his argument so powerful. He praises Kierkegaard to any and all thinkers, especially those idols of modern therapeutic reason, the psychoanalysts (Rieff, 1966; Marino, 2001).

> Modern psychoanalysts might learn much about the basic character of anxiety and its relation to human freedom from the greatest of Christian psychologists, Søren Kierkegaard, who devoted a profound study to the problem: *Der Begriff der Angst*. (Niebuhr, 1964: 44)

Niebuhr's basic and essential commitment to Kierkegaard's psychology is one of the things that keeps his argument both rhetorically persuasive and logically powerful (and in that order).

Following the tradition of Paul, Augustine, Calvin, Pascal, and Kierkegaard, Niebuhr emphasizes the anxiety at the heart of biblical psychology.

> The actual sin is the consequence of the temptation of anxiety in which all life stands. But anxiety alone is neither actual nor original sin. Sin does not

flow necessarily from it. Consequently the bias towards sin from which actual sin flows is anxiety plus sin. Or, in the words of Kierkegaard, sin presupposes itself. (250–251)

Niebuhr follows Kierkegaard on this point admirably and in so doing repeats the offensiveness of Christian dogma. It is this offensiveness which repels the understanding and modern reason and points to the importance of the leap, both for sin to occur and for one to believe that it does so occur.

> The anxiety of freedom leads to sin only if the prior sin of unbelief is assumed. This is the meaning of Kierkegaard's assertion that sin posits itself. (252)

Kierkegaard saw how anxiety produces both the vertigo of freedom and unfreedom. He also saw how this both makes and does not make sense. No one gets this point with greater clarity than Stanley Hauerwas:

> [I]f sin exists, it *makes some sense* to think that God exists. Niebuhr's project is to provide an account of the human condition that is so compelling that the more "absurd" aspects of "orthodox Christianity" – such as the beliefs that God exists and that God is love – might also receive a hearing. (Hauerwas, 2001: 120, emphasis mine)

However, Hauerwas should remove the scare quotation marks. The offense of the Christian doctrine of sin is that it is absurd from the standpoint of human reason and sensibility. One is only able to make some sense of it because they have and continue to leap moment by moment in sin and faith. But, the offensively stated doctrine and revelation fact on which it is based never go away. Thus, both sin and faith are possibilities, possibilities in and of anxiety.

One other place for comparison between Niebuhr and Kierkegaard involves the positive role of anxiety in faith for Kierkegaard. Niebuhr sees this differently:

> The anthropological consequences of this paradox [of revelation] are that faith in God's ultimate resolution of the contradiction in which man stands clarifies man's knowledge of that contradiction. He sees that his anxiety is due to his unbelief. (Niebuhr, 1964: 290)

This is a true but not complete paradox as Kierkegaard sees it. For Kierkegaard, anxiety plays a positive role as an educative factor for persons of faith (Kierkegaard, 1980). One is to grow in faith while one produces his own anxiety. This anxiety is never completely resolved nor transcended due to the sinful human condition of human being. Even persons of faith remain sinful and need God's anxiety-free grace. Only God is without anxiety and precisely where God is most passionately self-giving and loving. This is the absolute paradox that is scandalous to human reason but the peace that passes human understanding. If the Apostle Paul admonishes the believer to be not anxious (*Holy Bible*, Philippians 4: 6), it is nevertheless the apocalyptic gift that no believer can fully receive because he cannot be free from all anxiety. If God makes this possible and actual, subjectively one cannot completely see and understand it as such. Perhaps this is why Niebuhr is so well-known for his prayer seeking serenity in an age of anxiety, an age that continues to this day.

There is still anxiety in America and Europe and between them as well. Niebuhr and Kierkegaard help us partly see why this is the case today. In an apocalyptic age of anxiety such as we live in today perhaps these two finite and in some ways fragile thinkers can still enable us to face the uncertainties of our existence with hope.

References

Brown, Charles C. (2002) *Niebuhr and His Age*. Harrisburg: Trinity Press International

Fox, Richard (1985) *Reinhold Niebuhr: A Biography*. New York: Pantheon Books

Hauerwas, Stanley (2001) *With the Grain of the Universe*. Grand Rapids: Brazos Press

James, William (1958) *The Varieties of Religious Experience*. New York: Mentor

Kierkegaard, Soren (1980) *The Concept of Anxiety*. Princeton: Princeton University Press

Marino, Gordon (2001) *Kierkegaard in the Present Age*. Milwaukee: Marquette University Press

Niebuhr, Reinhold (1964) *The Nature and Destiny of Man. Vol. 1. Human Nature*. New York: Charles Scribner's Sons

Rieff, Philip (1966) *The Triumph of the Therapeutic*. New York: Harper & Row Publishers

The Holy Bible (RSV) (1953) New York: Thomas Nelsons & Sons

Contributors

Søren Hattesen Balle is a lecturer in English at Aalborg University

Brian Barlow is an associate professor of Philosophy and Religion in the Department of Humanities at Brenau University, Gainesville, Georgia

Andrea Croce Birch is Dean of the School of Fine Arts and Humanities and professor of Philosophy at Brenau University, Gainesville, Georgia

Dovile Budryte is an associate professor of International Studies in the Department of Humanities at Brenau University, Gainesville, Georgia

Heather Gollmar Casey is an assistant professor of Political Science in the Department of Humanities and Director of the Women's Center at Brenau University, Gainesville, Georgia

Steen Christiansen is a candidate in the PhD program in Cultural and Literary Studies at Aalborg University, Department of Languages and Intercultural Studies

Marian Dolan is an independent scholar and conductor in Naples, Florida

Camelia Elias is an associate professor of English at Aalborg University, Department of Languages and Intercultural Studies

J. Kay Keels is an assistant professor of Strategic Management in the Wall College of Business Administration at Coastal Carolina University

Mary Beth Looney is interim chair of the Department of Art and Design and an assistant professor of Studio Art and Art History in the Department of Art and Design at Brenau University, Gainesville, Georgia

Lene Yding Pedersen is an associate professor of English at Aalborg University, Department of Languages and Intercultural Studies

Charles C. Perrin is a PhD candidate in the Department of History at Georgia State University

Bent Sørensen is an associate professor of English at Aalborg University, Department of Languages and Intercultural Studies

Jean Westmacott is an associate professor of Sculpture in the Department of Art and Design and Gallery Director at Brenau University, Gainesville, Georgia